Culture and Development Series
No. 2

General Editor
Kapila Vatsyayan

Integration of Endogenous Cultural Dimension into Development

Integration of Endogenous Cultural Dimension into Development

Edited by

Baidyanath Saraswati

Indira Gandhi National Centre for the Arts
New Delhi

D. K. Printworld (P) Ltd.
New Delhi

Cataloging in Publication Data — DK

Integration of endogenous cultural dimension into development / edited by Baidyanath Saraswati.
(Culture and development series; no. 2).
Includes bibliographical references.

1. Culture and development. I. Saraswati, Baidyanath, 1932- II. Series : Culture and development series; no. 2.

ISBN 81-246-0089-9

First Published in India in 1997

Publishers
Indira Gandhi National Centre for the Arts
Central Vista Mess, Janpath, New Delhi - 110001

D.K. Printworld (P) Ltd.
Regd. office : 'Sri Kunj', F-52, Bali Nagar, New Delhi - 110015

Foreword

Kapila Vatsyayan

There can be no real exploration of the artistic experience, its diverse expressions and its power of communication without investigating the nature of the cultural fabric which ignites the creative energies. It was with this intention that the Indira Gandhi National Centre for the Arts initiated a number of dialogues on the cultural fabric in its Cross-Cultural Lifestyle Studies Programme. It endeavoured to measure the immeasurable under the aegis of Unesco-sponsored International Workshop on "Cross-Cultural Lifestyle Studies with Multimedia Computerizable Documentation", which brought forth very complex issues of measure, indicators and categories which would establish norms for comparison of cultures. It was recognised that while analytical studies could be done and should be done, it was necessary to recognize the very nature of the fluid dynamics of a culture. In the next seminar, the Indira Gandhi National Centre for the Arts went a little further in exploring what constituted Cultural Identity and Development. Undoubtedly, this is a world-wide debate and many conferences have been held both under the aegis of Unesco and independently. The IGNCA's Conference was different because it focussed attention on the nature of Cultural Identity through a discussion on the findings of actual pilot studies conducted in different parts of rural India. The proceedings of this Seminar constituted the First Volume, entitled *Interface of Cultural Identity and Development.* A stage had now been reached not only to speak of the Interface of Cultural Identity and Development, but also to suggest positive strategies for integrating all that could be understood by the term 'Indigenous Cultural Knowledge and Skills' into the processes and programmes of, what is called, 'Development'. These seminars brought together theorists as also people who had worked at the field level in different parts of Asia as also different domains of human activity. It was clear from the discussion, as is also evident from the papers included in this Volume, that most participants were of the view that there was need to re-think and, therefore, design appropriate cultural information models which could be used by the policy-makers and planners. Many amongst the participants were clearly of the view that some of the most creative aspects of human endeavour relating to his or her immediate environment, rearing of families, indigenous skills and techniques, were not fully used or positively employed in the programmes of socio-economic development. Thus, the indigenous cultural knowledge and the indigenous knowledge of skills become marginalised. Consequently, often the authentic Self of a culture is uprooted, alienated and disempowered. The experience of many Asian countries — Indonesia, Japan, Vietnam, Thailand, Sri Lanka and Korea — has brought to the fore the unnecessary tension which has been created between the dynamics of a uniform monolithic model of development and world-views and lifestyle as evident in the multiple models of social order still extant in many parts of Asia. The participants were also clear that a sizable body of information and knowledge regarding environment, natural resources, agro-techniques and much else is transmitted through verbal and non-verbal modes of communication. All this is either negated or not cognized in the evolution of policies on development by nation-states. There was unanimity on the view that the notion of development could not be restricted to measures of GNP and GDP or only economic development measured in terms of surplus money and power of purchase, but, had to include human-development so that the creative potential of each individual and community could be exploited to the fullest. No longer was it advisable to count human beings as economically-disposable units.

Many papers in this Volume refer to the need for integrating indigenous and modern technologies, modern science and ancient wisdom and practically all cautioned against the risk of deculturisation and cultural alienation.

Several authors in the Volume have suggested the evolution of plural models for a programme of sustainable development for diverse parts of the world. 'Decentralisation in planning', 'plurality of models', 'inclusiveness' of all sections of population were the key words of this discourse.

At a more fundamental level, these papers also ask the question: Can a world-view based on man's domination over nature sustain this Earth? These papers also question the very principle of uniformity of cultures or growth patterns of the human species. The recognition of diversity and of plurality within a universality of approach and possibilities of dialogue is the running-thread. The adoption of the principle of complementarity in its most scientific connotation and not conflict and linear progress, was recommended by all. A conclusion which was evident from the discussion, was that in most countries of Asia, the notion of viewing developmental sectors separate from non-developmental. sectors was both illogical and counterproductive. All dimensions of the human constituted development. A socio-economic man could only be truly productive if he or she was also a harmoniously balanced person recognizing difference and diversity. He could be creative only within a milieu of mutual interdependence and inter-connections and not in the competition of the market place.

The discussion at the Seminar, naturally, concentrated then on what constitutes modelling societies and how a society can be modelled? Many suggestions were put forth. Most advised against acceptance of derived uniform global models based on linearity on the one hand, and freezing of cultures as museum pieces in specific historical situations, on the other. There was a very lively discussion on what constitutes 'creativity','cultural heritage', 'empowerment of gender'. The participants pressed the need for the establishment of more meaningful networks of information and cultural communication within countries, nations and the world. Prof. B.N. Saraswati has touched upon the details of the discussions and the distinctive perspectives of many distinguished people. I hope that we have been able to bring together the different but important voices on a global issue. The moot question remains whether there is the inevitability of a global village and globalisation on the basis of homogenisation or whether each unique human being, individually and collectively, should have a global consciousness while being deeply rooted to his specificity with a respect of diversity.

Prologue

Francis Childe

The organisers of our forum have proposed that I speak of whether or not there can be an Asian Model of Development. Before I take up this challenge, I feel obliged to cite an old adage: 'The sage asks questions; the fool answers them'. So rather than try to provide any definitive answer — and thereby betray my own culture's traditional wisdom — I would like to suggest some possible points of view from which we may be able to give depth to the question of 'endogenous models of development', or what the United Nations has termed the 'cultural dimension of development'. And I would like to do this by asking you to consider how the enormous global problems facing humankind on the Earth today cannot be seen apart from *culture*.

The concept of culture is difficult to define — a liquid in an age of solids, as it has been described. However, we would not be far wrong if we were to characterise it as everything that we create, preserve, and transmit as a group, or — in a wider context — as a species. Such a definition has the advantage of encompassing culture both in the restricted sense of the arts, and in the broader sense of a 'whole way of life, material, intellectual and spiritual'. Culture, then, is something fashioned by humankind: it comprises all the expressions of our creativity, including language, science and technology, architecture, literature, music and art. It is an intimate part of the way we live, the way we think, and the way we see the world. It includes all our beliefs, attitudes, customs, and social relations. Culture transmits to us an intrinsic understanding of the way the world works, and leads us to see what is important within that world. In a word, culture represents our whole system of values, those conscious and explicit as well as those that are unconscious and implicit.

Culture seen in this light — our cultures — cannot, indeed must not, be viewed apart from the other great issues of our day, whether the destruction of the environment, the population explosion, or whatever. The global crisis facing humanity at the dawn of the 21st century is, more than anything else, a reflection of our collective values, behaviour and life-style. In short, we are, as a species, the agents of our own misfortune — and indeed, of the very Earth's misfortune.

Is it not a curious thing that, at the very time that our existence on the planet has become a threat not just to ourselves but also to the biosphere which spawned us, we have for the first time the means, if not the wisdom, to do something about it. So while humankind's collective presence on Earth has new-found global consequences, simultaneously there has arisen the possibility of our developing a global awareness of our situation and of the repercussions of our communal actions both for ourselves and for all elements of life in the world around us. Globalisation is a material phenomenon to be sure — global warming, for example, affects us all, no matter where we live nor from where the pollutants derive. But thanks to the power of modern communications technology and media, it also exhibits the intangible quality we call awareness of consciousness — what happens in Bosnia, or Rwanda, or even, for that matter, on the slopes of Mount Everest or the banks of the Ganges, is now immediately accessible, *as perception*, to people all over the world. The analogy of humankind as an infant, taking its first tentative steps, uttering its first words, becoming not only aware of itself but aware too of the world around it, immediately springs to mind and rings almost too true for comfort.

At the same time, this growing awareness of ourselves and of the world around us has had other, unforeseen, consequences. One of the most significant of these has been the rapid breakdown of old structures and control mechanisms — external in terms of political and economic structures, and internal in terms of shared values and codes of behaviour. This is accompanied by a lack — at least for the present — of coherent new structures, of new values and codes of behaviour with which to respond appropriately to the completely new situation in which we find ourselves. The result is that in many parts of the world, this uncertainty is attended by a kind of instinctive and frequently turbulent retreat into traditionalism, tribalism, and narrow ethnic or religious identities, where all the emphasis is on the difference between cultures and peoples, and none on their sameness. It is as if something old and massive is in its death throes, and something new and as yet undefined is struggling to be born in its shadow.

So the real question, or rather the *first* question, that we have to face may be that of the survival of human civilisation as we know it, as well as of a large part of the biosphere. As the old adage has it, 'Nothing focuses a person's mind so well as his (or her!) impending death'. I wonder whether we, as a species, understand that this may well be our collective situation today.

Now I would like to come back to what I said earlier: culture cannot, indeed must not, be divorced from the other great issues of our day. And I would like to illustrate this remark by examining two of the most pressing problems facing the world at the dawn of the 21st century — population and the environment — and the manner in which they relate to the culture, and cultures, of humankind.

The recent UN Summit on Population and Development held in Cairo brought home to the world as never before the scale of the human population explosion. The United Nations estimates that by the year 2050, the world's total population will reach somewhere between 8 and 12 billion people, from its current level of about 5.5 billion. The current increase is well over 90 million persons annually, which is equivalent to the entire population of Mexico. And while it took 125 years for the world's population to increase from 1 to 12 billion, the last increment of one billion persons was achieved in one-tenth of that time, in 13 years!

While human reproduction is clearly a biological function, there are also potent cultural imperatives at work. Everything associated with sexuality, marriage and childbearing has vital cultural and religious connotations that go far beyond the mere 'biology' involved. Every culture has definite teachings and norms in this regard, along with powerful inducements to behave in this way or that, and frequently also unpleasant sanctions for those who do not conform — not only in this world, but even in the next!

But in spite of this, the great majority of population programmes throughout the world have concentrated from the very beginning almost entirely on the technical aspects of family planning (provision of birth control devices, information on fertility cycles and conception, types of services, achievement of quantitative targets, etc.), while almost no attention has been given to the *socio-cultural* contexts in which such programmes are implemented. And yet religious beliefs, traditional relationships between men and women, family size and structure, marriage age, the status of women, taboos on the mere mention of sex (even in its clinical sense) in public or even in private, to name but a few aspects, are manifestly of crucial importance. As long and often bitter experience has taught us, family planning programmes are not merely a matter of providing contraceptive means and information: they touch the very fabric of the individual and of society and involve the most intimate physical, cultural and even spiritual levels of those concerned.

In short, family planning is essentially a programme of socio-cultural change. Or, to put it another way, the population explosion is not only a biological phenomenon; it is also without doubt rooted deeply in our socio-cultural norms and behaviour.

A second illustration of the integral relationship between culture and the state of the world in our time may be found in the relation between biological and cultural diversity. Not only are cultural and biological diversity intimately linked, we may even say that they are aspects of the same phenomenon: adaptation through diversity. Nature's response to different geographical and climatic conditions results in biological diversity, and thus a multitude of diverse species and life forms arise in adaptation to local conditions. On the other hand, *homo sapiens* is the only species living on the Earth today that has the potential to exploit every feasible ecological niche on the planet's surface, and this adaptability has been reflected in humankind's *cultural* diversity. In this way, not only the plants and animals but also the human cultural patterns that we find in the humid tropics are quite different from those we find in the Tundra or in the arid temperate zones. So, whereas nature produces different species (biodiversity) that adapt themselves to living in relative harmony within any given set of natural conditions, so too humankind develops different cultures (cultural diversity) that conform to local conditions using the same survival strategy of adaptation through diversification. Indeed, seen in this light, cultural diversity may well be a reflection of the very life principle itself.

Now, however, as modern industrial society (and its attendant values) has begun to exert its dominance over the most isolated parts of the globe, and over peoples and cultures that have existed for thousands of years in equilibrium with their natural environment, we are witnessing the rapid disappearance both of different life forms and of different cultures. As these distinct peoples and cultures disappear, so, too do the environments which sustained them. And as ecosystems disappear, so do the cultures which arose in them. In short, the loss of cultural diversity and of biodiversity are two aspects of the same event, or if you will, two sides of the same coin.

This linkage may go far deeper, in fact. It is precisely thanks to the enormous variety of species produced by nature that the Earth's ecosystem is able to respond and adapt to changing conditions, thus engendering a sustainable biosphere. Genetically speaking, and to borrow an appropriate metaphor, nature has learnt never to put all her eggs in one basket. The ecosystem's safeguard against a rapid change in external conditions therefore consists of plurality and diversity, and one of the most troubling aspects of the present accelerated loss of biodiversity is that nature — and the ecosystem as a whole — finds that its capacity to respond to the environmental changes being provoked by humankind is now being seriously compromised and diminished.

Here I would reiterate that something very similar is at work in the area of cultural diversity, and that we are now witnessing the rapid destruction of age-old cultures and traditions all over the planet to our extreme peril and that of future generations. Unlike modern industrial society, many traditional cultures existing up to the present from ages past still enable people to live in symbiosis with their natural environments. Such peoples and cultures have often been active agents in promoting the ecosystem's health and biodiversity. And it is within these traditional cultures that many now believe the seeds of a new culture — able and willing to live in creative harmony with its constituent parts — might be found. If the unique and particular understandings of humanity's different cultures are lost or simply reduced to the lowest common denominator, then it is clear that something precious, and perhaps even essential, for our collective survival will have been squandered. Their world-view, their values and their deeply innate respect for nature and life are the very elements that may form the basis of the profound change in attitude and behaviour that alone can engender a global culture capable of reacting responsively, and responsibly, to global change. A true, creative globalisation of culture, then, may more properly involve the induction of diversity into a common framework, where synergy (inclusion) rather than entropy (exclusion) is the operative principle. In short, it is not a question of achieving *either* unity *or* diversity, but rather of finding unity *in* diversity.

Humanity is at a great crossroads today. Our collective response to this conjuncture of forces and events will affect not only our own future but, as we are all beginning to realise, that of the entire biosphere. Either a new world will be born or the whole world, as we know it, may well perish. In any event, the old world cannot go on, for it carries within it the seeds of its own destruction: in other words, of its lack of sustainability.

In searching for the source of this new world or new world order, as it is sometimes called, we often have recourse to the fundamental ideals, first expressed in the 18th century, of inalienable human rights. What a powerful principle this is, and how strong has been its influence all over the world, perhaps never more so than today. But there is another side of the coin, for to claim rights without an attendant sense of responsibility — or duty, if you will — may be fulfilling *individually*, yet leads us only to the current *collective* relationship between rights — the great contribution of the West — and duties, the great understanding of the East. In a word, rights and duties are mutually dependent, just as are East and West.

And it may well be that it is only as part of such a relationship — between our unique inviolable nature as individuals and our collective responsibilities towards ourselves and all organic life on Earth — that life can have any real meaning.

Meaning implies relationship and can in no wise refer to one thing or part alone. Meaning comes from understanding the relationships of different parts to one another and to the whole. There can be no meaning for my life, or for our lives, except insofar as I, or we, relate to one another and to the whole. The very essence of meaning is this intimate, irreducible relation with the whole: the whole of myself; the whole of humankind; the whole of life on Earth. And yes, perhaps, the whole of Creation. Without this sense of relationship, our lives have no objective meaning.

Here I would like to quote President Vaclav Havel of the Czech Republic, who alluded to this very question in an address he gave recently in the Independence Hall in Philadelphia. President Havel spoke of the awareness of our being anchored in the Earth and the Universe — the awareness that we are not here alone, nor for ourselves alone, but are an integral part of higher, mysterious entities against whom it is not advisable to blaspheme.

This forgotten awareness is encoded in all religions. Cultures anticipate it in various forms. It is one of the things that form the basis of man's understanding of himself, of his place in the world and ultimately of the world as such. This awareness endows us with the capacity for self-transcendence.

Politicians at international forums may reiterate a thousand times that the basis of the new world order must be universal respect for human rights, but it will mean nothing as long as this imperative does not derive from the respect of the miracle of Being, the miracle of the universe, the miracle of nature, the miracle of our own existence.

Only someone who submits to the authority of the universal order and of creation, who values the right to be a part of it and a participant in it, can genuinely value himself and his neighbours and thus honour their rights as well.

It has often been said that knowledge is power. And indeed it is. But power, as we see so clearly in the world today, in and of itself is not only useless, but even dangerous. Knowledge, and the power that it spawns — especially in the field of science and technology — must be counterbalanced by wisdom, the very essence of which President Havel touches on in the short passage I have just quoted. And the well-spring of this wisdom is to be found in the most ancient traditions and cultures: in Taoism and Zen, in the understandings of the Hopi and the Maya Indians, in the *Veda*s and the Psalms, in the very origins of human culture itself. As a Tibetan monk told us recently, 'The state of the world today is nothing other than a reflection of our own inner world, and of our greed. If we wish to change the world, we must change ourselves'. Or, as Mahatma Gandhi once said, 'There is enough for everyone's need, but not for everyone's greed'.

It is this wisdom, based on a profound respect for nature, for one another, and indeed for the mystery of all creation, that we must rediscover, first in our own cultures, and then in the cultures of others. Only in this way can each and everyone of us make our own unique contribution to the emerging global culture — whose fate is far from certain, yet whose destiny we cannot but sense as being our own . . . both as a right and as a responsibility.

Contents

Introduction

Baidyanath Saraswati

It is all very well to talk about the 'global village'. It is wonderful to have a planetary network of communication. It is exciting to use the internet. But what if all this means the darker side of the dawn? The ultimate issue in the problematics are: What is the 'global village' like? What is its approach to human development? How is it related to 'untranscended technology'? Can we see ourselves and hear our voices in the new technocentric society? Can we distinguish the drop of water from the water of the drop? Can we establish external relations without developing internal relations? Would not globalization lead to sterile uniformity?

This collection of essays is the second of a series of IGNCA publications on 'Culture and Development', based on papers presented at a Unesco-sponsored expert meeting on 'Integration of Endogenous Cultural Dimension into Development', held at the Indira Gandhi National Centre for the Arts in New Delhi on 19-25 April 1995. These essays aim at: (a) conceptualizing culture, (b) planning cultural policies, (c) challenging development infallibility, (d) considering the cultural dimension, and (e) building cultural models. The present volume takes up some of the aspects of culture and development which were dealt with in the preceding volume, *Interface of Cultural Identity and Development.*

Both the volumes pose a long list of well-formulated questions. Questioning leads us to a state of perplexity, a very high state when something in us is awakened. We know that we do not know.

Conceptualizing Culture

Culture is a common word. Each culture defines itself in terms of its organic nature that distinguishes it from other cultures. Technical definitions, provided by philosophers, anthropologists, sociologists, and culturologists are numerous. Many of these academic definitions, which use the instrument of logos, are standardized models of the mind. The self-definition of a culture, which approaches mythos, is a moral message already integrated into society. The modern tendency is to reduce mythos to logos. The concern of this volume is to define culture in relation to development.

Unesco defines culture as a set of distinctive spiritual and material, intellectual and emotional characteristics which define a society or social group. In addition to the arts and letters, it encompasses ways of life, the fundamental rights of the person, value systems, traditions and beliefs (1982 Mexico Conference).

The importance of this definition lies in its globality, but it has certain limitations. It does not take into account the various manifestations of culture. Nor does it seem to offer an alternative. In fact, it is grounded in the Western world-view with subjective intention.

The authors of these essays have considered the various conceptions of culture at different levels of diversity. Their cultural backgrounds should have important consequences.

In the prologue, Francis Childe reinforces the Unesco definition from another angle. As is evident in the philosophical understanding, culture represents our whole system of values, those conscious and explicit as well as those that are unconscious and implicit.

We might go further still and lay stress on the multiplicity of perspectives on culture. S.C. Malik points out the error in anthropological-ethnographic knowledge: 'There is an inherent unidimensionality and linearity in the domain of objective rationality which blocks out experience (subjective and intuition). Understanding culture is not about information categories, it is a learning process that can only come in experiencing, and hence the linking of the inside experiencing world and the outside analytical one is crucial.'

Defining culture is terms of 'man in nature', Baidyanath Saraswati constructs fivefold conceptual types, namely 'dreamtime culture', 'cosmocentric culture', 'theocentric culture', 'anthropocentric culture' and 'technocentric culture'. Of these, the first three types maintain that life and culture originate dependently in the total context of divine nature which is changing and yet not changing. The other two types form a built environment disconnected with nature. Here the system of man and the system of machine are in conflict. Defined in this way the primacy of an essentialist conception of culture lies in its 'focus' rather than in its context. P.K. Misra takes the idea of cultural focus further when he writes that 'each culture is, in a way, unique. In the process of its growth it develops its own emphases'.

Minoru Kasai touches upon a crucial problem that could easily be the starting point for understanding culture in relation to development. He deals with it systematically: 'Tradition as culture,' he writes, 'has been used frequently as a simple contrast to development and as such has taken on almost a pejorative meaning. Traditionalism refers to a situation where one takes the past uncritically as a model for limitation. Thus, nothing new arises from tradition identified with traditionalism. This is a narrow and unhelpful understanding of tradition. Tradition in terms of cultural identity indicates the capacity of a society to maintain continuity, coherence and integrity, inspired and sustained by meaning. The slogan *wakon-yoasi* (Japanese spirit and Western science), which seems to show a rigid relationship between tradition and development and has inspired development in Japan, reveals a problematic and fatal condition of the modern world.'

New terms have been invented in other languages and cultures too, to take up the burden. Thailand, for instance, has coined *wattana-dharma* for culture, which, as Amara Raksasataya has mentioned, means 'development, growth or evolution from an original state, things that make a group grow, a group's way of life, order, harmonious progress of the country, and good moral standard of the people'. In India, the Hindu word *sanskriti* is used for culture, even though there is an inherent contradiction between the simple exegesis of *sanskriti* (from *samskara*, divine process of body cleansing) as the spiritual ordering of life and the conventional meaning of culture as man's cultivation of material objects. The precariousness of interpreting an indigenous word to fit into the shoes of an alien conception of culture is quite obvious, but this is a common experience flowing from the existential interpretation of a given context.

Conceptions of culture are valid in the contexts where they were originally conceived. There is no justification in extrapolating them. The 'modern' conception is taken as an incontestable given; it claims to stand for a 'reality' culture which presents itself in everyday life. The 'ancient' conception is re-introduced from outside; it allows itself to be discovered by others and shows itself as something unique. Since the old conception is not lived from the inside, the reconstructed elements hardly have a pattern of intelligibility. Believing that the old is 'unreal' in the contemporary perspective, experts and researchers insist on stitching the ancient and the modern together as something wholly new. Holism is fashionable; it is neither stable not consistent in itself. To aggregate the elements of cultural conceptions is to compromise with error.

Planning Cultural Policies

The conception of culture is made more explicit by showing the relationship between ordered human activities and the defined areas of social life. Culture has to find a balance when the great turning comes; it makes changes that are within its reach. But the real challenge comes from the ever-increasing interference from outside. A normal culture is concerned with its identity: being-in-its-body as its being-in-the world. Hence it adopts a set of cultural policies to strengthen its foundations and save its real identity.

Unesco has listed the following points to be emphasized in cultural policies: cultural identity; cultural dimension of development; cultural heritage; artistic and intellectual creation and art education; relationship of culture with education, science and communication, planning, administration and cooperation (the 1982 Mexico Conference).

The principles identified by the Mexico Conference are, for obvious reasons, addressed to its member states. While the spirit of the recommendations illuminates all nations, the governmental responses to the various components of cultural policies are unequal.

India's national cultural policy is still in a formative stage. To consider a practical policy for multicaste, multilingual, multireligious India is not an easy task. Rapid and drastic changes have led to homogenisation of life-styles, decay of multiple models of cultured expression, loss of community, erosion of individuality, and an increasing gulf between creative artists and thinkers and the rest. The thoughts of Ananda Coomaraswamy and Mahatma Gandhi, to which Ram Bapat has drawn us, 'should provide practical guidelines for linking cultural heritage with strategies for sustainable development'. But will India as a nation ever enter into the labyrinth of Gandhi's vision of self-government? Can a nation of traditional cultures compromise with a policy of maximum consumerism and minimum spiritualism?

In some cases, such as Thailand, where government agencies are directly involved in cultural promotion activities, as Raksastaya writes, ways have been found to valorize the new experience and to promote 'loyalty to the key institutions (the country, religions and the monarch), family and communal life, national and local tradition, language, discipline and values, virtues and ethics, way of life and folk wisdom, way of dressing, arts, tourism, and cultural development along with economic development'. An evolutionary sequence of cultural development, beginning from the natural state and going to the nation-state, is offered to demonstrate the forward march of the Thai nation.

Considering the *kairos* of culture, one cannot help saying that the modern nations engaged in the progress of high technology, industry, urbanization, socialization and intercommunication of all sorts of information, march behind the progress of humanity. The example of Japan is an eye-opener. As is pointed out by Kasai, in pre-war Japan development began under traditional auspices. It was possible and effective because of a deep respect for tradition among the Japanese. But, in connection with militaristic nationalism, tradition was exploited with the motive of building a nation-state. Subordination, manipulation and exploitation of tradition by excessive nationalism led to policies oppressive within and expensive without and to the tragic ruins of Hiroshima and Nagasaki.

Placing the nation above and beyond culture is a fatal mistake. Culture as a human invariant presupposes interdependence and mutual dependence among all forms of human life across the narrow boundaries of nations. There is even more: When cultural policies are governed by national policies, a downward spiral in the quality of culture follows. Cultures, or cultural communities, lose not only their freedom but also their ability for self-development.

Challenging Development's Infallibility

'Development' is a crucial expression of the New Age. For some it is the embodiment of economic progress, modernity, industrialization and science. For others, it evokes an esoteric or even bizarre perception of the contemporary world divided today into 'developed', 'underdeveloped', and 'developing' countries. The index of development is determined by growth in national production. But, as the truth reveals itself, in terms of human development those who are economically developed are culturally underdeveloped and those who are economically poor are culturally rich.

Unesco defines development as a complex, holistic and mutidimensional process, which goes beyond mere economic growth and integrates all the dimensions of life and all the energies of a community, all of whose members must share in the economic and social transformation effort and in the benefits that result therefrom. The principle is therefore proposed that development must be founded on the will of each society and express its profound identity (1982 Mexico Conference).

The ground reality is different. The development ideology announces itself and proclaims infallibility. Saraswati demands the exercise of critical thinking in which 'development appears more or less a separate construct governed by its own laws; it is a new culture, a new spirituality, a new path to salvation. The infallibility of development comes from technological advance taking a certain direction in which we acquire superior power of disorder over order'. But surprisingly, and not so surprisingly, the dilemma of development is denied.

This does not mean that people are unaware of the problem. Their harrowing experiences have been exemplified by several authors. P.K. Misra, for instance, points out that the problems posed by ageing in India have grown as a result of the development process itself. Sachchidananda draws our attention to the development experience among the tribal communities in India: 'In certain cases tribals have been hurt rather than helped on account of the development effort. In more cases it resulted in development for the few and destitution for the many. The experience of the pains of development is very poignant'. Ashish Bose's case studies of socio-cultural pitfalls in development planning show that there is considerable cultural illiteracy among policy-makers, planners, administrators and experts (Indian as well as foreign), which comes in the way of the success of many development projects launched with good intentions.

Briefly, the Asian experience of development is by and large barren and alienating. As Kadai describes it, 'Both the success and the failure of development raise a fundamental question about the meaning of life. This question is not confined to the Japanese but is a universal problem, because the success or failure of development have given man the power to destroy all life on earth. American native people (red people), are a tragic reminder of the violence of development. Today, success ideology of development cannot be accepted uncritically unless one is totally uprooted.'

Here we need only stress that faced with the modern development process, the 'democracy of the haves', or 'inner colonialism', or 'bureaucratic tradition', has created everywhere two nations: that of the minority haves and that of the majority have-nots. Further, the tendency of limiting development to the techno-economic field has reduced mankind to the status of a disposable commercial unit.

Considering the Cultural Dimension

The question of cultural dimension is a rather difficult one, but it is necessary to consider it if we are to open the door of emancipation from many of the problems of development.

According to Unesco, the cultural dimension of development embraces all the psychosociological components which, like the economic, technological and scientific factors, help to improve the material and intellectual life of the populations without introducing any violent change into their way of life or modes of thought, and at the same time contribute to the technical success of the development plans or projects. (*The Cultural Dimension of Development*, Unesco 1995).

There is a difference between a purely epistemological approach that defines culture in terms of the vertical dimension and a practical approach that seeks possibilities around the horizontal plane. Culture may respond to both situations differently, depending on the perception of development and the preferred world shaped by its own imagination. Some cultures may consider both the vertical and the horizontal dimensions; others may lay emphasis largely on the horizontal plane.

The distinctive nature of the vertical dimension of culture is considered by several authors. Keshav Malik, for instance, points out the unique nature of human organization: 'men without organizational power but only with the power of their spirit, heart or mind chart the longer path'. S.C. Malik highlights the significance of the mythic domain of culture by which 'humankind itself is animated and acts as a link between the inner dimension of spirit and the outer world of form'. Kasai considers the 'sacred reality as culture'. R.P. Misra emphasizes the 'reverence for all that exists in nature'. Saraswati refers to the aborigines' dreamtime culture, which has a 'spiritual understanding of nature'.

The horizontal dimension breeds the supremacy of the man of matter. The anthropic principle claims that the universe of man has no other structure than its own, and that culture is an unfolding within the human order of space and time. This seems to be the central concern but not the central experience of the authors of these essays.

The theme of development is treated at the local, national and international levels. Tan Chung provides a comprehensive survey of the socio-economic development of China in the light of civilizational dynamics. He holds the view that 'by attempting an endogenous development, China, or any nation, can't get away from exogenous influences — be they exopathetic diseases or exophilic blessings. Yet, it is in the context of globalization that there is the need to emphasise endogenous development.' Sang-Bok Han presents a Korean example of the integration of endogenous cultural dimension in socio-economic development, which "may be regarded, on the one hand, as a consequence of the combination of certain traditional cultural values, modern science and technology, and on the other as a consequence of the combination of non-rationality and rationality in terms of Western usage". R.P. Misra is of the view that if there is a possibility of a synthesis of the Western and the Indian paradigms of development, we must work for it and endeavour to operationalize it. Gandhi tried to do this in his own lifetime.

Meutia Swasono refers to the case of the indigenous population of Indonesia, consisting of various ethnic groups leading a variety of life-styles. Considering the fact that these 'local cultures' constitute development potential, she points out that 'neglecting these non-economic factors may cause development to become more expensive, socio-culturally ineffective, economically inefficient and wasteful'. Highlighting the importance of the local religion of Indonesia. Boedhihartono questions the credibility of the categorical terms 'indigenous', 'backward' and 'primitive', which are 'based more on the technological or civilizational level classification, though many of them are more generous, pacific and probably more honest, from the moral point of view better shaped and nurtured'. Based on realities in Vietnam, Ngo duc Thinh looks for a close relationship between 'local knowledge' and social development. In his opinion, 'to a modern society the local knowledge does not lose any of its scientific and practical value'.

Truly speaking, the authors of these essays do not give a prescription for development. What they discuss here is the state of culture in the context of development planning especially in the Asian nations. The purpose is not to condemn development efforts but to find a way towards integrating the cultural dimension into development.

Building Cultural Models

We are concretely aware that the method of development based on the experience of the industrialized world has not brought about either peace and harmony or alleviation of poverty. Nor has it ensured socio-economic equality or fostered value systems conducive to normal aspects of life. There is a need to challenge the ever-growing dominance of technocentric development. There is a need to redefine development in terms of culture, and not the other way round. There is a need to make man and man, and man and nature, live in relative harmony. There is a need to work towards a new way of thinking and acting. There is a need to move from the culture of consumerism to the culture of humanism. There is a need to build new cultural models which can tolerate the diversities of unity rather than enforce the unity of diversities.

We are convinced that the trend of globalization is threatening, its political consequences are far-reaching. A global network of communication means a global mode of thinking and acting, focusing on monoculture, monolanguage, and a common mind-set. Global commerce means a global consumer culture. A global consumer culture means sterile uniformity. A global village means the empire of a new elite — marketing and advertising people — dominating the future of mankind. The authors of these essays have different ways of describing this.

According to Bapat, 'globalization as it operates today is bound to threaten the plurality and diversity of all cultures'. Tan Chung identifies a trend in globalization that shows 'the hegemonic behaviour of certain great powers to monopolize the world market, to dominate the world development trends, to impose their own value judgements on the weaker nations'. He cites an obvious example of this: 'Both the Chinese and the Indian peasants share the worry that globalization would ultimately mean their marginalization from the mainstream of the country's development.' Saraswati also writes about this uneasy feeling of 'human cultures situated today in a technocentric framework of global interdependence created by a new kind of state system with multinational organizations' having market interest. Expressing dissatisfaction over the ugly and unjust state-centric development with global objectives, he pleads for *swaraj* (self rule) in development, as perceived by Gandhi: '*Swaraj* is complete independence of alien control and complete economic independence. It has two other ends. One of them is truth, the other is non-violence.' Making the setting of the problem explicit, he adds: 'If we aspire to *swaraj* in development, we must strive for *swadesi* (indigenous) development. If we aspire to a global village, we must set our house in order.'

Human hope confronts development. Experiments are made to offer an alternative to the Western model of development. P.D. Premasiri presents a case of the Sri Lankan experiment with the Sarvodaya model, based on Gandhi's philosophy of *sarvodaya* (upliftment of all). The hopes and the claims of the *sarvodaya* movement, inspired and led by A.T. Ariyaratne, are that 'it offers an alternative development model which is rooted in Sri Lankan culture and has a universal moral appeal. But as he admits regretfully, the day when such a philosophy and programme of development will win wide acceptance in Sri Lanka, to the extent of moving political forces to adopt it through constraints imposed by popular will and making a real impact at the national level, does not appear to be near'.

Sachchidananda introduces an experiment in alternative development carried out among the Santal, the largest tribe of eastern India. Giving the background of tribals coming under the sway of large industrial, mining and irrigation projects, he examines at length the activities of the Badalo Foundation. The success story of this non-governmental voluntary organization 'has shown ways in which the tribals in this area and other people can help themselves'.

Another success story is told by Sanjit (Bunker) Roy, who has dedicated his life to the cause of development through rural education in Rajasthan. Based on more than two decades of experiment, he presents a simple model called the Barefoot College, which "respects anyone who is prepared to work with his\her hands; anyone who is prepared to learn; anyone who is prepared to share skills and knowledge and treats others as equals; anyone who has no hang-ups, ego-problems and anyone who does not hide behind his\her degree to cover up incompetence, insecurity, and has the courage to say: I do not know and I am willing to learn". It is claimed that this model can be replicated wherever there are people from the rural areas.

Making a virtue of globalization and high-tech development, these simple isolated experiments may appear small and insignificant. But their success stories might well suggest the very symbiosis needed in our time.

As new experiments are introduced, an opportunity to build cultural models arises. Cultural models are not theoretical models; they operate in real life. In this context S.C. Malik raises several critical questions, claiming that cultural models provide a resource for making sense of experience; and that 'the notion of a cultural model is a way of describing knowledge that cannot in and of itself account for how this knowledge is used, even though it is produced from repeated experience'. Keshav Malik cautions that 'the emphasis in any model for human development, even when it tries to highlight material or institutional factors and frameworks, must not overlook or underestimate the fateful role of ideas and beliefs, that is, of reason as well as of unreason in the destiny of humanity'.

From the essays presented here what comes out clearly is a 'cultural information model' for Asia. By this we mean the codex, or the inventory, of fundamental themes and elements of culture forming, freezing and fostering human life in a particular social group. This model contains information regarding:

(a) process and extent of integration of endogenous insights, knowledge and techniques with exogenous modern science and technology, and the indigenous response to self-organizing and low-cost innovations such as biogas, solar energy, etc.;

(b) local knowledge of nature and the environment, of agriculture and other subsistence mechanisms, of health and healing practices, of social perception and population management, of rules, ranks and gender issues;

(c) textual and oral traditions, verbal and non-verbal modes of communication, linkage of formal (modern) and informal (traditional) systems of education, language and literature, and the role of religion in the integration of community life;

(d) nature and extent of decentralization of development planning and administration, contribution by people at the grassroots, NGOs, pressure groups, local or regional and trans-regional development agencies;

(e) people's sacred world-views, myths, rituals, and artistic manifestations;

(f) endogenous conceptions of the good life, truth, non-violence, freedom, equality, peace, and poverty preached by great religions and practised by such luminaries as Confucius, Buddha, Zen masters, Natsume, Gandhi, Vinoba and others who saw visionary schemes of human development; and

(g) people's experience of social and economic development under various political systems.

Finally, viewed in the light of the Asian experience, it must be said that the future of humanity will be determined not by turning the world into a technocentric global village of markets with fire-arms and industry, but by rebuilding a culture and faith in which the cosmic, divine, and human dimensions are suitably integrated.

1

Touchstones of Experience

Rethinking Cultural Information Models

S.C. Malik

> *. . . sound and silence would sound simultaneously; presence from absence and again its dissolution. . . . In that first morning haze India was a world without things; nothing was separated from another. There were no backgrounds, no spaces, no divisions, no fields which things were reclining and appearing. There was nothing in space and nothing in time. Nothing happened and it was all nowhere. All there was, was a pulsating presence: movement . . . perhaps an invitation to draw out of this a perspectival world the multitude of simultaneous perspectives that made it simultaneously present and absent. Perhaps it was an invitation to a birth. . . . The old Cartesian mind with neo-Kantian justifications had used the weak stomach to return to sanity, but there had been no birth. . . . My body and the world were in Euclidean space and in Newtonian time. . . .*
>
> **Antonio T. de Nicolas** (1976:xvi)

Humankind today faces a crisis at many levels, despite (or because) the magnitude of resources available as a consequence of tremendous technological and scientific growth. The idea of progress and development begins with the positivist-reductionist, empiricist and anthropocentric enterprise in Europe in the 17th century. Underlying contemporary challenges are certain unquestioned assumptions (e.g. rationality, linear time, subjectivity *vs.* objectivity, nature *vs.* man). Although outdated by Modern Science, these paradigms dominate decision-makers who continue to ignore many of the alternate world-views of indigenous non-Western cultures which are very relevant today. This is the perspective of interconnectedness, simultaneity and multilayeredness of reality; of a seamless whole, a continuum in which we — earth with its creatures and the universe — are all enmeshed within a Unified Force-Field, Energy or Consciousness. This overarching energy-field is expressed in various cultures through the mythic domain within which experiencing takes place, allowing for the psychic maintenance of socio-cultural variations, as is the case in India and other developing societies. This domain is crucial in understanding indigenous cultures; it is the source wherein lies our collective memory. Modern man has ignored this dimension at its own peril, although it is trying to create a new world order with the myth of history, the myth of materialism and the myth of science; believing as if together these will provide answers to all our prayers, to all our questions about existence. This seeking for answers — one's identity — in externalities alone has increased desperation and alienation; it has encouraged revivalism and fundamentalism. Clearly, this myopic unidimensional viewpoint has brought many diabolical scenarios for the planet and its creatures. Has not imagination and intuitive knowledge as experience, which is the essence of living cultures, taken a back seat?

Imagination literally means to form images which come to us from we do not know where. These are reappearances in individual minds of ancient and collective images. This mythic domain — call it Jungian archetypes — is the source of creative imagination which produces great works in the sciences, the humanities and the arts. This act of experiencing — including and transcending sensuousness — available to every human being, is not merely an individual creation, because the person within this totality acts as a vehicle for Consciousness. If fulfilling human potential is the goal of development in the long run, this becomes impossible in the present model of development, in the absence of the deeper knowledge which arises from the whole brain. Can happiness and fulfilling relationships be based on the mere pursuit of jobs, technological and social progress? Each one of us is aware of this intense longing to seek one's identity, which is possible only when there is an interiorization of this creative urge. It is here that primal myths expressed through various media take one back to primordial memory when Nature and Cosmos lived in miraculous harmony. Before proceeding further let us briefly examine how we know what we know.

How do we know what we know?

Most of our lives are governed by several unconscious assumptions absorbed during the socialization process. These hidden premises are what allow us to make sense of the world, to know what we know. To go into its source requires us to have an 'experiencing' encounter with the self and the other. This is imperative if we are to correct the suicidal path along which humankind is heading. It is crucial to ponder over what and how we communicate, feel, think and experience in everyday life.

Knowing and communication may be classified functionally into three interrelated spheres, namely (see *Figs.* 1 and 2):

(i) Concepts, Symbols, Images, and abstract thought.

(ii) Experiencing — feeling and emotions.

(iii) The overarching Be-ingness.

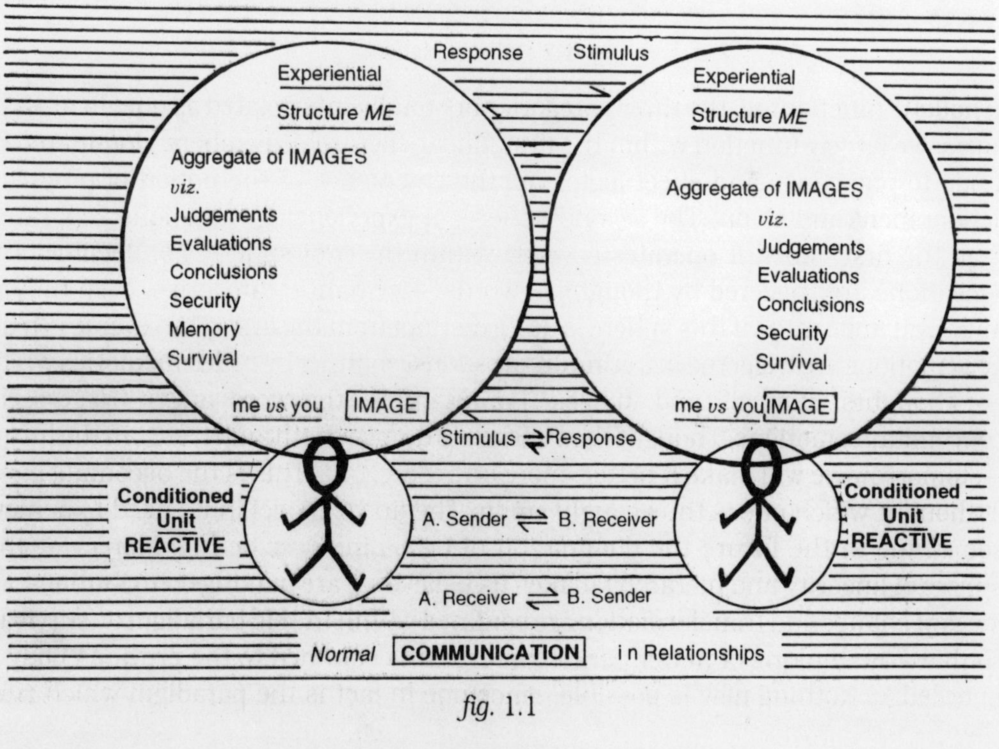

fig. 1.1

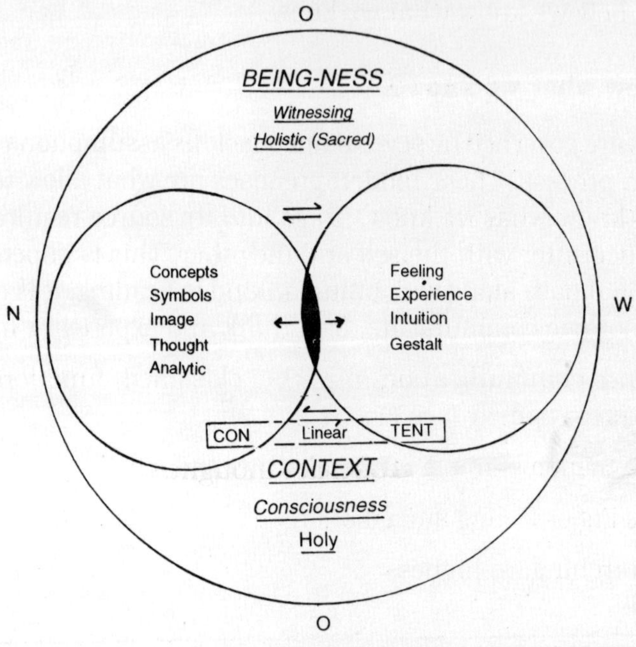

fig. 1.2 Holistic Model

In holistic functioning, the three categories are totally interrelated as one. In modern times, we largely function within the first, linear-hierarchical sphere, dominated by a one-to-one cause and effect logic, viz. the emergence of the notion of progress, development and so on. The second sphere, of experiencing, functions separately from the first, albeit it operates covertly within the first sphere, i.e., feelings and sensations are triggered by thought — words — semantic categories, even though initially it appears as if this sphere is quite distinct from the first. The reverse is true, i.e., emotions are triggered in a stimulus-response manner by coded memories which are thoughts, symbols and images. For example, the word anger triggers the concomitant emotions. Thought then wishes to do away with anger, etc., in the future — 'tomorrow we will make it better, more and more. . . . ' This is the becoming game of thought which one is thus caught up in. The linear model in its need to achieve something in the future the domination of becoming over be-ing. Moreover, this sphere of linearity and hierarchy makes us believe we are making contributions. All ideas of change and transformation are confined within the old paradigm of 'survival', so that any thinking of newer paradigms remains confined to the previous body of knowledge. Nothing new is possible, since one in fact is the paradigm which runs one's life. It is like living in a prison, imagining creating freedom outside by painting pictures within the prison, without leaving it. One thinks, believes in the illusion of experiencing the self and the other.

In order to experience the other, it is essential to be aware of one's own conditioning. Is it possible to do away with this conditioning? The first step is to be aware of this primary problem, since it is in the very understanding of this dilemma — the very limitations of the box — that the old paradigm disappears. In fact, the new and limitless cannot be understood intellectually. All this is only possible by dropping the old which functions within the context of a re-cognition. This process disallows first-hand experiencing. In this sense of re-cognition, all knowing of the new once again becomes the old. Thus, the old way is to be comfortable in the knowledge of the known. It does not allow one to be in touch with the Source, the Be-ing, which allows one to share, to be equally related to all of Creation. This kind of living is mere conceptual living, disallowing deep experiencing of the self and the other. In short, thinking about life is not living it, unless one sees that thoughts are subsets — material manifestation of Be-ingness — of the larger overarching category of Be-ing.

Thoughts are about the past and future reconstructions, about the becoming, which make us believe that we are alive. It is this becoming, this movement of thought which causes restlessness, this incessant seeking of what one has not got, away from what is — the experiencing in the now. It is from this wanting, desiring, searching for Utopias that the idea of progress and development emerges. It reflects the residues of incompletely experienced experience, or inexperienced experience. For example, this is why most of us easily recall painful and unpleasant experiences — thoughts about them — rather than the good and beautiful times; because the latter are complete experiences by themselves and have little residue as thought (merely stored as information, and not as a recall system). Hence, by this inherent logic, experiencing becomes a secondary feature, not a primary or experiential-existential state. This is what causes insecurity, which creates the need for constantly seeking new objectives. In this way is it that the behaviour of modern man is governed. As a consequence, this is how society is made up of insecure individuals who further create the concept of society that needs transformation. But can insecure individuals who make up society create a secure, peaceful and harmonious society? Thinking, limited within the paradigm stated above, has only further increased disorder and chaos. Of course, for a while there appears to be satisfaction, a feeling of achievement. But soon the old problems return, despite reaching the moon — so to speak, humanity continues to wrestle with the same old problems.

But what, one may ask, is Be-ingness? Be-ingness is not a thing; it is manifested in things. It may not be known conceptually, but experientially-existentially by a Self which transcends the boundaries of the limited person, a shadow of the Being. The reference here is to primordial reality, to experiencing *per se*, which does not arise out of any person. It is an impersonal experiencing that transcends both the experiencer and the experienced. The latter are peripheral and arise secondarily as shadows of the former. It is like listening to the commentary on a tennis or cricket match and believing it to be the match -- where action is taken place. The proof of Consciousness is that one is aware, and that it is symbolically known through the effects, the concepts, notions and ideas stored as memory.

True action lies in a kind of choiceless awareness. This implies the total functioning of all the three spheres, to be in the 'here and now' with no other purpose than to be aware, to be conscious, to be 'awake', to be 'alive'. This perception itself is action. In fact, this itself is the transformation which arises out of the eternal 'now'. While this is part of the 'Indian' heritage, it is also universal to many other cultures.

Mythic domain of cultures

Myths arise out of a broad base of the collective unconscious. There are, however, many meanings given to myths and their nature. A debate going on for many millennia concerns whether myths are distorted memories of historical events, or moral or psychological insights, and many other beliefs and speculations about myths. It is not possible here to trace these ideas in their historical setting. What one can say is that with colonial expansion new information was received about different peoples all over the world. By the middle of the 19th century, ethnologists and anthropologists attempted to deal with this new data in terms of some all-embracing new schemes of organization, viz. evolution of language, culture, and mythology, whereby the early stages were represented by various indigenous cultures within some value-laden theoretical ladder wherein mythologies were seemingly irrational obsessions of these peoples and the ancients — a prelogical, as James Frazer said, mode of thought that did not allow them to distinguish between Man, Nature and Cosmos. Even later Durkheim, with his functionalist approach to myth and culture, explained it in terms of social function, customs and attitude rather than by looking for deep philosophical meanings in myths. Of course Freud viewed myths as primitive humanity's disguised expressions of unconscious sexual and aggressive compulsions. Both Durkheim and Freud, who influenced most of the first half of this century, sought to identify religion with illusion and explain myth by reference to physical, social or psychological phenomena. Later it was realized that something was missing in this collective dissection, analysis and classifications of myths.

Not universally, but many psychologists, anthropologists and historians have abandoned this reductive approach. This radical new way of seeing myths as the doors to a realm of experience that was, and is, both real and profoundly meaningful owes much to the work of Carl Jung, who said, '. . . a tribe's mythology is its living religion whose loss is always and everywhere, even among the civilized, a moral catastrophe'. He saw myths as 'original revelations of the preconscious psyche, unconscious psychic processes . . . whole spiritual heritage of mankind's evolution born anew in the brain structure of every individual. . . . 'Jung was followed by Otto, Guenon, Campbell and Eliade — the latter refusing to see mythology simply as a study of economic, social and cultural meanings, emphasizing the primacy of the sacred in all traditions in the East and the West, among all peoples side by side and not in any evolutionary order in order to reveal and clarify their common motifs, archetypes of Jung, so that a universal pattern is revealed, e.g., rock, trees, rivers, and clouds are living parts of a living whole in which the Cosmos is alive and conscious, subject to the same intelligent force by which humankind itself is animated and acts as a link between the inner dimension of spirit and the outer world of form, i.e. every individual knew that his/her life was the embodiment of principle and purpose so that even the most mundane activity had an overarching significance because every act was performed not as a private act but as part of a Cosmic drama. In short, respect for the sacred was derived from an awareness of the creative process of Nature, and it implied a hesitancy to arbitrarily intrude on those processes in which time and space were themselves sacred.

Almost all non-industrial human cultures in the past and even today have had traditions of this simple yet magical harmonious attunement with Nature and the Cosmos. There is a mythic unity in the spiritual and religious realms; for repeatedly in America, Africa, Greece, India, Australia and so on, in different ways cultures have pursued this Cosmic unity in varied ways both metaphorically and literally. It is, in short, a sacred world-view which is devoid of any sense of sectarianism or dogmatism because there seems to be an understanding of the universal order and meaning of existence that guides one in relationship to social order, Nature and

Cosmos. Indigenous people have never assumed that Nature exists for the benefit of Man; rather, humankind owes a responsibility to Mother Earth and all its creatures — plants and animals. They in fact are apologetic for exploiting the earth for their food, and clearly see the Universe as aware and benevolent. In this sense, there has been a decline of humanity, for religions today appear as remnants of a formerly universal spiritual tradition which had the original sense of a sacred purpose. Hence, one sees uneasiness and restlessness despite all the technological and other achievements; this psychic and cultural neurosis is due to the lack of being in touch with an inner dimension which is so vital for humanity's nourishment. The emptiness is being filled, in vain, through personal achievement and material acquisitions, or by attempting to formulate new ideas albeit within the same dichotomous paradigm about Nature and Man.

The sacred world-view and mythology need to be resurrected, through acknowledgment of the principle of Consciousness in the Cosmos with a perspective of Holism which means that it is wholes that determine the design, function, and health of the parts, rather than the other way around. Modern physics, unlike classical physics, is recapitulating in many ways the ancient spiritual world-view of integral living. But in these new formulations, is it possible to discern any sense of the sacred? And, whatever the name given to this ultimate source — this universal ground of Being — it is no modern invention. Indigenous peoples all over the world were masters of holism long before this term was coined!

Let us consider the word myth and its possibilities. It functions as an internal image to guide actions; it acts as a suppressed premise, and is rarely made explicit. It is to this internal image that we give the name of myth. What is a scientific set, for instance? This is the myth of objective consciousness, i.e. that the mentality of scientists leans heavily on objectifying as the basis for explanation and prediction. In this view, science cannot go beyond the 'thinking-of-everything-and-everyone-as-object'; and thus, scientists 'certify themselves as experts . . . in the decision-making process generally employed in the "technology" '. While it is widely prevalent, Quantum Mechanics has gone beyond the general myth of science; the latter implicitly provides a useful, meaningful and sufficient way to cope with human experience, supposedly. In this way, the scientific mode of explanation has taken over the other two modes of explanation and acts as a large controlling image to govern all human experience. The main feature of such a definition is that neither of the other two explanatory modes are meaningful for human experience if science cannot deal with them; the dominance of the reigning Image-Myth or action is established. Thus human experience is deprived of the possibility of further self-expression and integration. In short, myth is a large controlling image that gives philosophical meaning to the facts of ordinary life: that is, which has organizing value for experience. Science and technology are not only a suppressed premise but have become a Fundamental Myth, a statement about dealing with all human experience. The same may be said about religion, magic and other sets of explanatory modes which lend themselves to this kind of examination.

The convergence of modern science and ancient insights

The viewpoint suggested above may be disturbing since it challenges earlier frameworks and unexamined certainties. The study of this area by many disciplines is inhibited by the essentially linear or non-contextual historical tradition that provides the presuppositions of scientific enquiry in the West. But these instruments of Western rationality are not applicable to other cultures, wherein rational principles are discoverable through their own world-view, i.e., a text within its own context, which is peculiarly non-linear or contextual. This is to be understood in the way complementary frameworks in Quantum Mechanics are created by different contexts of measurement — frameworks that are mutually exclusive (and therefore non-linear) but ordered to one another in a lattice structure (and therefore complementary). Complementary frameworks involve changes in the embodied subjectivity of the knower. Knowing about cultures therefore cannot be done with the head, on the conceptual soil of Europe, nor new models formulated about culture and development without sounding the death knell of this culture and civilization which is still a living body. The lived experience of such cultures seldom arises by describing the surface of their world; this knowledge must act, reflect, and communicate experiencing since it is this consciousness of man on which man counts and man must get hold of it in himself/herself.

The reference here is more to Western Thought which has become a cultural determination for all men. The first determination, for instance, in the problem of the one and the many, was the identification of the one with Thought; and the second was that this Thought was Being. This notion has become common to the individual both in the East and the West; that is, Be-ing identified with the word which proclaims in this fashion as able to control universal human behaviour, to this logic. But this will not allow us to reach the shores of other cultures which do not take Thought and Be-ing to be identical. It is possible to understand these cultures through the action and meaning given in their cultural 'texts', implicitly and explicitly; abandoning one's own theoretical knowledge, i.e. the starting point will be that Thought is a subset of Be-ing. The latter, for instance, is not an element in the conceptual system; it creates a reference to a domain of things, processes and events and exists independent of any human involvement. Be-ing is primal and as mentioned in Buddhist tradition, 'What is evident — *pratyaksam* — to men is concealed —*paroksam* — to the gods and what is concealed to men is evident to the gods'.

These ways of looking at the world may further be illustrated by the responses from philosophers of the West and the East, to the question 'What am I?' Socrates, as quoted by Plato, attempts to bring together the what and I of the question by trying to figure out the x-what and thereby have the answer to the dictum 'know thyself'. There would be a long list of each of the identifications given to the 'what' of man in the History of Western Philosophy — this figuring out the whatness of man or what it meant were it not for existentialism or phenomenology. But in every answer provided, the phenomenon itself was forgotten as meaningless. In this way the what became a strictly linguistic question, or some sort of an empirical problem which could be answered by adding up sets of empirically discovered characteristics or as a substance, etc. In contrast, in other cultures, it is not the what nor the subsequent possible identifications with the I which would give an answer to the problem, but rather the am-being of the question. What is being looked at is neither the whatness nor even the I as the source of enquiry but to go to the core of both the what and the I, i.e., existence itself, the am-being which every question-asking-subject is before he even bothers to figure out essences, or substances, whatever else becomes fashionable within a community to ask. In the modern world this dictum has become a question of achievement, of seeking self-identity, personality through several frantic steps of one order or another. This is the human-being-in-reality of Merleau-Ponty, of what Heidegger calls this priority of existence, or Sartre's 'existence precedes essence. . . .' and other phenomenological and existential approaches to philosophical anthropology.

The main point of this comparison is not to prove anyone nearer the truth than another, or to arbitrarily establish contact points between East and West. It is clear that man must realise himself as 'this' , 'that' , 'here', 'there' ; since, originally and finally, man-was-able-to-become one or another or several in an infinite repetition of this first affirmation of existence-as-capacity. It functions as the original 'space' out of which all form and name derive; as such, i.e. as original space, it is the container of all human possibilities.

Thus, one can say that there are two sources of knowledge — the indirect one (called understanding, imagination, etc.) and the direct one (called sensibility, perception, etc.); the two sources of knowledge are called 'nonsensuous' and 'sensuous' sources — neither better nor worse except in the manner of how we deal with the world. Instead of negating each other, these might be seen as complementary. In short, there are many ways of viewing the world and describing it without any one way being pre-eminent. If this is not the case in the modern world, it is because of certain preconceptual visions which are exclusivist and not inclusivist, and are adhered to dogmatically. The need is to transcend one's own framework. These two distinctive ways are available to man to view the world: the dominant 'commonsense-Classical-Physics viewing' and the 'Modern-Physics-Eastern viewing' of the world. Man's condition is such today that he is bound to use both viewpoints if he is to solve the problem of 'what-is-really-the-nature-of-things'.

Modern Physics and the Eastern world-view assume that whenever we are in search of anything, we are primarily in contact with a totality, the most 'real' aspect of any entity being the total pattern. Our perception of 'it' defies any atomicity or real identification. It is only secondarily that classification of individual entities is made possible, and for this we revert to ordinary symbolic manipulation. For example, one no longer says, 'Here is an electron', but instead, "Here is an area where the field is strong'. In this view, 'what is' appears as a quantum, a whole, a totality; the identifiable parts of this totality are artificially created for purposes of linguistic communication and conceptualization: they are artificial sub-patterns. The separation is totally false in relation to 'what is'.

The impact of this idea is to note that we are living in a continuum, in the present, where the distinction between living and dead, between moving bodies and bodies at rest, etc., no longer holds good. Man is now in nature, not seeing something distinct from himself. In this way we shall have to describe things in new and better ways, sometimes creating and selecting or abstracting. The human condition is such that both ways are essential, if man is to feel at home, and this is what complementarity means. 'It is not there are songs to be discovered but that the symphony was already there — sometimes in one note or in one song because both are necessary in knowledge. This freedom is necessary if one wants to stop reinforcing what one already knows'.

The historical accident of the discoveries of quantum mechanics and their relation to linguistic communication, complementarity, indeterminacy, and vision, makes our project of understanding cultures easier.

Culture, experience and oral traditions

Perhaps the greatest shortcoming in cultural studies is the hidden presupposition that our linguistic criteria are the only ones by which all men and cultures should be measured — the positivist view of language where the logic is universal irrespective of how the people use it. [The problem cultures face is not only to guarantee continuity but also to guarantee innovation.] The dialectical tension between continuity and innovation has given rise to the greatest inhumanity of one man against another, or one culture against another. Hence culture is yet to be discovered; and what we constantly face is the plurality of perspectives with which a culture has to contend and somehow guarantee equal rights so that culture may live in continuity and innovation. It is essential therefore that we do not presuppose what Culture is before we discover it. Culture is always incomplete, always on the move; this making gives it a certain indirection as an open phrase hanging in mid-air.

The knowledge we formulate about the 'other' is filtered or refracted through the knowledge we have built for ourselves, i.e. we are interpreters of cultures and can observe 'others' only through our own cultural and experiential biases. But this is not all so subjective, for at any given time there are accepted norms of what knowledge is conceived to mean, i.e. knowledge of the 'self' and of the 'others' come together in terms of some subjective and creative understanding: say, about new sights, sounds, rhythms, silences, feelings and tastes amidst many other cultural paraphernalia. Theoretical issues may be raised asking, Is it possible to talk about shared experiences that exist in the absence of being part of the local culture, language comprehension and so on? This means that a consideration of methodology, evolving a new framework, becomes necessary in terms of the anthropology of experience. This does not mean that language is not important in that culture and that they are not linguistically sophisticated. It is just that in the natural flow of interaction, especially in music and dance and so on, there is something behind the words — a hum of another kind — which takes into account a large sensory inventory which cannot be frozen into the written word that becomes the so-called ethnographic record. The human approach to a cultural model just encompass all 'experience' even if in terms of categories — taste, smell, sound, shape, colour and so on. Moreover, while linguistic categories may be gradually learnt, cultural learning may have to be picked up through sheer participation — doing the right thing at the right time, by feeling something beyond language that give some meaningfulness and vibrancy before these are classified and explained away. One can of course only attempt to approximate to verbal and non-verbal experiences in terms of the shared experience as a participant-observer, and as far as possible it is to share emotions. Maybe there can be a lived understanding of the situation, event and process. Primarily, I must feel and learn to express my own experiences.

We need to consider our model along these lines; the multiplicity of perspectives. Modernism has imposed a single perspective in dealing with human language and human culture. Cultures have to be seen as a whole, linguistic or otherwise. It is to see the presuppositions and criteria on which life is grounded, to discover a different way of viewing and listening. This perspectival vision thus does not rupture the continuum between thought and action, viewing and action. To reduce and measure man by the image of his thought carries inevitable consequences: for one thing, what is not an image, a thought, is outside of man, a mystical power, a god or a devil; while whatever is human must of necessity be only that which appears or is an image. For another, the only possible role for man to play in a world grounded on thought is to systematically reduce and control all his possibilities to the reality offered by the image; it is to condemn man to a programme of desensitization through the reinforcement of his belief of sensation. Through this identification, the bodies of man and woman have grown sick and live in mortal suffering. The integrating way to see this in many cultures is to put an axe to this tendency, so that all perspectives are kept alive simultaneously.

The question may be asked, how is one to include such recent and ancient ideas into anthropological knowledge of cultures? Normally governed by Newtonian-Cartesian notions, cultural information continues simply to be gathered; it is then embodied in words and applied in the relevant areas through new technologies wherever the 'quality of life' is to be altered. But since quality (lacking a human face) is equated with statistics, and despite the availability of tremendous resources, hitherto unimaginable psycho-social disasters have hit humankind. It has been overlooked that most social experience about cultures is not beyond language, both 'theirs' and 'ours'. Cultures are not things, objects, theoretical frameworks. The error lies in the production of anthropological-ethnographic knowledge which has ignored experience, personal and social. Language categories fragment the experience of both the 'self' and the 'others', i.e. there is an inherent unidimensionality and linearity involved in this domain of objective rationality which blocks out experience (subjectivity and intuition). The contention here is that this need not be so in any exclusivistic terms, as both domains are crucial for understanding cultures in general and specifically in India.

Clearly, the spoken or written word — prose — involves one of the senses, and not the other senses (say, smell, touch, feelings, sight, rhythm and so on) which express vividly what cultures are all about, especially Indian civilization. It is dominated by oral means of transmission of heritage where songs, music, dance, poetry — the Arts in a broad manner — are important. While this point is easily accepted, the question asked may be about its relevance and of how to show what means and methods are to be evolved at both the theoretical and applied levels to build information models which will allow us to put across such creative understanding of any culture. The first step is to rethink earlier axioms and assumptions of the research involved. An awareness of the issues and seeing that such fusion is possible between the two poles, is itself an important step in contributing to methodological frameworks. This is the only way to incorporate inputs which become suitable for including endogenous cultural dimensions into the idea of development. The latter may be restated and defined as the growth of creativity of human potential — the being of man — rather than merely the advancement of science and technology which in developing nations is considered by those who matter to not only be the answer to our prayers but an explanatory concept which tells us about all of existence, even lived experience!

The making of cultural information models is only possible when cultures are experienced comprehensively; the internalization of the holistic social and cultural experience is crucial since it allows one to move beyond conceptual worlds of people, to a totality that comprises thoughts, feelings and emotions. In fact, this is the only way which allows for a fuller understanding of both cognitive and embodied knowledge. Understanding cultures is not about information categories; it is a learning process that can only come via experiencing. This is especially true for India. Of course, field workers have been aware of the discrepancy between what is observed and what is recorded. But is it possible to change the route radically by researchers and decision-makers if meaningful inputs are to be made into the notions of culture and development even though it appears that time has already run out for most of the world?

The centrality of the methodological issue is on how to deal with this flow of intersubjective human experience without dehumanizing it in presenting any cultural model. This linking of the inside experiencing world and the outside analytical one is crucial, and once this proposition is accepted other avenues will open up in the ethnographic understanding of cultures.

There are problems, of course, of definitions, concepts and theoretical models which need to be evolved. The approach suggested here is an integral one, a holistic view of the totality of cultural transmission. The importance of global cross-cultural framework — this may be true for this subcontinent also — is clearly a movement beyond normative, prescriptive and ethnographic description of written forms which allows for expanding cultural links in a worldwide perspective. In short, it is no longer possible to work within old dichotomous boundaries, viz. primitive/civilized, industrial/non-industrial, tradition/modernity, written/oral and so on, emphasized in the Western sense. Oral and written interaction is part of a whole human communication system in which a number of different media and processes are involved. The notion of pure forms is practically and theoretically no longer true in understanding the long continuity of a civilization like the Indian one. This perspective allows one to focus attention on comparative questions about historical and specific approaches to cultures — local, regional and all-India ones. The emphasis is thus on the multilayered nature of the transmission of human expression — especially on audio-visual, verbal, artistic and literary forms; the anthropology of social experience reflecting a multiplicity of interpretive approaches that are not fixed within binary divides.

Cultural models provide a resource for understanding, for the negotiation of understanding, in short, for making sense of experience. Cultural models cannot be taught exclusively by linguistic means but must be acquired through embodiment, through the heart — the notion of a cultural model is a way of describing knowledge that cannot in and of itself account for how this knowledge is used, even though it is produced from repeated experience. In this context several critical questions may be asked, and these are as follows:

1. What are the concepts, definitions of orality, traditions (is there a time limit of tradition?), verbal, audio-visual texts?
2. What is patterned communication in tradition, in myth, ritual, oral history and literature? Is there such a thing as a neutral text?
3. What are the problems related to collection of data, observation, equipment used, analysis of data, and other ethical and social issues involved during field work?

4. In this seamless area of speech, idea, action and performance that make up living where there is no clear-cut 'object of study', how do cultures express their ideas, emotions and actions in both formalized and oral ways? Are not both ways, empirical and theoretical, Western and Eastern, verbal and nonverbal, to be taken into account? Is there any universal category applicable throughout Indian civilization, or elsewhere?
5. Is orality transmitted by word of mouth alone, or is it also referring to nonverbal — artistic performance, paintings on rock, monuments, sacred places, etc. — media as opposed to literacy defined in the modern sense? In this sense, is not oral tradition on 'open' system compared to the literate one since it is not restricted and receives knowledge from many other senses and sensibilities?
6. Does not this means of communication refer to group identity since the process of handing down is related to a collective memory bank with methods of recall, of particular cultural groups *vis-a-vis* another group in terms of some generalized tradition of context, myths, genre and so on?
7. Do current definitions seem true, and is the term 'folk' to be restricted to rural, traditional non-literate people, in contrast to modern urban populations who themselves have no verbal arts worth studying and are gradually becoming illiterate through the media of movies, television, etc., without becoming creative as they are passive receivers only?
8. What is the information base of specific cultures characterized by oral traditions? What, in this context, is theory about Memory — *sruti* or *smrti*? Is it automative, is there mere recall, or does it involve change by individuals, both in terms of cultural-specifics and the brain itself in terms of scientific laws, and what is remembering both as rote and creative and reorganizational recall? Is there a stream of verbatim recall in terms of style, content, or form? And who in a culture is trained to do this memory transmission? Is there not an ideology and process involved in the preservation of records of memories? Who are the experts and specialists involved in this process, and can these be identified?

Conclusion

Various routes from social experience to anthropological knowledge have been explored and discussed above, questioning both local and anthropological concepts. This tour reflects different poles of experience, stressing process at the expense of structure and knowledge as a creative field rather than as a solid construction. The objectivity approach has been replaced by more sensitive forms of studying and by a much wider use of the senses in ethnography. The ethnographic experience cannot be taken at face value but must be studied in its sensational depth. In real life, knowledge, so often isolated as cognition in theory, is not independent of emotion. Emotions, consequently, belong to the realm of rationality. Individuals are not only defined by their space but are also its defining consciousness — thinking implies caring. Scientists also architecture a particular space with its own vectors of direction towards the desirable, if these have generally been silenced. Most often the scientific space has been conceived of as wholly unemotional; it has been flattened into a place. We can no longer live by Cartesian rules but only by its illusions. The goal of the ethnographer is established on a much wider basis of experience, which again transforms the nature of the objects studied. They are somehow subjectified, and we have to understand how this does not detract from their reality. The main condition of knowledge is still related to individual field work, which cannot be conceived of independently of the subject; there is no experience apart from the experiencer, no knowledge without a knower. The idea of dissecting a dead body, experimenting on it as a clinical view of science, has to be given up as a model — it is not a lived experience. One of the results was the splitting apart of body and mind, which we have had to straddle. Realizing the impossibility of equating lived experience with dead bodies, anthropologists face a methodological problem acknowledging the corporeal fields of people. The reference is to that larger space with which every individual is inextricably linked by way of the physical, sensing and moving body. Whatever the words used, we need to recognize that the apparently theoretical problem of uniting mind and body as the locus of action is itself constituted within a specific discourse that separated them in the first place. Anthropology must learn to question the conditions for experience and it cannot continue to accept a radical discontinuity between theoretical and practical knowledge — or, for that matter, between mind and body. The origins of this false ontology have to be traced and understood before a new way and vocabulary is found for dealing with lived experience that was broken in two only in theory.

The shift in scientific theory pioneered by Galileo, and to which Cartesian reason was intimately linked, transformed the idea of a unified Cosmos embodying the Ideas of the World, of which humans were but fractions (and representations).

Instead the world became recast in mechanistic terms; moral virtue and self-mastery were transformed in the process. The mechanistic approach dissociated human from nature, as it were. This dislocation also implied a uniformation of time which dissonated with the ordinary experience of density and emptiness. During the 17th century reality was recast as a machine, a precise clockwork rather than an arhythmic living body.

With Descartes moral resources became firmly within ourselves; outer points of orientation were evaded, and the entire inner/outer dichotomy took on a new meaning. Scientific explanation was cut loose from moral vision; the former became a question of correct representation, the latter of individual firmness of will. The very notion of 'idea' migrated from Cosmos to person; its ontic sense was translocated to an intrapsychic world. Ideas became something one had 'in the mind'. There, it became a means for objectifying the world, including the body. As a cultural model it had its own motivating force — we are accustomed to the mind and body distinction. And it is this metaphysical dualism that has ever since been reflected in the subject-object dichotomy as basic to our knowledge of the world. However, this violates both the classical ontology and the ordinary experience of embodied understanding; the need is also of dissolving the Kantian distinction between pure and empirical knowledge.

Just as culture is meaningful only to someone in particular, not in some emotionless state of reasoning which we share in some cross-cultural sense, the agent of scholarship is a living person, not just the mind. Field work is thus essentially an intersubjective experience; sensations, feelings, and emotions demand a certain degree of personal involvement — what it means to be in pain, hungry, joyful and so on. In short, there is no way of understanding people except through one's own experience and power of imagination.

The dualism of mind and body, on the other hand, implies hierarchy, an implicit scheme of evaluation; it calls for disengagement from world and body, i.e. a rationality not defined by order of being but by the standards by which we construct orders in science and life. Anthropology has grown thus within a field defined by Cartesian co-ordinates; culture and society were studied from 'above', so to speak. But can we know except by way of our own presence and questioning? Since knowledge is profoundly embodied, understanding can only be achieved by way of involvement — the lived experience of the anthropologist. The capacity for understanding is not solely located in the mind; pure reason, as opposed to imagination, is not the locus of rationality. Human rationality is profoundly imaginative; it is a capacity for ordering representations, for making sense of unprecedented experiences, and for acting upon them in meaningful ways. Meaning is not a fixed relation between sentences and objective reality, as objectivism has it. Meaning does not exist in itself within the fixed co-ordinates of an abstract place; it is always meaning for someone in a particular social space.

The desire for fixed standards in science is challenged by the frightening indeterminacy of experience, social experience as the starting point for anthropological reflection. To understand the interplay between social processes and cultural knowledge, the model set by Enlightenment natural science is of limited value. The search for the One Truth in the Many is at odds with the relativist experience of anthropology. The point is to dignify subjective experience, not to deny reality; to appreciate imagination, not to disregard reason; to honour our differences, not to underestimate our common humanity. Within this view of anthropological practice, there are no facts without value, no reason without emotion, and no knowledge without experience. In this way the particular conditions of knowledge also become shared experience among anthropologists.

References

Finnegan, Ruth, 1992, *Oral Traditions and the Verbal Arts*. London.

Hastrup, Kirsten and Peter Hervik, 1994, *Social Experience and Anthropological Knowledge*. London and New York: Routledge.

Malik, S.C., 1989, *Modern Civilization: A Crisis of Civilization*. New Delhi: Abhinav Publishers.

——, 1995, 'Matter Is Consciousness'. *Prakrti*, New Delhi; IGNCA & D.K. Printworld.

——, 1995, 'Holistic Science and Consciousness'. *Prakrti*.

——, 1995, *Re-conceptualising the Sciences and the Humanities – An Integral Approach* New Delhi: Manohar and NMML.

——, forthcoming, 'Interface of Science, Consciousness and Identity'. New Delhi: IGNCA.

de Nicolas, Antonio T., 1976, *Meditations through the Rg Veda: Four-Dimensional Man*. New York: Nicolas Hays.

2

Cultures and Development

Guideline Questions

Baidyanath Saraswati

There are more than three hundred anthropological definitions of culture referring to various aspects of human life. Development originally stood for lineal progress, growth, advancement, increase of income and a right to gain it or an improvement in the quality of life as a consequence of one's achievement. Unesco has redefined both terms to provide the framework for the concept of the cultural dimension of development.[1]

Along with development the word 'culture' is used in several different connections such as cultural development, cultural dimension of development, and culture and development. Each of these expressions has a different ideological implication. Unesco was the first to link the terms culture and development, and again the first to raise the question of the cultural dimension of development.[2]

Ideologically, the modern concept of development emerged during that epoch in the Western intellectual tradition known as the Enlightenment — the period between the late 17th century and the French Revolution. The rationalists of this age gave the first formal definition of culture as an instrument evolved by man. The Enlightenment filled man with the presumptuous idea that he himself was the creator of his cultural destiny and that his cultural progress was dependent upon his rational efforts to perfect himself and his institutions.

The anthropological definitions of culture and the Western concept of development are totally irrelevant for the living traditional cultures of any part of the world. In the Sanskritic tradition of India, the term culture is contested by *sanskrti* (divine process of body cleansing, moral ordering), and development signifies *vikrti* (distortion) or *hrasa* (degeneration).

To take refuge in an alien definition of development is quite absurd. It is not the private sensation of the intellectual definition, unshared by the rest, that can demonstrate to another what it signifies in the real life situation.

The five parts of this presentation form a pattern of thought in regard to cultural freedom, that is *swaraj* (self-rule) in development.

Denying the dilemma of development

Modern man is dazzled and blinded by the image of development as something inherited from advancing technology. Development is more or less a separate construct, governed by its own laws, a sanctifier, a cultural marker. For the so-called technologically backward countries, it is a new culture, a new spirituality, a new path to salvation.

Man today is no longer Earth-bound. His aspiration to conquer the Sky, the City of God, does not seem to be far from realization. But where is he really going? There is a Zen story about a monk who was galloping down the road with his robes flapping in the wind. An old farmer, sitting on the gate, yelled out as the monk clattered by: 'Sir, where are you going?' The monk shouted back: 'Don't ask me, ask the horse!' Development culture rides a lion, not a horse.

What does the contemporary celebration of Project Global 2000 show? Is it the hope of an evolutionary leap, the new man, the new age, the new space, the new culture? Or is it the fear of a holocaust, depression, world wars, the arsenal of nuclear weaponry, widespread pollution, acid rain, toxic waste, and deforestation? Or is it a prayer to protect us from the horrors of hunger, broken homes, ethnic cleansings, apartheid, genocide, ecocides, and other threats to human security? Or is it the propitiation of Mother Earth, who is becoming tired and exhausted? Is this a celebration of progress or a terminal crisis?

Technological advance is taking a certain direction in which we acquire superior power of disorder over order. Can the *bhasmasur*[3] technology build a normal civilization? It may be that the rest of mankind is not aware that Technology (with a capital T) has brought the world to a deadly point from where there is possibly no return. But why can't scientists and intellectuals understand this plain truth? Do they think that the death of human civilization is inevitable? Are they aware in what sense man is progressing, and what sort of cultural death he is facing? Do they hide a deep inner terror of death? Why do they deny the dilemma of development?

Defining culture in terms of man in nature

To make sense of this dilemma it is important to understand the true nature of human culture.

The Western definitions of culture centre around an interminable debate on *cultura ex natura* and *cultura ex cultura*. Theoretically, the main contention lies between the organic and the superorganic views of culture. The organicists claim that culture consists in the forms and processes of behaviour which man acquires through his innate potentialities. And hence it is a subjective or personal attribute — a state, or quality, attributed to an organism. The superorganicists, on the other hand, hold that culture is the objective product of man's cultivation of the natural objects of his environment. And as objects or artifacts exist independently of the organism, they are described as superorganic. It is also claimed that the superorganic products are endowed with efficient power, that is, they make or develop themselves according to their own natural laws.

No one would suppose that either of these two views would be common to all human beings. Yet these are after all man's own explanations of himself. Can one rule out the possibility of discovering non-human views about humans in the future? The idea seems ridiculous. But it is against the spirit of science to deny such a possibility. However, relying on the human perception of reality, we may ask: Is biological man alone by himself and with himself? Is he a cultural being of a single form? Is he the creator of culture in the true sense? Can object be detached from subject? Is art independent of the artist? How do humans apply art to nature?

Creativity has a wide range. Culture as a kind of creativity is dependent on its 'maker', who turns towards it in many ways. Hence there are several different forms of culture. These can be broadly grouped as:

1. Dreamtime culture, which has acquired spiritual understanding of nature through dreaming, that is the *alcheringa*[4] awareness, the most expressive aboriginal mode of knowing the language of nature.
2. Cosmocentric culture, which recognizes the vital significance of cosmic elements in the making of biological and cultural man.
3. Theocentric culture, which considers dissociation from the phenomenal world in favour of the divine eternal world as human perfection.
4. Anthropocentric culture, which makes man the measure of all and teaches a path to progress which is external to nature.
5. Technocentric culture, which worships technology in the belief that higher possibilities of man lie in affluence which is largely and necessarily a function of advancing technology.

Of these the first three forms maintain that life and culture originate dependently in the total context of divine nature, which is changing and yet not changing. The path of human perfection lies within it: man living in harmony with nature. In the other two forms of culture there is a built environment, disconnected with nature, where the system of man and the system of machine are in conflict. In a chaotic system, any small difference between two identical systems will grow rapidly. The hallmark of chaos is that two motions diverge exponentially. If the superorganic products are endowed with efficient power, what would safeguard human life? If the system of the machine develops itself, by its own laws, how can a technocentric man set his choice between good and evil? How can he be the measure of all? Wouldn't it be illusion?

Determining the nature of social truth

Biological truth is universal. The difference between the quick and the dead is self-evident. Hence it is relatively easy to comprehend.

Social truth is far more complex. It is essentially a model or a description of reality rather than reality. The relationship between the social description of reality and the real system it purports to represent raises deep issues. For instance, with the power of the machine and all the wisdom of science, half of the world's scientists are currently in war-related industries. Every minute two million dollars are spent on the production and use of armaments. Resources are being squandered, while millions of children die of malnutrition. The theory of parallel worlds — the world of man and the world of the machine — as stated before, has developed out of the psychical peculiarity of human actors. Modern man talks about lineal development but moves in the opposite direction. He preaches democracy and practises domination and discrimination. Lying is peculiar to man.

Turning to chaos and uncertainty, the following kinds of questions can be raised: Was the original relation between biological and social laws benign? If so, what makes modern man destroy the web of natural relationships? If not, what is that which has so far sustained the human world? The question before humanity today is not *whether* life will survive. Rather, it is *what kind* of life that will be. Is it not true that as a citizen of Earth modern man has become dysfunctional? Does this truth apply to all living societies? Is human nature the same everywhere? Do all humans perceive ugliness and beauty, good and evil the same way? Is there nothing other than the beautiful and the good that they love?

There is no ready answer to any of these questions other than one based on the diversity of human nature and culture.

Demanding a preferred world

Based upon a social truth, each human group forms a preferred world shaped by its own imagination and values. This preferred world is determined by the alteration of state caused by internal and external forces.

How can one comprehend the complexity of the preferred world of a self-organizing culture that coexists with nature? Considering the global concern and various development strategies, to what extent have traditional cultures the freedom to form a preferred world?

By contrast, how can one trust a parasitic culture with citycraft (of which warcraft is a part) that builds on advancing technology and affluence-servicing science? How can a moral order be established by other than moral restraints? How can a sane social order operate without strict preliminary discipline? How can there be peace in the world so long as even one man is violent?

Modern science and technology have generated an intense interest in a global perspective. But what does this globalization aim at? Can one become national without being local, international without being national, universal without being global, and again global without being local? How can one talk about a global ethic without having concern for the man suffering next door? What kind of global vision is that which enforces a dominant techno-economic system which reduces people to the status of disposable economic units?

The preferred world of modern man is woven by the technocentric system. Is there no alternative to this system? If there is none, how can it be said without qualification that we live in a preferred world at all? Can one grow in this system without losing one's original identity? Is the system of the machine capable of giving birth to a just and humane civilization? Why do we call it a preferred world? What determines the preference? Is it the consideration of the good and the beautiful? Does it mean that whatever is not beautiful and good must necessarily be ugly and bad? Or is there something in between? Can these questions be correctly answered by mere intelligence without the language of the heart?

Developing without a centre

Human cultures are situated today in a technocentric framework of global interdependence created by a new kind of state system with multinational organizations. This engenders an uneasy feeling. The moot questions are: What will be the structure of the global village? Who will be the controller? Can the inherent conflict between an exploitative Western and a harmonious Eastern approach to nature and culture be resolved by the promise of a shared global ethic and the prospect of a developed techno-economic system? If humans are themselves controlled by technology, who will fulfil the promise?

In its 1993 report,[5] Unesco made several pertinent observations on the problems of development. Briefly, it says: Development is not a neutral concept capable of universal application. Its proclaimed intentions are only very partially translated into actual projects. Development is technically characterized by limited duration, global objectives, predominance of economics, fragmentation of action, and the reduction of cultural aspects to education and the elimination of illiteracy. Development documents are based on a macro-economic or macro-social scale of observation which presupposes a search for regularity rather than diversity in every field. It follows classical methods of planning and data qualification, and stresses activities that can easily be audited. The distance between the decision-makers and the population concerned determines the nature and content of development programmes. The participation of the population in its own development never extends beyond purely local limits, the 'vertical' or institutional channels of communication, either distorting some of the data from the field or watering it down en route. The decision-makers consult their peers, not the 'field', before determining their broad programme of future action.

Following on this there arise two sets of questions. The first set highlights further the ugly and unjust state-centric development. In matters of modern development what is true and what is false? Is development a flagrant mistake? Is the rhetoric of development nothing but a tool of persuasion for those intent on deception? Why does the state make a fetish of literacy? As Gandhi said, 'what better book can there be than the book of humanity?'[6] Is it not true that foreign languages in education have caused incalculable intellectual and moral injury to Asian and African cultures? Is it not unnatural to cultivate intellectuals in the garden of another culture? Can true development come through the state department of numerology? If decision-makers sit in an ivory tower and distort the facts of development, what empowers them to impose on the common man an insufferable interference with the freedom of culture? Must we seek to get the better of state-centric development, which is by nature hurtful? Or should we tell the emperor that he has no clothes?

Swaraj in development

What is manifest in the Unesco document makes it plain that the greatest need of our times is *swaraj* in development. The second set of questions relates to the guiding principle which makes development profitable. Is it sensible to speak of a single world order based on state-centric technology? Is it not more realistic to develop endogenously, slowly and independently without a centre? Isn't small beautiful? Aren't self-organizing cultures the noblest and the best? Is it not amazing today that the 'elephant' is asking the 'ant' for food? Is there nothing in traditional culture that can play a positive role in an alternative type of development? Is it possible in a technocentric system of development to safeguard distinctly defined cultural identities? Is industrialization necessary? Can a nation be called developed where the rich have a store of things which they do not need, while millions are starved to death? Have the developing countries the freedom to choose between the traditional moral order and the modern technical order? Can cultures be created without freedom of choice? Can *swaraj* in development come about through untruthful and violent means?

For our guidance, then, let us make use of Gandhi's concept of *swaraj*: 'To get *Swaraj* then is to get rid of our helplessness. The problem is no doubt stupendous even as it is for the fabled lion who having been brought up in the company of goats found it impossible to feel that he was a lion'.[7] Such is the state of the ancient cultures with great traditions which are now condemned as 'developing countries'.

Gandhi defined *swaraj* as the essence of man: 'So far as we are removed from *swaraj* we are removed from manhood. A proper manifestation of all our powers is not possible without *swaraj*'.[8] '*Swaraj* is not meant for cowards, but for those who would mount smilingly to the gallows, and refuse even to allow their eyes to be bandaged'.[9] '*Swaraj* is for the awakened, not for the sleepy and the ignorant'.[10] '*Swaraj* is our birthright. No one can deprive us of it, unless we forfeit it ourselves'.[11]

For Gandhi *swaraj* means a just society and an all-round development: '*Swaraj* means ability to regard everyone as our brother and sister'.[12] 'Do not talk of winning *Swaraj* without making a fair return to the villager for the daily exploitation to which you subject him'.[13] 'There can be no *Swaraj* by non-violent means without communal unity'.[14] '*Swaraj* is not absence of rule'.[15] '*Swaraj* is complete independence of alien control and complete economic independence. It has two other ends. One of them is truth (*dharma*, religion), the other is non-violence (moral and social upliftment). Let us call this the square of *Swaraj*, which will be out of shape if any of its angles is untrue'.[16]

If we aspire to *swaraj* in development, we must strive for *swadesi* development. If we aspire to a global village, we must first set our house in order.

Notes

1. The 1982 Mexico conference held by Unesco declared:

   [Culture] comprises the whole complex of distinctive spiritual, material, intellectual and emotional features that characterize a society or social group. It includes not only the arts and letters, but also modes of life, the fundamental rights of the human being, value systems, traditions and beliefs'.

   [Development is] a complex, comprehensive and multidimensional process which extends beyond mere economic growth, to incorporate all dimensions of life and all the energies of a community, all of whose members are called upon to make a contribution and expect to share in the benefits. . . . Development should be based on the will of each society and should express its fundamental identity' (Arfwedson 1994).

2. Unesco Report, June 1993.
3. In the Puranic tradition of India, there is a myth of Bhasmasur: Once a demon went on performing penance for a thousand years. Pleased by his penance, Siva appeared before him and said, 'Ask a boon'. The demon replied, 'Lord! If

you are so pleased, grant that I may be endowed with the power of reducing anyone to ashes merely by putting my hand on the head of the prey.' Siva said, 'May it be so'. Now the demon wanted to test the efficacy of the boon forthwith. And as he was about to swoop down on Siva, his benefactor, standing right there, the God of Death took to his heels in utter desperation. The demon started chasing him. Eventually, filled with fright, Siva approached Visnu for protection. Thereupon, the God of Preservation assumed the form of Mohini, a charming woman, and sat under a tree where the demon Bhasmasur eventually came in search of his prey. Infatuated by Mohini's beauty and charm, he proposed that she make love with him. Mohini replied, 'I am a dancer, you can get my hand only if you match me in dance.' Bhasmasur agreed and began dancing in great excitement. Following Mohini's dancing gesture, he lifted his hand higher and higher until it touched his own head and reduced him to ashes instantly.

Strange as it may appear, instead of asking for beneficence such as deathless existence for himself, the demon prayed for a boon that could only destroy. But it is not so strange, because by asking such a boon the demon had virtually usurped Siva's greatest power. And thus when the boon was given, the Great God of Death and Dissolution himself became utterly helpless and miserable.

The myth of Bhasmasur is a pointer to the human condition of our time, when man has already granted the boon to demonic technology. Technology today is chasing man; man is no longer controlling technology (Saraswati 1989).

4. The Australian aboriginal outlook on the universe and man is shaped by the conception of *alcheringa* of the Arunta or Aranda tribe. Europeans have called it Eternal Dream Time. The term relates to sacred, heroic time long, long ago when man and nature came to be as they are; but neither 'time' nor 'history' as we understand them is involved in this meaning. It stands for totem or the place from which the aboriginal spirit came; and it also explains the existence of a custom, or a law of life, as causally due to *alcheringa* (***see*** Stanner 1990). This term is used here for all aboriginal cultures which are characterized by *alcheringa* awareness.

5. Unesco Report, June 1993. ***See also*** the diagram: Effects and Costs of the Contemporary Development Crisis (Leander 1991).

6. *Selections from Gandhi* (Bose 1948:251).

7. *Mahatma* (Tendulkar 1969, Vol.2:19).

8. *Ibid.*, Vol.2:262.

9. *Ibid.*, Vol.2:346.

10. *Ibid.*, Vol.5:27.

11. *Ibid.*, Vol.4:29.
12. *Ibid.*, Vol.2:51.
13. *Ibid.*, Vol.2:252.
14. *Ibid.*, Vol.5:27.
15. *Ibid.*, Vol.4: 31.
16. *Ibid.*, Vol.4:114.

References

Arfwedson, Anders, 1994, 'Introduction'. In *Culture and Development: World Day for Cultural Development.* Paris: Unesco.

Bose, Nirmal Kumar, 1948, *Selections from Gandhi.* Ahmedabad: Navajivan Publishing House.

Leander, Birgitta, 1994, 'The Forgotten Dimensions of Development'. In *Culture Plus.* Paris: Unesco.

Saraswati, Baidyanath, 1994, 'The Indian Vision of Technology: An Interpretation of Myths and Traditions in Pottery-making'. *Technique and Culture,* No.14.

Stanner, W.E.H., 1990, 'The Dreaming'. In W.H. Edwards, (ed.), *Traditional Aboriginal Society: A Reader.* Melbourne: The Macmillan Company of Australia.

Tendulkar, D.G., 1969, *Mahatma: Life of Mohandas Karamchand Gandhi,* 5 vols. New Delhi: Publications Division, Government of India.

Unesco, 1993, *The Cultural Dimensions of Development: Towards a Practical Approach: Compendium of Methodological Experience of Taking Cultural Factors into Account in Development.* Paris: Unesco.

3

China Under the Impact of Modern Civilization

Problems for an Endogenous Developmental Model

Tan Chung

In this presentation I try to survey the Chinese developmental model in the light of civilizational dynamics. I will first give an overview of the Chinese scene, and then take up a few issues for specific discussion. As China is a huge country and her problems are equally vast, numerous and complex, this presentation has become fairly long, yet with important issues I may fail to cover.

I

Napoleon once described China as a sleeping giant, and hoped it would remain so lest the world might be shaken by it. Today, this sleeping giant has not only waken up, but is bending on her internal development in a scale and dimension exceeding what it had been doing in history. The entire world is watching what China is doing domestically because whatever happens there might have an universal impact.

China, like India, was a developed country before the 18th century when the rest of the world remained less developed. The emergence of the modern civilization and the powerful impact of Western colonialism and finance imperialism condemned her to a developing country for one whole century. After 1949, the People's

Republic of China (PRC) launched a feverish movement to regain China's position in the family of nations as a developed country. This feverish movement for making China "*fu*" (rich) and "*qiang*" (strong) was a successor to the May Fourth Movement (1919) which has driven home a conviction that the evil roots of China's humiliating defeat by the western powers lay in China's own age-old traditions. Unless China totally broke away from that tradition there would be no prospects for the emergence of a new China.

The first generation of the leaders of the PRC operated on this premise; and worked hard to destroy the old and build up the new. Destroying the old was easier than building up the new as there was no suitable example to emulate. In many aspects, the PRC adopted the Soviet model, particularly the "Economic Planning" system which is now called by the Western economists as "Command Economy" This has brought a drastic change in China's way of life.

In the past, China was like the USA — a vast country with abundant resources welcoming people of various ethnic origins to settle there to develop its economy. There were two kinds of scenarios of government rule. A benevolent kind was to maintain peace and levy less taxes. Economy could prosper under such regimes. Another kind was the government's involvement in constant warfare, and had to pass on the burden to the common people. Life became miserable under such reigns. Thus, the Chinese history had projected a time-tested rhythm that grassroots initiatives were precious in developing a prosperous life in the country.

The PRC leadership ignored this rhythm initially, and tried to make the state power the sole locomotive for the country's economic development. In this process, the grassroots initiatives were destroyed. There were some isolated examples of people under a highly regimented management system maintaining great enthusiasm in developing production. But the People's Communes, by and large, could register very slow economic growth, and the state owned industrial enterprises proved to be highly inefficient and uneconomical. However, the country succeeded in keeping a high spiritual culture with revolutionary zeal. Social evils like prostitution, drug addiction, black money etc. were unheard of. Of course, because of the want of transparency, many ugly things, particularly corruption and petty crimes committed by those who held power, were hidden under the carpet.

Then came the post-Mao era of reforms and opening up of China to the outside world. The post-Mao leadership under Deng Xiaoping gradually diluted the economic plans of the state and loosened the state control on grassroot economic activities.

This change brought about positive results in economic development. In the last 15 years China's economic growth was nearly 10 per cent a year on an average, which was not only unheard of in China's history, but was also outstanding in the post-World War era, when Europe lingered around 2-3 per cent of growth rate.

Another fundamental change adopted by Deng Xiaoping's leadership is to erase the abstract dichotomy between socialism and capitalism. Socialism during the Mao era was conceived as "*Xing wu mie zi*" (Uplift the proletariat and exterminate the bourgeoisie). Deng Xiaoping felt that China should emulate all good examples which could develop the productive force. While economic planning, to him, was not exclusively socialist, market economy was not exclusively capitalist either. Market economy was just a "method". "If it serves the interest of socialism, then it belongs to socialism. If it serves the interest of capitalism, then it belongs to capitalism." Deng Xiaoping, thus, created a new conception in China's development orientation. "He destroyed the adherence to economic planning, and also broke the taboo on market economy," commented Hu Sheng, President of the Chinese Academy of Social Sciences.[1]

China has had one and half centuries of interface with the modern civilization since the Opium War (1840-42). This interface has experienced some twists and turns. In the beginning China tried to reject modern civilization but failed. Then, a leftist movement rose under the influence of the anti-current of modern civilization, i.e., Marxism, and launched an attack on China's own traditions. Then, China, during the post-Mao era ceased to embrace communism too tightly, and developed a soft corner for the capitalist economic pattern of development. Today, China wishes to have the good things from both the mainstream and anti-current of modern civilization — to emulate the market economic system from the mainstream capitalist world, and to adhere to socialism which is an inspiration from the anti-current of modern west.

Deng Xiaoping raised an important slogan "Building up socialism according to Chinese characteristics". His approach is also known as pursuing the "Chinese road towards socialism". Such a policy symbolizes China's quest for an endogenous pattern of development. During the Mao era there used to be the slogan: "*Gu wei jin yong, yang wei Zhong yong.*" (Employ past experience for the benefit of the present, and employ foreign experience for the benefit of China.) Outwardly, there seems to be a contradiction between China's providing herself as a market for foreign trade and investment and her strong desire for enhancing her own enlightened self-interest. One Chinese scholar, Li Yi'ning, a professor of Beijing University, tries to find a logic in this contradiction by describing it as a strategy of "exchanging market for technology" (*yi shichang huan jishu*) — meaning to have the benefit of the latest foreign technology implanted in China by allowing foreign enterprises to enjoy the profit of Chinese market.[2] Li Yi'ning is one of the avant-garde economists in China who have gone quite beyond the framework of Marxist political-economy. He is one of the members of the think-tank for the present PRC leaders, but not all his proposals have been accepted for implementation.

Here is the involvement of a fundamental problem concerning national self-reliance and international globalization. Both in India and in China there has been a strong opposition to the encroachment of transnational interests into the domestic economy to hamper the growth of the national industries. What Deng Xiaoping and his followers among present-day PRC leadership have been doing is an experiment based on either a self-confidence that China's national industries will emerge a winner in the on-going globalization, or a fatalistic mentality that without participating in the globalization China will not take off in the fierce international competition. Li Yi'ning and others who see the right logic in such an experiment seem to reflect a complex mentality of both this self-confidence and fatalistic mentality.

One element of urgency for China to embrace globalization is the time factor when both the developed countries and the Newly Industrialised Countries (NICs) are eager to shed their labour-intensive industries. China has seized this opportunity to take over the "sun-set industries" of Hong Kong, Taiwan, and other countries to become the processing zone of the world for shoes, electronic toys, garments, cheap watches, etc. Such "sun-set industries" do not augment self-reliance to China's modern development. But, China has, at no time, ignored the need of developing her own manufacturing and other industrial capability to be able to stand on her own as a modern power. It is estimated that there were three major waves in the last 40 years of importing advanced foreign technology into China. The first wave took place in the 1950s when the Soviet Union helped China to build up her heavy industrial base. The second wave took place in 1978 when the government led by the transitional leader Hua Guofeng hurriedly signed huge contracts with Japan and Germany to modernize its steel industry to the extent that the country failed to digest the intake, and had to cut down the import by paying compensation to foreign companies. From 1983 there started the third major wave, and in three years 3,000 plus new technological items were imported.

But, many of such items were repetitions, amounting to a waste of precious foreign exchange.[3] There were even isolated instances of China-made machinery being bought back as advanced foreign technology. In all, China's industrial capability is commendable after four decades of hard work in development. In the Mao era, when the Western world imposed an embargo on China, she could make a series of breakthrough in science and technology by using the reverse technology. China could develop its own atomic energy, aeronautic and air-space industries, etc. China has now the largest manufacturing industry in the world, and is fairly advanced in certain fields of technology such as rocketry, nuclear, underground mining, bridge building, etc. But, on the whole China's technological level remains three or four decades behind the leaders of the world. According to American standards, most of China's factories are junk yards. China can't throw the obsolete equipment away, but is trying to renovate them into semi-state-of-the-art conditions. It is a poor country's development course to modernization.

China has an ingenious programme in developing her own science capability called "*Xinghuo jihua*" (Spark Programme), drawing inspiration from Chairman Mao's famous saying that "A single spark can start a prairie fire". This Spark Programme was initiated in 1986, aiming at introducing scientific research findings to industrial units, agriculture, animal husbandry and other areas of productivity. There is another programme called "863 Programme" instituted in 1986 to develop high tech by indigenous efforts. This was supplemented by the "Torch Programme" in 1988 for marketization of the achievements of the 863 Programme. Over the years, there has been a brain-drain in China with young scientists going abroad and failing to come back. The PRC govenment has announced special incentives to attract them to return to the motherland. This step has created a discrimination between homespun scientists and sea-water-drunken scientists, thus becoming an invisible encouragement for more brain-drain.

The "Special Economic Zone" and its younger sister, "Economic and Technological Development Zones" are special features of post-Mao China's new economic development. The government grants a special policy to such zones to allow them to import foreign technology and investment. The philosophy behind the establishment of these zones is termed "*Yin feng ru chao*" (Making a nest for the phoenix to enter) — foreign investment is the "phoenix". The "Special Economic Zones", particularly Shenzhen, was a topic of great controversy. Many veteran leaders wept after visiting the place — feeling that their revolutionary martyrdom and heroism had been cheated, and no one would have shed blood for the communist revolution if they had known that capitalism and exploitation would have been brought back through the back door. There were fierce internal debate about whether such zones belonged to the socialist or capitalist family. In 1992, Deng Xiaoping, the designer of such zones, visited them and reaffirmed their contributions to the country. He also appealed to fellow Party comrades to postpone the debate for a decade or so to let history judge whether such an invention had any justification. Today, such zones are no longer in the limelight as the whole country has virtually become a huge "Special Zone" for opening up to the outside world.

What China presents today is a very dynamic, fluid, complex, and in certain sense, chaotic picture of embarking on the course of development. China was a developed country in the past. Chinese were great inventors, and have always had an aptitude for expanding production. Such basic orientation and talent of the Chinese people are the major factor for China's fast economic growth now that the government spares no efforts to encourage grassroot initiatives. However, China's past development and prosperity is one thing while the development and affluence in the modern civilization is another. England and other European countries had taken three centuries to build up the edifice of modern prosperity. America has taken less time, but also about two centuries. It would be impossible for China to flog-leap into the brave new world. In many ways, she has to advance steadily like a tortoise, if not a snail. There are many problems and obstacles on her future road.

The greatest difficulty in China is the size of population. The Chinese government is always proud of the fact that with only 7 per cent of the earth's cultivated land, China is feeding 22 per cent of humankind. But, behind this proud proposition is the great strain as well. In the first place, there is tremendous population pressure on land which has to produce enough to sustain all these people. Second, with the application of modern technology China's limited agricultural land does not need more than a fraction of this huge population to attend to it. During the Mao era, people were just whiling away time in non-productive pursuits under the management of the communes. Today, the majority of Chinese population — those who live in the countryside — have to fend for themselves. They will starve if they while away their time. But, when they want to take up production sincerely there is not enough work for most of them. Two situations have risen. In the better developed areas, people have invested in village and township industries (like India's cottage industry) and succeeded in absorbing the surplus labour from the plantation industry. There are even some areas where all the rural population have been absorbed into the secondary and tertiary industries, leaving the primary industry, i.e. plantation, to imported labourers. But, these are only isolated examples. Overwhelmingly large parts of China's countryside have developed a surplus labour force without full employment. In some areas, this surplus labour has started to spill over to the affluent areas or the big cities to find odd jobs. In the last six, seven years, such movements have assumed alarming dimension in what is called "mingongchao" (waves of job-seekers). There are several tens of millions of such job-seekers flowing from the poor villages into the big cities and affluent coastal areas today which is a serious destabilizing factor in China's socio-economic life right now, and, in course of time, would become a political destabilizing force if the trend is not timely checked.

China is, paradoxically, a big country without sufficient land for her agricultural development. One-fifteenth of the land masses on earth belongs to China which amounts to 9.6 million square kilometres. Country-wise, China is the third largest on earth in size, but population-wise, her per capita possession of land territory is only one-third of the average of the world population. Then, large tracts of China's territory are occupied by deserts, glaciers, rocky mountains and plains, and high altitude cold areas unfit for agriculture. China's per capita arable land is one of the lowest among countries whose population is above 50 million — only slightly higher than Japan and Bangladesh. China's per capita agricultural land is only half of that of India and Pakistan, and only one-ninth of that of USA. Worse still, because of rapid industrial development, there has been a sharp reduction of China's agricultural land. This reduction couples with a high rate of population increase. For instance, in 1993, the total loss of agricultural land in China amounted to 9.37 million mu (a mu is about 1/6 of an acre) which was as large as the total agricultural land of Qinghai province. While the agricultural land of the size of a province was lost, the population increase in 1993 was about 16 million which was three times of Qinghai's population. Under such dual pressure on agricultural land — diversion for non-agricultural use and population increase — the per capita share of agricultural land would be reduced to 0.6 mu (i.e. 0.1 acre) fifty years later. And there would be hardly any agricultural land visible for an average Chinese in the end of the 21st century if such a development continues.[4]

Erosion is another cause of the loss of agricultural land which, too, threatens China's future development. As Mr. Li Ruihuan, one of China's top five leaders, observed:

> Another deep crisis faced by the agricultural land of our country is the grave erosion of the soil, leading to the deterioration of our ecological environment. Now the total area of erosion of soil amounts to 1.3 million square kilometres, the total area of desertification is 176,000 square kilometres. Every year large tracts of cultivated and grass lands are swallowed up. If we don't take effective measures, by the year 2000 we are going to lose 1.8 million square kilometres of soil and will have 0.2 million square kilometres of land being turned into deserts.[5]

Connected with the loss of agricultural land is the scarcity of water resources in China. As Li Ruihuan observes:

> The special feature of the topography of our country is having high land in the west and low land in the east, creating the loss of large quantity of water. The distribution of water resources is tilted towards the south, resulting in frequent floods in the south and general drought in the north. Particularly during the rainy seasons there is a serious imbalance among areas. We have drought and flood happening in different places at the same time, or in the same place at different times. In the past 2, 000 years, there occurred 1,600 great droughts, and 1,300 great floods in our country.[6]

Li Ruihuan added that in the vast north-west there was a vast area of 2.96 million square kilometres which comprised 31 per cent of China's entire territory. The potential farmland resources here was 32.3 per cent of China's total. The area was rich in sunshine. Many of the places could be turned into fertile agricultural lands if there was water.[7] Right now, there is serious thinking about making some major alternations of China's water distribution systems. One scheme is to make Yangtse River flow into Yellow River. Another is to bore a water tunnel through the Kun Lun Range and make Brahmaputra flow into Xinjiang.[8] The second scheme, if implemented, will affect India and Bangladesh as Brahmaputra is shared by the three countries. The first scheme would not affect any other country, but it would mean to merge the world's fourth largest river (Yangtse) and the seventh largest (Yellow) and make the largest river system of the world.

The deterioration of ecological environment which has been touched upon by Li Ruihuan deserves serious attention. The number of Chinese household is too large to be supplied with electricity or cooking gas. Burning coal and firewood is still widely practised. While coal burning generates carbon monoxide, burning firewood tends to destroy the existing forest coverage. A new ecological threat is the acid rain. The rainfall area with precipitation containing less than 5.6 pH has increased from 1.75 million square kilometres in 1985 to 2.8 million square kilometres in 1993. It occurs in southeast China where factories are concentrated, and has a tendency of moving northwards and westwards.[9] There is avoidable pollution created by ignorance and want of health regulations. In Jiuqi village, Taoyuan county, in Hunan province people wash their insecticide implements in the pond where fish is also bred. In course of time, the fish which gradually developed their immunity have become live carriers of poison. Peasants who eat such fish get poisoned and even get killed for want of immunity.[10] Modern culture itself contains danger to life if people don't have scientific knowledge and consciousness. There are a lot of man-made disasters in China because of such ignorance, and neglect of safety measures. Such ignorance-induced pollution or calamity will continue for some time until the level of education in China reaches the safety mark.

When the humankind enters the 21st century modern civilization will turn softer and softer. The battle of economic development will no longer be fought on the ground. It will be fought on the computers in the game of system science — networking in information gathering and employing information for profitable ends. Human resources will assume great importance in the future scheme of development. China and India are the largest reservoirs in the world of human resources. But, human heads are not automatically the human talents needed for the future. Ordinary human heads have to be converted into talented human heads. Education must be placed on the agenda right now if India and China are to stand in the front row of development in the 21st century.

Coming to the subject of education in China, we have the shocking statistics revealed by Li Ruihuan, in his speech addressed to an all China educational conference in Beijing in January, 1995. He said that Chinese, on an average, is exposed to systemic education for only 5.4 years. He also revealed that the Chinese population's per capita share of government expenditure on education comes to only US $ 12.92 in a year as against the average figure of $ 42 among all developing countries.[11]

There are various remedies for the deficiency in education. Allocation of more funds is one of them. However, in a developing economy like China, and a country of China's population size, even spending one US dollar more on education for every Chinese would mean an additional government expenditure of 10 billion yuan (equivalent to Rs. 4-5 billions) which is a large burden for the exchequer. Of course, as education is so vitally important for future development, not spending large sums on it is unwise and myopic. But, there are still limitations to such a spending.

How education can develop smoothly and healthily in China's current honeymoon with the market economic system is a question which has received serious attention. One problem is whether education should be pushed into the market economy or not. Chinese education, particularly higher education, is now under a double assault by the new emergent socio-economic order of the market system. In the first place, the overwhelming number of educational institutions in China are government owned. They are subjected to the same pressure as the government-owned enterprises in industry and other fields are subjected to, viz. finding their own resources and fending for themselves. The prestigious Beijing University, for instance, is saved from bankruptcy only because of its establishment of a business concern called "Beida Fangzheng" which supplies a software to modernize Chinese printing press — a major invention by one of the University professors. While the University has been saved by this master stroke of commercialization (with Beida Fangzheng Company contributing to one half of its annual expenditure which the Ministry of Education fails to meet), commercialization has already eaten into the vitals of life of the University. University teachers take the first opportunity to "go commercial", and every University department sets up a commercial wing to earn some extra income to cater for the welfare of their own staff. While certain departments like scientific subjects and law can prosper, departments like "Eastern Languages" (with Hindi, Urdu, Sanskrit, etc.) have to envy their *nouveau riche* sisters helplessly. All this results in a degeneration in the teaching ethics of the University. On the other hand, the students of the University have, by and large, lost their interest in studies. Their morale is hard hit by such unpalatable fact: they had worked hard through all-China competitions just to enter into the No. 1 educational institution which now looks like an apology of China's modern culture of commercialization, while many of their fellow students who were the residues of academic competition are now successful entrepreneurs — darlings of Deng Xiaoping's China. Beijing University is just an example to show how China is dangerously heading towards destroying its educational institutions.

There is another dangerous tendency of trying to turn education into a commodity, and educational institution into a market. There is a serious ignorance of the nature of education on the part of the Chinese zealots for marketization. The importance of education lies in its being "an invisible hand" as one Chinese scholar terms it. Of course, in the market economy there is always an invisible hand, i.e., the market lever which decides the success or failure of an enterprise. However, one should not ignore another invisible hand which regulates the human ethics and morality — the hand of education. Education, thus, should be understood as a different productive base which should have its autonomy from the market forces, although it should be relevant to the market needs.[12]

Apart from educational institutions, there are other means to achieve an improvement of mass education. The rapid development of audio and video communication networking has already drastically revolutionized the educational process. Today, classroom education which the educational institutions offer are serving only a narrow purpose of qualification creation. The quality of the education and the quality of the receivers of education are less important than the papers which these institutions offer. You may be a genius and a person of exceptional information and intelligence. But, you do not get a job which you deserve if you do not have a university degree. On the other hand, you may be the most unintelligent and uninformed among your generation, but because of your excellent paper qualifications you get into the ranks of the social elite.

In the 21st century this paper-qualification-oriented education will die its natural death because of revolutionized methods of evaluation talents, of selections of managers and administrators. Future education is also moving away from classrooms to remote-sensing education networks through radio and television waves and optical cables. This is both good news and danger signal to humankind. I shall come back to this problem later.

Similar to education, Chinese literature has also received a fierce assault from the force of marketization. I must briefly introduce the background before discussing this issue. Chinese literature was a huge state-owned industry during the Mao era. The majority of Chinese "writers" were, and still are, on the payroll of the state. In the meanwhile, except the illegal underground press, all the publishing houses are state-owned enterprises throughout the history of the PRC. The profession of Chinese "writers" is a curious creation. Many of the "writers" have been posted to the literary arena to engage in literary creation which was described by Stalin as the "engineering of human soul". There are also many writers who first emerge by their own creative genius, and, then, get enrolled as a "writer" either in the provincial Writers' Union, or in the all-China Writers' Union, both of which are semi-government organizations. Such writers get paid even if they don't write or publish. But, they become famous with enhanced income and social status if their names see printing in the state-owned publishing world. In the past, these writers had an easy task of propagating the government policies which gave them enough themes to write about. Today, the state no longer gives them readymade themes, and has asked them to write according to the needs of the emerging socialist market economy.

Many writers feel that the "Modern Period" of Chinese literature has come to an end, and a "Post-Modern Period" is unfolding itself. There is great confusion in the literary scene. Commercialization has deeply affected the popular taste, the writers are widely divided in their responses to the changing literary taste. Some of them have quickly shifted to vulgar and sensational staff and earn lots of royalty. Shenzhen, which is the leader of China's Economic Zones, has been staging "Manuscript Auctions" by contemporary writers.[13] Others who don't want to stoop so low are having a hard time to survive as respected writers. Some few writers have become business entrepreneurs and continue to create. On the whole, the literary scene is a jungle full of weeds — very few flowers, let alone immortal works.

A serious problem of the health of China's endogenous development is how to tame political power and let the economic growth ride on it for steady galloping towards prosperity. Historically, China has had the largest bureaucracy for ruling over a population from 1/5 to 1/3 of the humanity which has chosen to live under the Chinese political umbrella for the last two thousand years. The Chinese bureaucracy is a monster of two thousand years of life. It was and still is a necessary evil to safeguard the unity and integrity of the country. But, it is a great burden of the *ancien regime* which should not be carried into the 21st century.

During the Mao era, China had carried this burden when she adopted the Soviet model of the "Command Economy". This further heightened the abuse of political power in all the spheres of the country's life, and created the phenomenon of what may be called the "dislocation of power" (*quanli cuowei*). There were three ramifications of it. The first was the "Monopoly of Power", rendering China into a huge factory. The second was the "Misplacement of Power", making the government manage what should have been left to the people to manage. The third was the "Alienation of Power", facilitating the infiltration of political power into economic arena. It was the third ramification which could easily generate corruption.[14]

China still suffers the top-heavy pattern of governance today. All the changes of the present Reform Regime, good or bad, originated from the central government. Any dilution of the implementation of the centre's decisions in a local setup is frowned upon. An appending evil of this top-heavy system is the absence of public supervision of the government officers' doings. The age old "guan benwei" (officers rule the roost) tradition is still well entrenched. Such a government-officer-oriented social trend is churning out what is termed "Power Fetishism", clinging to power as the short cut for amassing personal wealth on the part of the corrupt government officials.[15] A Chinese scholar observed:

> However, during the great tide of commodity economy and the transition of administrative system from the old to the new, we have some Party and government officials using the power within their control to infiltrate illegally into the commodity economy, which has, thus, created the phenomenon of corruption, of a collusion between officials and businessmen, employing power to run business, transacting power with money, using power for personal gains . . . this not only runs counter with the demand that the socialist state mechanism must serve the economic base, but also creates a sharp contradiction with the principle of equal exchanges of the commodity economy and the mechanics of the market economy. Because of the intrusion and effect of political power serious unequal exchanges have been created in the economic arena. This will produce an inestimable corroding effect and destructive effect on the developing commodity economy and the market economic mechanism which is now being built.[16]

II

There are some specific issues facing China today which are a universal phenomenon. I shall highlight a few for a brief discussion, using the Chinese example to see the fundamental problems of our modern civilization. I am quite conscious that the moment I step beyond China I am on an unsure turf, and my conclusions may carry certain bias due to want of deep understanding of other civilizational developments. But, I shall venture into this part of my presentation to elicit criticism and help from fellow-participants to enhance my own understanding.

The first issue I wish to raise concerns the equilibrium between the Western domination and the promotion of China's native characteristics in her future development. China's quest for an endogenous developmental model tends to encourage the revival of her traditional values. China's ruling elite has begun to re-examine the merits of Chinese traditional thinking according to Marxist analysis. Some scholars have even gone beyond the Marxist framework to appreciate the positive aspects of Confucian ethics and spiritual order. Since the supreme leader, Deng Xiaoping, could go beyond the Marxist framework to embrace market economic system, these scholars who now covertly or even overtly propagate the restoration of the Confucian spiritual superstructure are having freedom to do so.

Many scholars feel that the traditional Chinese value systems occupy a major place in China's future spiritual arena. This arena will be dominated by two Western cultural guests: Marxist political ideology, and Darwinist rationalism. The ideal mainstream of Chinese culture should be a three-in-one synthesis, according to some thinking, i.e. socialism, scientism, and Chinese traditional virtues. Today, such a synthesis is vaguely visible in a blurred picture in China's superstructure. There are various sub-currents and anti-currents in China's cultural arena.[17] Among the sub-currents we have regional life-styles such as "Shanghai culture", "Guangdong culture". A kind of "Yuppie culture" is also emerging championed by young entrepreneurs. The "Hong Kong culture" and "Shenzhen culture" are also appearing as these two places are China's windows for the opening towards the modern developed world. There are also "smoking culture" and "prostitution culture" which have attraction for certain sections of the society along the coastal areas. While there are attempts to exalt the art and style of smoking, there are also literary creations highlighting historical prostitutes as lovable and even admirable specimens of human beings.

Tradition versus modernity is a theme particularly vital but complex to tackle in such age-old civilizations like India and China. On the one hand, one need not be a Marxist to concede that humanity is always on a unilineal course of civilizational evolution, that the present is more advanced than the past. On the other hand, it is also clear to many, including sensitive Western thinkers, that there is a spiritual decline of humankind which, if unchecked, will create a universal civilizational crisis. There are many happenings in the modern era which cannot be called human progress. For one thing, two world wars were fought in the 20th century with such mass killing never witnessed in human history. While the cold war has just ended, the world is still holding dangerous nuclear weapons which can destroy the earth many times over. While money is not available to buy milk for millions of babies born in Africa and Asia, the governments are spending US $ 130 million a year on the production of human-killing weapons. For another, in many Western societies, the family institution is on the verge of total destruction while humans are retrogressing from monogamy to free and unrestrained copulation like the primitives or even beasts. By destroying traditional values, China has now exposed herself to both the progressive and retrogressive trends of the modern civilization. A few years ago, some left (or call them "ultra-left") intellectuals raised the alarm of "spiritual pollution" (*jingshen wuran*) and wanted a nation-wide campaign to counter it. This was stopped by Deng Xiaoping, fearing that it might disturb the smooth development of Chinese economic reforms. Deng's soft pedalling the degenerating Western cultural influences has resulted in serious erosion of morality in China today, particularly among those who were born and brought up during the Cultural Revolution — people who have never been systematically indoctrinated by healthy education and revolutionary ideology.

Let me take up a case of the ground reality as an illustration of cultural degeneration in the context of tradition versus modernity. We know that in historical times the Tarim Basin was lush green. Today it is mostly dry and barren. This has figured in one of Li Ruihuan's above quoted speeches as well.[18] Desertification has had a tremendous growth in the last two thousand years in Xinjiang in China, and the Taklamakan Desert in the Tarim Basin covers an area of 327,000 square kilometres which is 2.27 times the territory of Bangladesh. More unpleasant is a report about the phenomenon of "increasing desertification day by day" (*ri jian shahua*) of Xinjiang's culture today. The report says that when you visit a book shop you see on the shelves a plethora of unhealthy vulgar publications which bring discomfort to the mind. When you turn on the television or radio, good programmes are like soothing streams being drowned by the ocean of sand. When you watch the cruel executions of violence on the silver screen you wonder how there could be such human hatred against each other. When you hear the pop albums blaring out such lines like "Let me for once having enough love", you feel you are listening to the last cry of someone who is going to die in the next moment. Why can't love be enjoyed by a human heart enduringly instead of the momentary feeding of a hungry sex beast?[19]

Xinjiang is what modern foreign scholars call "Chinese Turkistan" and what ancient Europeans call "Serindia", meaning China-India (The first syllable "ser" stood for "Seres" or "Serica", the ancient Roman word for "The Land of Silk", i.e.

China). Scholars and tourists can still find remnants of ancient Buddhist monuments in Xinjiang which suggest the existence of a highly developed and sophisticated spiritual culture in this land more than a thousand years ago. It was the records of those days which depicted the Tarim Basin as a greenland on the track of the famous "Silk Road". This name "Silk Road" (alternately "Silk Route") was given by a German sinologist, Albert Herrmann, in 1910. It would have been more appropriately called "*Dharmaratna Marg*" (Road of the Jewels of Truth). The great Taklamakan Desert in the heart of the Tarim Basin did exist at that time. Many Chinese pilgrims who had trodden on it believed that ferocious goblins resided in the desert, and devoured human beings and animals who passed through it. But, what these pilgrims did was to trace the skeletons of those devoured by the goblins so that they could find their path to India — the "Land of Buddha".[20] Many Indian monks did the same in a reverse direction to reach China to disseminate Buddha's message of enlightenment, non-violence, and universal love. Without such selfless spirit and self sacrifice of ancient Buddhists of China. India and many Central Asian nationalities there would not have been the "Dharmaratna Marg" and "Serinda". It is the fallacy of human evolution that the ancients built cultural edifices in the desert while the modernists turn cultural greenland into a desert.

This brings home the maldevelopment of modern civilization. On the one hand, there has been tremendous material advancement in Xinjiang, in China, in other parts of Asia and the world; on the other hand, there is retrogression in moral standard and spiritual culture everywhere including Xinjiang as we have just seen.

Scientists have noticed the depletion of Ozone Layer around the globe. This Ozone Layer is earth's shield to protect human bodies from the damage of harmful rays. Spiritually, culture is the invisible Ozone Layer that protects human souls from harmful rays from the cesspool of iniquity. Desertification of culture is more harmful to humankind than that of the ecological environment.

Interesting statistics show that Xinjiang ranks as one of China's largest homes for centenarians. According to the 1990 census, 894 centenarians were discovered in Xinjiang among whom 814 were Uighurs. We know that there were only 8.6 million Uighurs according to the 1990 census figure. This means that for every ten thousand Uighurs, one has lived more than a hundred years. According to analysis, the sources of the Uighurs' longevity comes from their life style. First, their daily diet consists of wheat, rice, carrot, onion, cabbage, mutton, in addition to a lot of fruits, i.e. water-melon, melon, fig, walnut, peach, date, apricot, grape, mulberry. Second, they don't smoke, drink very little alcohol, refuse to eat the meat that is not from freshly killed animals by the cut which lets out their blood (the *halal* food for all Muslims). Third, they drink tea with milk and with a sprinkle of goat's or mare's butter. Fourth, they are a tension-free people, fond of singing and dancing, physical labour, helping others etc.[21] In other words, it is the preservation of the endogenous life style which is the secret of long life for the Uighur race, and for other ethnic communities who can preserve their endogenous virtues.

This endogenous life style in Xinjiang, in other parts of China, in India, in many developing countries is being endangered by unhealthy trends of modern civilization which are being popularized by the mass media, particularly movies and television programmes. As I have alluded to earlier, television programmes will replace classroom teaching as the most important means in popularizing education. It would be dangerous if the field of television and other visual media are dominated by commercialization. Visual media induced crimes are not only a perennial feature of the USA but are on the increase in India, China, and other Asian countries. In the award-winning Chinese movie, "Red Sorghum", the hero is a rapist, and the theme song of the film is the rapist's joyous expression when he chases the heroine of the film and rapes her in the field. Today, you go to any city or town in China, you hear the tiny tots singing this song merrily which is not only sickening, but has a dangerous impact on the healthy growth of morality in China.

One notices that in India it is the cosmetic industries which control the mass media, in China it is the food processing, brewing, and tonic medicine industries which have an upper hand. When you just watch Chinese television you may gain a misconception that Chinese are a sick race, or are deficient in healthy food in their daily diet, whereas it is just the other way round. But, they are many Chinese who are crazy for tonics, and, at one time, the free medical services of China became the back door for the distribution of tonics. Powerful cadres and respected elders still gather a huge stock of tonics as gifts that they don't need at all. This brings us closer to the subject of AIDS (Acquired Immunity Deficiency Syndrome). AIDS is a terrible disease which not only takes away the lives of those who, for their own indulgence in unhealthy social behaviour, have suffered its affliction, but also kills those who are entirely innocent — getting it through birth or blood transfusion. AIDS symbolizes the wrong direction which modern civilization chooses to develop. It is a punishment for the sin committed by the humankind for their obsession with materialism. It is the most materialistically oriented societies which are worst affected by such a deadly disease. Scientists have been trying hard to combat this deadly enemy of humans through laboratory research. But, in my opinion, this is not the remedial solution. In the first place in the absence of rigid monogamy and strict discipline in sexual life, AIDS cannot be eliminated even if it eventually becomes curable. In the second place, even if AIDS is eliminated, another deadly or deadlier punishment will be on its way against human obsession with materialism without the accompanying high spiritual culture as an antidote.

To go a step deeper into the problem, the occurrence of AIDS to humans is because of ACIDS, i.e. Acquired Cultural Immunity Deficiency Syndrome. We can see clearly that the phenomenon of cultural desertification which I have alluded to earlier is created by the poisonous wind from the Western world. This wind has come to Xinjiang and other parts of Asia after turning many Western communities and societies into cultural deserts. In USA, television is called the "idiot box". The new generation of America is called "Generation X" which is deeply poisoned by this Idiot Box. There are 40 odd commercial channels of American television which (except a couple of them being devoted to Christian programmes) rarely impart any moral education and spiritual culture. This X-Generation is daily poisoned by the advertisements enticing them to eat more junk food, to indulge in more luxuries, to participate in the gambling games with culture only as a disguise, to the scenes of sex and violence — but seldom telling them how to become morally healthy and spiritually noble human beings, how to choose their future careers, how to combat social evils, etc. This is the generation whose minds and souls have already undergone desertification. Since there is no strong spiritual force to combat this cultural poison in USA, the American society is already the victim of ACIDS. In fact, ACIDS and AIDS are two heads of the same monster. Just chopping off the head of AIDS it can grow again in another form. Only after chopping off the head of ACIDS will the monster be killed once for all.

AIDS is an exopathic disease. It does not grow from the endobiotic development or maldevelopment like obesity, hypertension, tumour, tuberculosis, diabetes, etc. America was AIDS-free a few decades ago, and the disease has come to the USA from Africa. ACIDS is also an exopathic disease, and modern America is one of the sources of it. Both these aspects have connections. America is a land wedded to freedom and openness. It is the greatest sanctuary for the human birds of all different ethnic features of the world to feather their own nests without restrictions and discriminations. The American way of life is not endogenous. It is a universal creation which has forged into a powerful exogenous acculturation force.

America is the best specimen of modern civilization, while the harmful part of modern civilization is the worst endopathic disease for pre-modern societies. Modern civilization is strong in modern science, but weak in philosophy, in moral values, in spiritual enlightenment. Modern science has achieved wonders in examining the exterior of the universe, getting the true picture of the twinkle twinkle little stars which exist light years away from the humankind. However, modern science still gropes in the dark about human body's own internal rhythms and functioning. The more modern the gadgets that subject the human body to echographic or radiographic examinations, the more confused are the pictures that appear. This is because a human is 50 per cent material and 50 per cent spirit. To find out the dynamics of human spirit we have to design different research methods and laboratories.

The best defence against AIDS and ACIDS is to emphasize the endogenous development of a country, a community, a society. In the Chinese context, this means combating Commercialism and Mammonism which has not yet become an important agenda in China's developmental strategy. There is a Chinese saying: "Ren wei cai si, niao wei shi wang." (As the birds die in the quest for food, humans die in the quest for money). If this saying becomes a universal truth, the "economic animal" which a human being is will be reduced to a slave of Mammon. This was a theme which Jiang Zemin, the Chairman of the PRC, advocated against at an all China conference on mass media in January, 1995.[22]

Commercialism is a complex subject which a non-economist like me may not be able to do justice with. The dilemma of China today is that while the leadership has tasted the forbidden fruit of commercialization and marketization and want them to take China to a higher level of economic development, it has also noticed the danger of the inundation of Commercialism and Mammonism. There is a dichotomy in the situation concerning the socio-economic development of China today.

I seem to have said too many bad things about commercialization, and about the USA which exemplifies commercialization. But, I am not blind to the virtues of the USA and the US model of commercialization. See the facelift which commercialization has brought about in China. In the Mao era when commercialization was frowned upon life was dull, and the developmental front was a drab scene. In the last 15 years, China seems to have suddenly awakened from a monotonous slumber, and every body, everywhere is crying for development.

So many high rise buildings, flyovers, factories, motor cars and motor cycles, etc. — as if all have suddenly appeared from nowhere. It is commercialization which has created such a developmental explosion. USA is no doubt a benign model for China to leap forward to a higher stage of economic development.

However, there is no denying the fact that Commercialism and Mammonism erode all spiritual values, and degenerate the cultural fabrics of a society. At the root of Commercialism is the paramountcy of self-interest of the individual. In the USA and other capitalist countries self-interest is balanced with the norms of a civil society, with civic courtesy and civic ethics harmonizing the social life. China under the Mao regime had made hundreds of millions of bird-cages to keep the bird of egotism in place. In the post-Mao era the cages are open, and individual egotism flies all over. Without the civic norms, they fight each other without any law of games, and some birds become vultures. People with better resources abuse the political power to advance in fortune seeking. A few talented reach to the top relying on their own merits, but few of them can avoid greasing the palms of the checkposts by compromising their conscience. Many others who don't have the means to get rich through proper channels resort to cheating, counterfeiting and other unethical means towards the goal of personal prosperity. China, in the last 15 years, has suddenly become a classical example of "every road leads to Rome" — never mind the immorality along the roads. While counterfeit drugs kill the lives of human beings, counterfeit fertilizer and insecticide damage the crops.

Whereas in the USA such things can't easily happen it takes time for the Chinese authorities to regulate industrial production and commercial behaviour. During the Mao era, China was miraculously honest with almost no theft. Today, petty theft is rampant, pickpockets have a field day, gangs of robbers operate in crowded trains. How is it that overnight a puritan society has suddenly become so outrageous? The sudden liberalization of egotism which I have just alluded to is, no doubt, at the root of the change. But, there are other factors — the absence of rule of law, the want of civic ethics, etc. In a word, it will take a few decades, if not longer, for China to build up a civil society like that functioning in the USA and other advanced countries. But, even in the USA, Japan, Italy, frauds, hoaxes, and economic crimes are not infrequent occurrences. Individualism, selfishness and indifference to collective interest and to the affairs of fellow human beings are the fatal weakness of a capitalist society, no matter how perfect is its civic order. Capitalism, essentially, is a moral disease. By emulating capitalism, China has contracted this disease in no small measure.

Another irritating phenomenon in China today is the absence of courtesy. Even foreign tourists can't tolerate the arrogant attitude of some of the public service personnel although they generally treat foreigners far more courteously than they do their fellow countrymen. Not that Chinese are arrogant as a race. Individual Chinese do impress their foreign friends as most amiable and modest. The arrogance is the residue of the traditional heritage — a tradition of "officers rule the roost", as alluded to earlier. The concept of "public servant" is alien to Chinese culture although the slogan of "*wei renmin fuwu*" (service before self) was the loudest slogan during the Mao era. Placed in any tiny position like a sales person at a counter a Chinese instantly feels his or her importance which generates arrogance. Another factor contributory to this arrogance is PRC's cadre system. All those who have been cadres, big or small, have a sense of pride of belonging to a revolutionary organization which rules over China. In Indian traditional parlance, they are a kind of "Brahmins", while those who are outside the cadre are called "qunzhong" (the masses) — a term which also connotes "those who are less revolutionary conscious", thus in an inferior status. Although the revolutionary spirit among the cadres is much diluted today, the arrogance attached to it has not totally disappeared. There is also the phenomenon of an "in-group" scenario which exists in all countries but particularly in China. There is an "in-group" affinity which is the source of affection, cooperation, courtesy, and even self-sacrifice — all not available for others who are not included in the "group". In China, so also in India, one generally gets things done through "*guanxi*" (literally "relationship", in reality "connections") and avoids the toil of standing in the long queue as well as the irritation at the public counters. In this way, the public counters are for the "mass", i.e. those who have no "guanxi" — no strings to pull. Naturally, they have to be the recipients of arrogance of the "in-group" oriented Chinese service personnel. In other words, where there is no "guanxi" there is arrogance and the accompanying irritation. If China can Americanize in this respect as fast as possible, half of her social tension will disappear.

Superstition smacks of ignorance, but superstition brandished in Commercialism makes it look more ridiculous. In China, like in India, people can spend money to get their favourite numbers of the allotted telephones. The people of Guangdong province which is full of *nouveaux riches* would spend money to get number "8" and to avoid number "4". This is because, in their dialect (the Cantonese), the sound "fa" for "eight" is homonymous to the word for "getting rich", while the sound "si" for "four" is homonymous to that for "to die". In the past, the ancient Chinese used to burn some paper symbolically for the dead, wishing that the departed souls would not be short of money to spend in Heaven or hell — a custom which must have spread from India to China. Now, people spend enormous sums to ask the Buddhist temples or individual suppliers to make paper-made houses, motor cars, refrigerators, sofas, etc. and burn them during the funeral. This is the custom which has prevailed in Hong Kong for many decades, and is now getting widely spread in neighbouring Guangdong province. This custom has completely lost its original touch of symbolism, but becomes a stupid indulgence in superstition and pomp and show. Here is another example of how the development of material culture can pollute the spiritual culture.

Tackling "poverty" has become an increasingly important universal subject. The general approach is to increase growth coupled with some forcible measures of equitable distribution of soicial wealth. The world developmental strategists first fix an arbitrary criterion of US $ 300 as the "poverty line", and, then, try to mobilize resources to help those segments to increase their annual income to cross this line. So far, such a strategy has not achieved much success. Those who live under the "poverty line" are on the increase year after year. Out of 5 billion people of the humankind, 1.3 billion are living below the poverty line.[23] This is a problem which cannot be solved by the modern culture of development.

We must first understand the nature of the problem. World-wise, humans today have increased social wealth many times more than the increase in world population. During pre-modern times people might have been poor, but there was no "poverty" problem. "Poverty" is a modern institution — the legitimate child of modern civilization. For instance, the poor people in ancient India and China ate very little food, and dressed very shabbily according to modern standard. Their hygienic conditions were bad in comparison with modern standard. Yet, poverty was not such a glaring problem as it is today. To begin with, people, rich or poor, were living on the same scale and mode of material consumption. The difference between the rich and poor lay only in the quantity and quality — eating the same kind of food, using the same means of transport, i.e. their own legs. Today, the affluent segments of humankind travel by jet planes while those who live below the poverty line can't even get near the airport to look at the exterior of the planes. And, so much food is thrown away from the air services that could feed many who cannot even get such luxurious leftovers. And the paper used up by an international flight can be enough stationery for a rural school for a whole year. Some of such rural schools in India and China don't even have blackboards and slates, let alone paper for the students to write. In eating, the dog food for the pets of the rich is more than luxurious delicacies for poor human beings. In China, before 1979, a household had an income of only few hundred yuan for a year. Then, in the beginning of 1980s, there was the new phenomenon of the *nouveaux riche* called "wanyuanhu" (Ten thousand yuan households) which made headline news. In recent years, there has been a phenomenon called "wanyuangou" (Ten thousand yuan dogs). Some of the *nouveaux riches* in China now spend ten thousand yuans or more to buy famous European species of pet dogs, while there are several tens of million of Chinese today whose annual income is below 400 yuan. This is the true nature of "poverty"! Today, in certain Chinese circles where Commercialism and Mammonism have become people's deities, "Ten thousand yuan households" no longer arouse admiration and excitement, but "Ten thousand yuan dogs" do. In other words, in a section of Chinese society, the rapid economic development has made human dignity below that of the dogs. What a degeneration!

We see here clearly that "poverty" is not a phenomenon of want. It is a social disease. We must first cure such human disease before we can tackle the problem of "poverty". I am glad to see that some municipal governments in China, like Beijing, have started administrative measures to discourage the development of this "dog culture". However, such a "dog culture" is only the symptom, not the pathogenesis of the disease. The pathogenesis lies in the deficiency of spiritual culture. All what we have discussed earlier — cultural desertification, ACIDS and "dog culture" — are from the same root cause. The other side of the coin is Commercialism and Mammonism. Commercialism and Mammonism are the cancer-causing agents for our cultural body. They are worse than narcotics.

China's national minorities suffer a good deal in the development of globalization. As the Nagas in India resist strongly the building up of a railway through their territory, minorities have their rights to live according to their own liking. In China, no minority community can resist the wheel of modernization which has rolled into all the remote nooks and corners of the country. Natural economy does not survive anywhere in China now. But, the demolition of the self-sufficiency economy does not necessarily mean an improvement of economic conditions in the minority areas. The main difficulty is that many minority communities can't establish modern economic enterprises on their own after their rights of self-sufficiency were taken away from them. There is the need of capital, technology, personnel, infrastructure and transportation and other services all of which have to depend upon exogenous aid. Destruction of the endogenous economic system in the minority areas without exogenous aid is a mockery of modern development. As a result, some minority areas in China can't even survive without urgent relief measures. In 1994, half of the minority families of the Baise Zhuang Autonomous Perfecture in Guangxi province had no food, nor warm clothing to pass the winter. The central government, provincial government, and prefecture government had to rush 9 million kilograms of foodgrains, 550,000 pieces of quilts and cotton quilted coats for their survival, in addition to 1.48 million yuan (about 6-7 million rupees) for them to invest in various production projects.[24] Here is an instance of both the PRC's efficiency in its protection of the minority communities as well as its failure in developing all the minority areas into prosperous modern societies.

III

I should conclude now by returning to the theme of endogenous development for China's future. I have dwelt much upon the fact that China's national development is symbiotic with the development of modern civilization of the world. By attempting an endogenous development, China, or any nation, can't get away from the exogenous influences — be they exopathic diseases or exophilic blessings. Yet, it is in the context of globalization that there is the need for emphasis on endogenous development. The fundamental logic behind endogenous development is to recognize the heterogeneity of modern civilization. It is wrong to think that west or USA is the sole origin of modernity. Modern civilization is the joint contribution of all the peoples, of the first or second or third world. However, there is also the unmistakable tendency of some nations trying to impose their own value judgements on other nations in the name of modernization. Emphasizing endogenous development bears relevance to a resistance against such hegemonic tendency of modern development.

Globalization is a subject of much controversy among academic circles. We might detect two different developing trends in globalization. The first trend is what I have just now alluded to: the hegemonic behaviour of certain great powers to monopolize the world market, to dominate world developmental trends, to impose their own value judgements on the weaker nations. The second trend is the genuine demand of all the nations, peoples, ethnic and cultural communities to come closer towards one another, and build up a *Jambudvipa* (universe) of co-prosperity, amity, and harmony. Obviously, no one in the developing world would vote for the first move, but everyone would try to contribute to the healthy development of the second dynamism.

To return to China's development, we also see the existence of binary opposites. The opposites are not unrelated to the opposite dynamics which I have just stated. On the one hand, there is a strong desire on the part of China to march hand in hand with other developing countries to build up a millennium of universal co - prosperity. On the other hand, she has to struggle against the imposition of other nation's will on her developmental course. There is a new dimension: if China becomes a world power (which is very likely) would she also behave like a hegemonist in the international affairs? Right now, of course, China has a large share of the world's population below the poverty line. So, from the viewpoint of the entire Chinese nation, it is in her interest to march hand in hand with other developing nations — otherwise she will never achieve her national salvation from backwardness and want.

One important issue concerning the dichotomy between endogenous development of China and the exogenous influences of modern civilization is how to modernize China's vast rural areas and bring modern civilization to Chinese peasants who comprise 80 per cent of China's population. Europe never had such a problem in its modernization process. In the 18th and 19th centuries, England could afford to destroy her primary industry — agriculture — because she had colonies to supply plenty of agricultural products. America started its agriculture as an industrial enterprise, and never has had a large portion of its population solely dependent on agricultural income. Only India and other Asian countries have acute problems of developing agriculture, and uplifting the living standard of the peasants.

There is a slogan in China that "Agriculture is a strategic industry. Foodgrain is a strategic material." It is now realized that China's 1.2 billion mouths have to be fed by the yield from Chinese fields. If China's countryside is poor, 900 million of her population are sufferers. On top of it, China is a country famous for peasant rebellions. In the last four decades, Chinese peasants have been strong supporters of the PRC because the Chinese communist movement, particularly its armed wing, essentially belonged to Chinese peasantry. The majority of PRC's leaders and cadres at all levels in the past were peasants, and the majority of the membership of CPC are still peasants.

In the last few years, Chinese peasants have been very unhappy for many reasons. First, the new changes take place mostly along the sea coast while peasants in the interior are still as poor as before. Secondly, modernization is always a trend in favour of the secondary and tertiary industries. Industrial products, commercial profits, and service charges are all more lucrative than the toiling in plantation. The country's reforms, particularly the price reform, leave all products in the jungle of market competition where agricultural products always have a disadvantage. The result of the reforms is the hike of prices of fertilizer, insecticide, and agricultural implements much higher than the increase of prices of agricultural products. Peasants have found it unprofitable to produce. Disparity between rural and urban incomes which has been reduced for some years is again being increased, and has reached as high as 1:2.53 (urban population earning two and half times of the income of the rural population) according to 1993 statistics. To add injustice to injury, the state planning has proportionally reduced its rural input. Investment in agriculture which was 10.69 per cent of China's total investment in 1978 has occupied only a poor 2.2 per cent in 1993. In the last two years, the government has been trying to mobilize more resource onto agriculture, and adopt all possible measures to stabilize the enthusiasm of the farmers, particularly the grain and cotton growers. But, how to carry the huge peasantry of China to future prosperity remains a serious problem in China's development.

India, too, has a similar problem. Both the Chinese and Indian peasants share the worry that globalization would ultimately mean their marginalization from the mainstream of the country's development. In other words, modernization has its innate dynamism against the agricultural society which China and India have inherited for three thousand years. Endogenous development in China (also in India) means to protect the majority of her population from the onslaught of the anti-agricultural exogenous force of modern civilization. To do this and still embrace modernization is like having the cake and eating it.

Another exogenous tendency carried by modernization to China (also India) is to erase the characteristics of national minorities which have existed in China for more than a thousand years. If the minority culture is merely backwardness, there is no need of even crocodile tears for its extinction. But, China has always been a collective of diverse nationalities and cultures. Minority cultures have played an important role in enriching Chinese cultural life. The Manchu culture, for instance, has contributed greatly to the development of the Beijing dialect (which is the standard language of China today) and the Beijing Opera. Today, the popularity of Beijing Opera has been overtaken by Jazz in Beijing itself because of modernization. Incidentally, Jazz itself was and still is the cultural asset of the minority — the African Americans. This community has the most awkward fate in the USA today.

On the one hand, almost all the great singers and athletes who have won glory for America are "blacks" and many of them are heroes of millions of American "whites", while one-fourth and more of African American youths are languishing in jail. The latter phenomenon is the marginalization of the minority society due to the Social-Darwinist force of modernization — Survival of the fittest. In China, this force of Survival of the fittest is being patted by the authorities which leads to many state-owned enterprises going bankrupt, causing problems to hundreds of thousands of their workers. If the majority nationality cannot protect itself from the onslaught of marginalization, how can the minorities in a much weaker position protect themselves. China should prevent her minorities to go the direction of the African Americans. Otherwise, there will be no endogenous model in her development.

There is a theory anticipating China to break up after the exit of the supreme leader, Deng Xiaoping. Minority areas, particularly Tibet and Xinjiang, figure in this hypothesis. I think there is no likelihood that this will happen. China will hold, and will be in a strong position after the return of Hong Kong and Macau to the motherland. Then, mainland China will be in an even stronger position to get Taiwan closer to its orbit. Taiwan's independence and China's break-up are supposed to be linked up. I think both can be avoided if the PRC leadership plays its cards tactfully and attains success in developing the economy and enhancing the living standard of all its nationalities.

If everything goes well, many models will develop inside China. Right now, there are two distinguishing themselves. One is the Guangdong model, and another the Su'nan model. The first is exogenous in nature and tilted towards private enterprises, while the second is endogenous in nature and tilted towards collective developmental programmes.

Guangdong province is situated in the Pearl River Delta which is now one of China's golden triangles. Guangdong is the homeland of the majority of overseas Chinese in Southeast Asia as well as other continents. As blood is thicker than water, when the Chinese diaspora enthusiastically responded to Deng Xiaoping's new economic policy to invest in China, they naturally put most of their eggs in the Guangdong basket. Guangdong also has an important linkage with the developed world, i.e. Hong Kong. From the early 1980s onwards, Guangdong and Hong Kong have started merging into one integral economic zone with the Hong Kong capitalists and transnational companies dominating the scene. Today, virtually all the chimney-smoking industries of Hong Kong have moved to Guangdong, making Hong Kong a city of office premises, and the nerve-centre controlling the next door industrial bases at Guandong. The Hong Kong-China border immigration posts are now overlooking the heaviest road traffic of the world, and most of the trucks bear both the Hong Kong and PRC Guangdong registration plates (one white and another black for easy differentiation). Hong Kong has not waited for 1997 to integrate with the motherland. It is already inseparable with Guangdong now. People are saying that Guangdong is the 5th "small tiger" of the Asia-Pacific region (after South Korea, Taiwan, Hong Kong, and Singapore), which is not an exaggeration. There is a delicate relationship between Beijing and Guangdong. On the one hand, the central government has purposely allowed Guangdong to go a step ahead to stimulate a rapid economic growth of the entire country. On the other hand, there are reports about the semi-independent attitude on the part of Guangdong province in carrying out the central government's decisions. In this relationship there is the scenario of a spoiled favourite child. Right now, there is no sign of rebellion of the child who is still a favourite bathing in the affection of a joint family.

The Su'nan (southern Jiangsu province) model is made up of ten odd counties under the jurisdiction of three cities, Suzhou, Wuxi, and Changzhou. There are some similarities of Su'nan with Guangdong. It is situated in the Yangtse River Delta (another golden triangle of China) with China's biggest city, Shanghai, as its neighbourhood. Su'nan has, from history, been the most prosperous countryside of China. Cotton textile industry was first established here in the 14th century. It has since become China's textile centres specializing in both cotton and silk fabric productions. It was because of Su'nan that Shanghai became China's textile centre in the 19th and 20th centuries. Su'nan was one of the first Chinese countryside to respond to Deng Xiaoping's new economic policy. The peasants there initially pooled their savings and started establishing industries in the villages. They gathered information about the international markets, designed suitable consumer goods, imported latest machines, and produced garments, knitwear, shoes and other light industrial products for the overseas market. They employed foreign experts (many of them Chinese), and even went abroad to start new ventures. With such epoch-making enterprises, Su'nan has 2-3,000 village factories enjoying international reputation. They form an important foreign exchange earning sector of China's small-scale industries. An additional feature of the Su'nan model is the protection of agriculture by its new rising industry. Because of the collective ownership of assets, the local leadership see to it that adequate funds are allocated to the development of agriculture so that there is ample supply of food and raw material. As I have said earlier that agriculture is the mainstay of endogenous development in China, the Su'an model ensures this endogenous interest. Perhaps, it is in the Su'nan model that we can ultimately find the solution of modernizing China's countryside without first destroying China's agriculture. If every Chinese province can be developed like Su'nan, China will succeed in carrying her 80 per cent of peasant population to the modernized future without making them suffer.

Among the affluent components of the Su'nan model, the Huaxi Village of Jiangyin County is most famous. It has achieved a per capita income level higher than that of the four "Asia-Pacific Tigers". The unique feature in the development of this village is that there are neither *nouveau riche* households, nor "poverty households". Su'nan is a typical model of coprosperity. Developing spiritual culture is another special feature of the Su'nan model. Sizeable investment has been put into the establishment of "cultural palaces" where the workers and peasants can have a healthy recreation during week ends and after work on week days. Such a model has transformed the countryside into many newly built towns some of which are even more modern than many big and medium cities of China. Because of such a developing pattern, a phenomenon has occurred which is described as "Peasants become workers but not going to the cities; peasants leave plantation but not leaving the village."[25] Like Guangdong, Su'nan today is crowded with foreign investors and tourists. Airports have been built on agricultural lands to facilitate international travellers. Limousines are a common sight, carrying both foreign guests and also natives — bumpkins who 15 years ago knew only cycling. It is in this Su'nan model in which we see the future of a healthy endogenous development of China. If there is any place in China where there is genuine socialism, it is in Su'nan (also in other areas where the Su'nan model is followed).

Already in the limelight is the rapid development of Shanghai which is designed as the "dragon head" (*longtou*) of the entire Yangtse river valley. Both the central government and the municipal government of Shanghai (the richest city of China) are investing heavily in infrastructural development of Pudong area — the new Shanghai. The ambition of all this is to revive Shanghai's position of the biggest city and industrial, commercial and financial centre in the East during the 19th century — as built by the Britons. When this dream comes true (which may take 50 to 100 years), China will have both Hong Kong and Shanghai to form a hub of economic development of the Eastern Hemisphere, echoing with Tokyo, Osaka, and Singapore. While Hong Kong will remain a capitalist paradise for at least 50 years after the 1997 takeover, Shanghai will essentially belong to the socialist arena of China — the socialist version of Hong Kong. When Shanghai becomes the Dragon Head, Su'nan and a larger area (including the entire Jiangsu province, in addition to neighbouring Shandong and other provinces) will emerge as the body of this new socialist dragon in development. Meanwhile, when Hong Kong and Macau return to the motherland in 1997 and 1999, south China (centering around the Pearl River delta) would become China's bridgehead to integrate all diaspora developmental initiatives for an international and interzonal development which would be exogenous in character. The Shanghai-Su'nan endogenous and the Guangdong exogenous models will vie with each other for supremacy: while China marches along the road of endogenous development, she will progress further towards globalization. In the long run, China will still be a unity of diverse models like it is today. Perhaps, the confusion and uncertainty will not be as great as at present, if we re-examine the same issue after five or ten years. By then, we shall already be in the 3rd millennium of our common era. By that time, I hope China, India and other countries of the world will become more united in their joint march towards the milliennium of coprosperity.

Notes

1. ***See*** Hu Sheng, "Shenme shi shehuizhuyi, ruhe jianshe shehuizhuyi?" (What is socialism? How to construct socialism?), in *Xinhua Wenzhai* (Xinhua Digest Monthly), Beijing, No. 8, 1994, p. 11.
2. Li Yi'ning, "Zhongguo jingji gaige yu shichang qianjing (China's economic reforms and market prospects), in *Xinhua Wenzhai*, No. 12, 1994, pp. 44-45.
3. Gu Honghong, "'Yinjinchao' pingshuo" (Comment on "Import waves"). In *Liaowang* (Observation weekly), Beijing, No. 53, Dec. 31, 1990, pp. 16-17.
4. All these statistics were given by Li Ruihuan, a top ranking Chinese leader, in his speech delivered to the 7th session of the 8th Chinese People's Consultative Conference on July 1st, 1994. ***See*** *Xinhua Wenzhai*, No. 9, 1994, p. 1.
5. *Ibid.*
6. *Ibid.*, p. 2.
7. *Ibid.*
8. *Ibid.*
9. *Renmin Ribao* (People's Daily), Beijing, Jan. 10, 1995, p.5.
10. *Ibid.*, Jan. 5, p. 2.
11. *Ibid.*, Jan. 15, 1995, p. 1.

12. Zhang Renjie, "Dui 'jiaoyu ying shiying shichang jingji xuyao' zhi zai sikao" (The rethinking on "Education should cater for the needs of market economy"), *Xinhua Wenzhai*, No. 12, 1994, pp. 147-48.
13. Zhang Jun, "Lun 90 niandai woguo wenxuede zouxiang yu xuanze" (On the direction and choice of the literature of our country in the 1990s), in *Xinhua Wenzhai*, No. 9, 1994, p. 115.
14. *Ibid.*, Bao Xinjian, "Lun woguo xingzhengtizhi gaigede shuangxiang mubiao jiegou" (On the structure for the dual targets of the administrative reforms of our country), p. 10.
15. *Ibid.*, No. 8, 1994, Bai Enpei, "Laogu shuli Makesizhuyi qunzhongguandian" (Firmly estabilsh the Marxist mass perspective), p. 19.
16. Bao Xinjian, *loc cit*, p. 11.
17. Zheng Hangsheng, "Guanyu dangqian wenhua fazhan moshide jidian sikao" (Some thoughts on the developmental model of present Chinese culture), in *Xinhua Wenzhai*, No. 9, 1994, pp. 150-52.
18. *Ibid.*, p. 1, text of Li Ruihuan's speech. Li said in his speech on July 1st, 1994 that "Because of the destruction of the ecological environment, the prosperous Silk Road of the Tang Dynasty and the greenlands of our vast west has become a vast desert."
19. This is the summary of an article by Xiao Lian entitled "Shamo yu qingquan" (Desert and clean stream), in *Xinjiang Ribao* (Xinjiang Daily) published in Urumqi, Nov. 23, 1994, p. 3.
20. ***See*** famous pilgrim Xuanzang's (602-64) description in his biography authored by his disciples Huili and Yanzong. ***See*** Wu Bolun, *Chuanbo youyide sichouzhilu* (The Silk Road which spreads friendship), Xi'an: People's Publishing House, 1983, p. 80.
21. Li Qingshan, "Weiwuer laoren changshou tanyuan" (An inquiry into the sources of the longevity of the Uighurs), in *Xinjiang Ribao*, Nov. 26, 1994, p. 5.
22. *Renmin Ribao*, Jan. 20, 1995, p. 1.
23. Mahbub ul Haq, "Towards a better social order", in *The Economic Times*, Feb. 27, 1995, "Insight".
24. *Renmin Ribao*, Jan. 2, 1995, p. 3.
25. Zhang Qinde, " 'Su'nan moshi' de qishi" (The revelation of the "Su'nan Model"), in *Xinhua Wenzhai*, No. 7, 1994, pp. 10-11.

4

Indigenous Cultures in the Development of Indonesia

Meutia F. Swasono

Many countries have different population compositions. In some countries, newcomers go beyond indigenous people, both in numbers as well as in social-economic advantages. In others the composition is balanced, while in still other countries, the indigenous people represent the majority.

Indonesia with its five large islands, Sumatra, Java, Kalimantan (Borneo), Sulawesi (Celebes), Irian Jaya (west of Papua Nugini) and thousands of medium-sized and small islands, is a country whose indigenous people represent the majority of the population. The concept of *indigenous people* has to be traced back in history (Koentjaraningrat, ed., 1984).[1]

Since the Hindu era, which marked the historical period of literacy, people from different parts of the world continuously came to Nusantara, the vast archipelago stretching from Sumatra to Irian Jaya, mostly for trade or for the spread of religion. The Dutch were leading among European traders and established themselves as the colonial power in Nusantara for about three and a half centuries. It was then called The East Indies, at first under the Dutch East Indies Companies (VOC) and later under the Dutch colonial government. After national independence in 1945, the Dutch East Indies were internationally recognised as the Republic of Indonesia.

During the colonial period the Dutch East Indies government divided the East Indies population into three categories: European/Dutch citizens; the *Vreemde Oosterlingen*[2] (foreign easterners); and the *Inlanders* (indigenous people). Unfortunately the last had a 'backwardness' connotation.

After Indonesia's independence, the *Vreemde Oosterlingen* were given the choice either to apply for Indonesian citizenship or to choose Dutch or other citizenships. Through this process, Indonesia recognises two kinds of citizenship, the *warganegara Indonesia* (Indonesians) and the *warganegara asing* (foreigners). Thus the Indonesian population consisted of the indigenous people as well as the former *Vreemde Oosterlingen* and their descendants who had chosen the Indonesian citizenship. Culturally the former are called the *pribumi*, 'natives of the country' while the latter are called *non-pribumi*, those whose ancestors came from other races and countries.[3]

The indigenous cultures in development programmes

The brief introduction has described the 'indigenous population of Indonesia' as the *warganegara pribumi* (native Indonesians), consisting of various ethnic groups spread all over the country. Each considers a place in Indonesia as its land of origin, where it maintains ancestors' graves and major cultural heritage. Progress and development have increased their socio-economic and socio-cultural mobility, and some of them live in the metropolitan and large cities and small towns while some others remain in the villages and in remote places and islands, leading a variety of life-styles and living patterns. A small portion of the indigenous population who live in remote or isolated places are known by a special term, *masyarakat terasing* or 'isolated people', since they have chosen to live in the deep forest, the mountains, or the swampy areas, far from modern life (Dept. of Social Affairs 1992).[4]

In some countries indigenous people are considered minorities in their own motherland and become the less privileged. In Indonesia, on the contrary, all citizens, both the *pribumi* (including the isolated people) and the *non-pribumi*, have equal rights as per the Constitution of 1945. The Constitution recognises human rights and provides special attention to the poor, including the less privileged and the isolated populations.

When Indonesia proclaimed its independence in August 1945, the Government of Indonesia strove to regain the dignity of the people, to emerge in glory from the scars of colonial oppression and humiliation through national development plans and efforts. The 1945 Constitution, Article 32, states: 'The Government shall advance the national culture of Indonesia'.[5]

All *warganegara* have full and equal rights to progress,[6] and at the same time to preserve and develop their own cultures and regions. They have the rights to decide their own destiny with dignity. The goal of the government is to provide the means to strengthen their own cultural resilience so that they have the capacity to overcome helplessness and dependency. The peoples' cultures represent identity and existence, sources of confidence, security, comforts and order, rendering participation and sharing. National development has gradually taken into consideration the needs of the diverse people, empowering their cultural potentials and overcoming cultural barriers. The development planners, after 25 years' experience, have learnt that development implementation should not necessarily be conducted in uniformity, as that would discourage local acceptability and creativity.

There are several examples in which development programmes have paid deliberate attention to local cultures, such as the development of village life in Bali as well as in Sumatra, particularly the village life of the Minangkabau ethnic groups.[7]

In 1968 Indonesia started a national family planning programme. Through a process of trial and error, the government realised the significance of understanding the variety of kinship systems in the Indonesian population. As a result, several different approaches have been applied to people with unilineal kinship systems and those with bilateral ones.

People change through their cultures. Studies on cultural response and stimulus have recently been encouraged to assure that the implementation of development plans yields higher effectiveness and gains people's acceptance and participation. Local art, as well as local cultural heritage, have long been utilised as media for effective communication. In the national family planning programme, the puppet show (the *wayang* performance) has been used as an effective means of delivering development messages.

Similarly, in Aceh, on the northern tip of the island of Sumatra, the *didong* art has been used to encourage positive competition among the villagers bounded in the village's moiety, in executing the government's development programme.[8]

Regarding the development of people living in remote places, the initial goal has been to raise their standard of living. One of the efforts has been the building of resettlement areas for them, to make them more exposed to educational as well as medical facilities and other resources for development.

Another effort has been shown in the improvement of the people's houses in accordance with standards which reflect the philosophy of the indigenous people,[9] whereas the former policy was to build houses in accordance with the development planners' own (etic) view of modern and reasonably acceptable houses. This effort has not proved to be sufficiently successful, as the people often need more time to accept the modification of the house designs and structure (Swasono, *et al.*, 1994).[10]

It cannot be denied that in the past, the cultural dimension had not been fully integrated in the development strategy. There were some records of development failures which were due to ignorance of the cultural potentials and barriers of the indigenous peoples. Such ignorance led to the implementation of development projects which often distorted their cultural knowledge and also created an attitude of rejection towards further development programmes.

However, the implementation of development plans which have been made on the basis of past experience, sometimes through trial and error, continues. If we accept the fact that local cultures and value systems have to be acknowledged as an integral substance of development, this means that the approach to development policy has become culturally more and more participatory and emancipatory.

The *Program Inpres Desa Tertinggal* (Presidential Program for Backward Villages), a national programme to combat poverty recently implemented, shows that development planners have been learning from experience. A direct attack on poverty through development from the grassroots level, the people's self-confidence, bottom-up initiative and motivation as the driving forces behind the productivity in the poor and economically stagnant villages, have to be utilised as the operating forces to trigger development. The development planners have realised the importance of local and indigenous cultures in selecting and implementing programmes for eradicating poverty (Mubyarto, 1994).

A similar attitude has been observed in research projects, especially those proposed and carried out in the past few years. For example, in accordance with the plan for construction of highways and sub-district roads penetrating isolated areas, the Department of Public Works is now offering a research project to gain understanding of the cultures of the isolated people in the respective areas, as the basis for finding ways and alternatives to assist them in adjusting themselves to the rapid socio-cultural changes which may come about during and after the completion of infrastructural development projects such as highways, bridges and feeder roads.

In developing the standard of living of the isolated people, formerly the main policy of the government was to remove them from their old dwelling places within the forest, especially when the areas had been earmarked as natural reserves. The people were given new settlements of standardised houses and areas for cultivation.

However, recently a government agency has proposed a new approach in the development programme for these isolated and scattered people. Rather than removing them from their original places, where they have been living for centuries, and causing them to become low class people dependent on development agencies or other groups and newcomers in the resettlement areas, it would be better to give them a position as the 'guardians' of the forest, to prevent it from devastation. By using their cultural knowledge in preserving their environment, such a position will give them an important role to play in society which would increase their dignity among the other groups of Indonesian citizens, thus conforming to what has been stated in the Constitution of the Republic of Indonesia.

There have also been new ideas proposed concerning the people living near and on the sea. As an archipelagic country, Indonesia has many ethnic groups with maritime cultures. Some of the old policies of development suggested moving them to resettlement areas inland. A new approach proposes that they be given facilities to explore the sea and to develop sea-related activities, such as sea cultivators developing seaweed agriculture, fish, shrimp and other sea products, as well as activities in sea trade. They should be encouraged to preserve their maritime culture, the folk wisdom which they inherited from their ancestors. The government should help them with necessary facilities.

The need for understanding indigenous culture: the Mentawaian case

Although development programmes were planned after giving attention to indigenous cultures, there are still many reports revealing the failure of these programmes due to neglect of local cultures. Some other reports mention the urgent need for taking into account local cultures in future development programmes, which was not done in the past (Sumodiningrat 1995; Susanto 1994; Universitas Bung Hatta 1992).

Anthropological reports comprehending the success of culturally oriented development programmes are still insufficient. Much more has to be revealed by anthropologists to provide development planners and agencies with inputs for better planning and implementation of future development programmes.

However, the failure of programmes is not always due to the neglect of local cultures. It is because of the development planners' wrong perceptions about progress and also because of their inability to recognise and translate the real needs of the people. The macro and centrally oriented development planners are, on the one hand, inclined to neglect local details, and on the other, are not fed sufficient information for understanding the core of the local culture and its potentialities. This often causes a complete absence of understanding of people and failure to anticipate their responses (Swasono 1994). It also prevents a good rapport with those who have to be dealt with. A people-oriented development approach starts its failure from here.

A description of the culture of the Mentawaians, an indigenous people in Siberut Island, west of Sumatra, the failure of the newcomers there and that of the development agencies in understanding the core of their culture, and the situation it creates, is cited as an example.

The Mentawaians, as an isolated people, live as cultivators in the forest in the hinterland of Siberut Island. The newcomers, consisting of several ethnic groups, mostly Moslem Minangkabau and smaller numbers of Javanese, Bataks, and others, live in the coastal areas as traders and civil servants.

The Mentawaians manage their life in two areas. The first is the *uma* or the main village, with its large house (also called the *uma*), surrounded by the people's private or *lalep* houses. The second is their fields in the forest, usually located at a distance of a half-day walk from the *uma*, sometimes farther.

The *uma* is the place for religious activities, where the villagers, who are mostly related through patrilineal clans, gather for ceremonial purposes. There they show their existence as a community and fulfil their spiritual needs through the performance of life-cycle ceremonies as well as the *punen* (a sacred period of resting and for performing taboos). The *sikerei*, the traditional religious leader, leads the religious ceremonies.

It is within the *uma* large house that the sacred objects belonging to the clan are kept and are taken care of by the *sikerei*. It is also here that the souls of the deceased are temporarily placed during the death ceremonies, before the *sikerei* 'sends' them to their eternal place in the other world.

A *sikerei* is honoured not only as a spiritual leader but also as a traditional healer who cures many kinds of diseases based on naturalistic and personalistic aetiologies.

The *sikerei* also leads a life-cycle ceremony marking the acceptance of a baby into the patrilineal clan. Child-rearing is done by parents, but when the child is old enough to learn he will enter the next phase of socialisation under the guidance of the *sikerei*, who will teach him about his ancestors, their traditional beliefs, and the ways to cure diseases with traditional medicinal plants available in their environment.

The fields cultivated in the forest are the places where people produce their crops for subsistence. A field is also the place where a young couple goes for several days and upon returning to the *uma*, announces their decision to be husband and wife. It is also inside the forest that a husband and wife go for their most private relationship in their very private spot.

The *sapou* house in the field is the place where the birth of a baby takes place, in order to prevent other people from seeing the woman during childbirth. Only the woman's mother and her husband are allowed to be present to help with childbirth.

Under the *sapou* houses, which are built on wooden piles, people breed their pigs. Until today, a pig has several important cultural functions.[11]

As the Mentawaians live in patrilineal clans, there is still another leader, the *rimata*, who manages problems concerning *adat* (traditional customs), *adat*-law, customary law and other non-religious matters. He is also the one who decides when a *punen* should be started and ended.

Thus the Mentawaians acknowledge two centres of life based on their cultural concept of space. Each has its own cultural meaning based on the people's values and norms which are deeply rooted in their culture: the *uma* as the centre of spiritual life and the symbol of togetherness; and the field in the forest as a place for reproduction and production.

The *uma* represents the 'sacred' life while the field in the forest represents the 'profane'. The *sikerei* is the religious leader in the *uma* where ceremonies are performed, and the *rimata* is the leader of the community in non-religious matters.

The design of living and the design of time in the two centres of life are also based on this cultural concept of space and time. It is in the *uma* main village with the *uma* large house where the people perform religious ceremonies, and it is in the field that they produce staple food and breed pigs and reproduce (having sexual intercourse and delivering babies). Based on their design of time in the two centres of life, there is a time for working, producing crops and breeding pigs, the ceremonial animals, in the field, for hunting and collecting forest products, as well as for gathering sago and fishing in the forest and its rivers. On the other hand, there is a time to stay in the *uma* main village for religious resting (*punen*) and for performing taboos.

In daily life, they need long blades and other simple agricultural tools for production. They need pigs, porcelain plates, frying pans, and bed-curtains as dowry for creating a family.

As they live a very simple life, with not much clothing, they have their own concept of wealth. Their household tools and possessions may be limited and simple, but they spend a large amount of money received from selling rattans and *gaharu* (aloewood) not on a number of economic investments available in the area but for buying *adat* property (long knives, bed-curtains, different sizes of cooking pans, and pigs), on dowries and for paying fines in cases of misconduct.

Their reluctance to abandon their fields far inside the forest for possible economic opportunities in non-agricultural jobs in the coastal areas has been based on their cultural division of space and the design of living and time carried out in each space throughout the year. Furthermore, their reluctance to move to the coastal areas has been stronger due to the unpleasant relationship between the Mentawaians and the newcomers, who do not understand their culture.

It is also understandable why the Mentawaians disappointed the development agencies. They did not wish to respond as they were expected, i.e. to live in the resettlement project prepared for them, which was located far away from the *uma*. On the other hand, they have accepted resettlement projects built near their *uma*.

In the same manner one can understand why until now the people have been very enthusiastic about tourism, cordially welcoming the foreign tourists who come there regularly to explore the beauty of their environment, their dwelling place and their way of life. The enthusiasm arises from their perception that the tourists appreciate their material culture and their way of life, whereas such appreciation is nearly absent among the coastal people.

Therefore, if one hears the disparaging comments of the newcomers and development agents that the Mentawaians are 'lazy', 'big spenders for little fortune', 'unintelligent', or 'backward', 'limited in their basic needs', all of these are actually a stereotype given to them due to a lack of understanding and misperception of their cultural values and norms, their conception of time and space, and their expectations.

Worst of all, the stereotype often induces unpleasant treatment by the newcomers on the coast.[12]

The Mentawaians' problem has been caused by the newcomers' lack of understanding of the core of the local culture, so that the organisation and application of development programmes did not cover their role and participation. In fact, the life of the Mentawaians in general should be understood from their emic view, not from the etic view of the newcomers.

The description of the problems faced by the Mentawaians shows the importance of the understanding of an indigenous culture by outsiders, 'modern' people so that a good relationship and social integration, which are very important for the existence of a nation, can be maintained. The function of the indigenous people has to be acknowledged and they have to gain some respect from modern society.

National unity and cohesion

In the case of Indonesia, the participatory role of the anthropological profession in development planning and its implementation has not been sufficient. The publication and distribution of their research findings, from which the development planners and the executing development agencies can comprehend the cultural potentials and barriers in development programmes, are still limited. National development would be meaningful for Indonesia only if it strengthens the unity of the diverse people of the nation.

The Indonesian motto, 'unity in diversity', will transform itself into strong national unity and cohesion if the cultural identities of ethnic groups are mutually respected. As an economist has put it, the understanding of local cultures is believed to be conducive to national mutuality and enhances national unity and cohesion. But he further stated that if there is a danger of national disintegration, it will come from economic inequality and social jealousy, from the growing developmental gap between Java and the outer islands, and between the less developed eastern region and the rapidly developing western region, not for ethnic and cultural reasons. One cannot, however, ignore the fact that integrally embodied in the economic development problems of Indonesia are socio-cultural ones (Swasono 1992).

With respect to Indonesian unity, the cultural dimension meets the economic one, i.e. the problem of economic inequality. Both meet the political dimension, i.e. the past history of Dutch oppression and the *pancasila* ideology[13] as the basis for development.

Conclusion

There have been cases of ignorance of local cultures in the fields of development planning and implementation, and the Mentawaian case is only one of them. Similar kinds of ignorance have also been found in Marunda (the coastal area in north Jakarta), in the hinterland of East Kalimantan, in Jayawijaya (the highlands of Irian Jaya), in some of the transmigration settlements in the outer islands, in resettlement areas for relocated people, and in the Moluccas. Similarly, the Madura case (the prevention of the construction of a bridge connecting Madura island and Java) reflects the cultural (religious and aspirational) ignorance towards the Maduranese. These cases create a very ironic phrase, 'paradise for outsiders, hell for [the] indigenous' (Abdillah 1995).

As for the role of anthropologists, it will be their task to reveal more of the cultures of ethnic group where development programmes are to be implemented. It will also be very important to give a more decisive role to anthropologists in action programmes, so that the cultural problems that might come from the field can be identified and overcome. Through this process, the people's resistance to change could be transformed into positive participation.

In the last 25 years, the development experience has met with obstacles and sometimes failure. This has been due partly to cultural factors integrally embedded in the development process. The academicians seem to confirm this fact, as they found it necessary to strengthen and to give new substance to the study of development anthropology.

It is important to take note of a development milestone when the Minister of National Development Planning, in his speech on 15 April 1995, introduced a new development paradigm in which he stated that progress is achieved in the form of stronger self-reliance, and this is loaded with cultural matters. Some economists even believe that genuine development should bring not only 'economic value-added' change but also 'cultural value-added' change.

It has been accepted that local cultures constitute development potential. Neglecting these non-economic factors may cause development to become more expensive, socio-culturally ineffective, economically inefficient and wasteful.

Notes

1. Archaeological findings indicated a number of dwelling places in several stages of the pre-Hindu era, as well as migrations from the eastern and the western parts of the archipelago since that time. Those people and their descendants were regarded as the early dwellers of the Nusantara, the Indonesian archipelago. Coming from them are the large number of ethnic groups found in Indonesia today.
2. The Vreemde Oosterlingen consist of people of Asian origin, mostly Chinese and Arabs. They were given an important role in commerce by the Dutch.
3. Although considering themselves *warganegara Indonesia* through Indonesian citizenship, the *non-pribumi* still maintain some of their old cultures, such as kinship system, some cultural values and norms, and religious beliefs. However, through a long process, acculturation of their culture with the *pribumi* cultures existed.
4. The number of the *masyarakat terasing* is relatively small, about 1.5 to 2 million, compared with the whole Indonesian population which consists of 185 million people. The group itself is divided into three categories: nomadic people, semi-nomadic people and permanent isolated people, in terms of their dwelling places as well as economic subsistence.
5. The elucidation of this article is as follows: 'The ancient and indigenous cultures which are to be found as cultural heights in all the regions throughout Indonesia are part of the nation's culture. Cultural efforts should lead towards advances in civilization, culture and unity without rejecting from foreign cultures new materials which can bring about the development of or enrich the nation's own culture, as well as to raise the height of humanity of the Indonesian nation'.
6. The Constitution, Article 26 (1) states: 'Citizens shall be persons who are native-born Indonesians and persons of other nationality who are legalized by statute as being citizens'. Article 27(1) states: 'Without any exception, all citizens shall have equal position in Law and Government and shall be obliged to uphold that Law and Government'.

7. The traditional Balinese village is a community whose members are united by a common custom called the *banjar*. The *klian banjar* is the head of the community. This system has been known in Bali since more than a century ago. In accordance with the Law No.5/1979, a newly formulated system of village administration has been applied throughout the country, where criteria are set by the Government of Indonesia, and the formation of a village has to meet standard requirements based on these criteria, on its size and population. The *kepala desa*, abbreviated as *kades*, is the administrative head of the village. He or she is the lowest in rank of the authorities of the national bureaucracy and is responsible for implementing the government's national development programmes in his or her village.

   Based on the intention to develop the people without neglecting their culture, the existence of the traditional *banjar* has been maintained, especially for preserving Balinese culture, whereas the administrative *desa* represents the government's bureaucracy. However, in implementing development programmes, the informal leader of the *banjar* is also given some role, so that the formal and informal leaders of the village can cooperate in many circumstances.

   Similarly, the traditional Minangkabau unit known for centuries has been the *nagari*, a community based on customary law, led by the *penghulu*. Through Law No.5/1979, the territory of the *nagaris* were divided into several administrative villages, each led by a *kepala desa*. However, until today the existence of the *nagari* and the *penghulu* as the head of the *nagari*, the informal leader, is still acknowledged, especially for solving the problems of the people's customs, dealing with all aspects of the Minangkabau matrilineal kinship system and social organisation (Koentjaraningrat 1984). Both the formal (*kepala desa*) and informal (*penghulu*) leaders often cooperate in executing development programmes in the village.

8. Gayoland in the province of Aceh and its villages are divided into moieties. The *didong* art belongs to the Gayo ethnic group. Competitive performances of the *didong* art are often shown by groups of artists of two villages, each belonging to a different moiety. Through the harmony of the lyrics, songs and artistic movements of the *didong* performance, each village tells of the progress it has made, and the audience is able to evaluate which group has been better in performing the art as well as in the implementation of the government's development programmes (Melalatoa 1982).

9. The modification of the style of the houses in the resettlement areas for health purposes has been done following the style of the people's traditional houses, considering their cultural concept of space, the style as well as the materials, instead of following the styles of modern houses.

10. As in the case of the Dani people in Irian Jaya, although the people have not

yet fully accepted their new houses, they seem to be able to accept public facilities such as primary health care and local hospitals which were built adapting the style of the traditional house.

11. A pig is given to the bride by the family of the groom. It is also a means of exchanging goods and food products, as well as a mode of payment for services, school tuition and payment for traditional training of a child given by the *sikerei*. Lastly, it is also one of the properties given as a fine for misconduct among family and clan members.
12. As an example, the newcomers to the coast pay a very low price for all field produce sold by the Mentawaians. Since the general idea in the area considers the Mentawaian culture as more 'backward' than the 'newcomers', the people are economically 'subdued' in relations with the newcomers.
13. The *pancasila* ideology consists of: (1) belief in the One, Supreme God; (2) just and civilised humanity; (3) the unity of Indonesia; (4) democracy which is guided by the inner wisdom in the unanimity arising out of deliberation amongst representatives; and (5) social justice for the whole of the people of Indonesia.

References

Abdillah, Kafil Yamin, 1995, 'Paradise for Outsiders, Hell for Indigenous'. *Indonesian Observer*, 1 April, p.3

Department of Social Affairs and The Research Institute of the University of Indonesia Joint Research Team, 1992, *Kenyah di Kalimantan Timur* (The Cultural Concept of Space of the Kenyah Dayak in East Kalimantan). Jakarta: University of Indonesia

Department of Social Affairs, 1992, *Profile Pembinaan Masyarakat Terasing* (The Profile of the Isolated People Development). Jakarta: Directorate of Isolated People Development

Koentjaraningrat, ed., 1984, *Manusia dan Kebudayaan di Indonesia* (People and Cultures in Indonesia). Jakarta: Djambatan

Melalatoa, M.J., 1982, *Didong: Kesenian Tradisional Gayo* (Didong: The Traditional Art of the Gayo). Jakarta: Dept. P & K

Mubyarto, ed., 1994, *Profil Desa Tertinqgal Indonesia 1994* (The Profile of Indonesian Backward Villages 1994). Jakarta : Aditya Media

Universitas Bung Hatta, 1992, *Pembangunan Mentawai Berwawasan Lingkungan dengan Pendekatan Sosial-Budaya* (The Ecology-Based Development of Mentawai with Socio-Cultural Approach). Padang

Persoon, Gerard and Reimar Schefold, 1985, *Pulau Siberut: Pembangunan Sosio-Ekonomi,*

Kebudayaan Tradisional dan Lingkungan Hidup (Siberut Island: Socio-Economic Development, Traditional Culture and Ecology). Jakarta: Penerbit Bhratara Karya Aksara

Sairin, Sjafri, 1995, 'Dimensi Sosial Budaya Dari Program Transmigrasi' (The Socio-Cultural Dimension of the Transmigration Program). Jakarta: mimeo

Sedyawati, ed., 1995, 'Konsep Kosmologi dan Lingkungan Alam: Tinjauan Keanekaragaman Budaya dan Perubahan" (The Cosmological Concept and the Environment: Cultural Diversity and Changes). Jakarta: mimeo

Sumodiningrat, Gunawan,1995, 'Konsep Tata Ruang Dalam Kaitannya Dengan Pengembangan Desa' (The Concept of Regional Space in Village Development). Jakarta: mimeo

Sunaryo, Astrid S., 1994, *Usaha Pemberantasan Kemiskinan Dengan Pendekatan Sosial dan Budaya* (The Efforts of Attacking Poverty with Socio-Cultural Approach). Jakarta: Gramedia

Swasono, Meutia F., 1991, 'Proyek Pembangunan, Pemindahan Kampung dan Stres pada Masyarakat Marunda Besar, Jakarta Utara' (Development Project, Village Relocation and Stress in the Community of Marunda Besar, North Jakarta). Jakarta: unpublished doctoral dissertation

——, 1994, 'The Mentawaian Culture and Its Relation to the People's Health". Jakarta: mimeo

——, Ukke R. Kosasih and Sri Murni, 1994, 'Masyarakat Dani di Kecamatan Kurulu, Kabupaten Jayawijaya, Irian Jaya: Adat Istiadat dan Pengaruhnya Terhadap Kesehatan' (The Dani in Kurulu Sub-district, Jayawijaya District, Irian Jaya: The Custom and Their Effects on Health). Jakarta: mimeo

Swasono, Sri-Edi, 1992, *Dari Daulat Tuanku ke Daulat Rakyat* (From Master's Sovereignty to People's Sovereignty). Jakarta: University of Indonesia Press

Tirtosudarmo, Riwanto and Roosmalawati, 1995, 'Pembangunan dan Perubahan Sosial di Minahasa: Sebuah Pengamatan Awal dari Luar' (Development and Social Change in Minahasa: A Preliminary Observation). *Antropologi Indonesia*, Vol.18, No.51, pp.108-15

5

Local Religion and Traditional Healing Practice

The indigenous minority groups of Indonesia

Boedhihartono

It is widely recognized that many have great concern for societies which live in remote areas and are categorized as being indigenous: indigenous minority, minority ethnic group, 'primitive', 'backward', isolated from the civilized world, 'uncivilized', prey to the surrounding communities, and possibly on the verge of extinction. Critiques from different sources have come of the efforts of many Third World countries which are trying to modify the socio-economic or socio-cultural status of these people. Many are considering that the governments of the Third World are replacing the white colonials against 'backward' societies (***see*** Penz 1993). The idea of integration, progress, sharing benefit and development proposed by the Third World governments is considered to be disadvantageous to the life of the 'backward' societies. Deihl and Gordon (1987) blamed the transmigration programmes as having a tragic impact on the Irianese and the Irian ecosystem.

At last some authors (***see*** Bodley 1982, for instance) have proposed socio-political solutions or ideas which are in their opinion suited to the interests of the 'backward' people.

This paper does not aim to argue about the possible differences, neither on the idea of socio-economic or socio-cultural changes, nor on the political solutions many have proposed for the problems of those societies classified as 'backward'. The author is only presenting an idea on possibly a more rigorous approach to the problem of these people which would not hurt any parties involved.

Clarification of terms

It seems proper to first define some terms applied to the minority groups concerned or indigenous minorities, which in the author's opinion do not properly fit reality. The terms 'backward' and 'primitive' are seemingly based more on the technological or civilization level classification. It is not fair to classify indigenous minorities as backward and primitive, because many of them are more generous, pacific and probably more honest, from the moral point of view better shaped and nurtured than many of us.

It does not seem proper also to address them as indigenous people, because most of the Third World citizens are themselves indigenous. They all live side by side. Some of the indigenous people or ethnic groups within a nation are direct users of the products of Western civilization. They are socialized to Western education and they are becoming intermediate societies between the 'civilized' and the 'uncivilized'. The position of the intermediate groups is not always convenient. They face criticism and prejudice from both sides: the traditional community members of the nation and the foreigners. Among the traditional community members are the isolated minority ethnic groups living in remote areas. In fact, there are differences between various indigenous groups: first are those which live in the urban areas (***see*** Boedhihartono 1993 for the Jakarta case); second are those who live in remote areas far from the civilized world but practise occupations which support the country market system; and the third are those who are totally devoid of any contact with the outside world and are independent of the market system.

Facts in the Third World show that there are minority groups still living with great dependence on their natural surroundings, practising a simple exploitative technology and independent of the market system. These people, who still live in a state quite attached to nature, are preferably described as MANS (more attached to nature society), rather than categorized as backward, primitive, tribal or anything else.

Contrary to the position of MANS are those societies which achieve a state of living less dependent on nature (LANS — less attached to nature society), and which are the product of acculturation achieved by a part of the indigenous people during the colonial period: the adoption of Western culture.

Contacts between indigenous peoples and the West during colonialism and the successive independence (liberation) of Third World societies have intensified the process by which MANS become LANS. Particularly if we refer to the fact that many have considered that the progress to be achieved is measured by the degree of technological achievement imported from the West, the change from a subsistence economy to a market-oriented economy and the change from the traditional mode of production to the modern mode of production.

The significance of indigenous religion and the practice of traditional healing to the integrity of MANS

A systemic approach to MANS culture is important to enable us to propose proper measures for supporting their existence. Such a systemic approach in dealing with MANS is only possible if we understand all elements of culture, interlinked in a complex network, which characterize a society. The religion or the belief system and the practice of traditional medicine both form the institutionalized effort of keeping a society's members in a state of equilibrium.

Different ethnic groups in Indonesia have their own local systems of belief or their own religions: the Kataringan of the Ngaju Dayak, the Sabulungan of the Mentawai people, the Pelbegu of the Batak, the Sunda wiwitan of the Baduy people, the Kepercayaan of the Javanese, the Taluk To Dolo of the Toraja people in Sulawesi and other different animistic beliefs spread out even to the level of tribal groups in Indonesia.

Case examples will be described here to show the importance of the local religion of the Baduy in west Java and some notes on the traditional healing practices of the indigenous people of Kalimantan, Sulawesi and Irian Jaya.

1. At the western tip of Java there are people still living in a small society, which is recognized as the Baduy. They practise slash and burn cultivation and rely on dry rice as their staple food. The Baduy live in a hilly limestone formation on which the topsoil layer is quite thin. The only technology fitted to these conditions is seemingly the slash and burn cultivation, without any form of surface soil

modification. The use of a hoe is considered to mutilate the soil surface and is taboo to the Baduy (Boedhihartono *et al.* 1994).

The Baduy daily life is cyclical according to the seasonal rhythm. They plant their dry rice once a year. Members of the society are forbidden to adopt a new technique of cultivation, to plant a new variety of rice from outside, and to cultivate imported crops (they refuse to plant cassava — *Manihot esculenta* — and the marketable clover tree). One is prohibited to go on whatever form of transportation, to own and utilize any form of industrial products, to stay overnight more than one night in the house of an outsider, to marry more than once, to divorce, etc.

Most recent reports (daily *Suara Pembaharuan* 1995) mention that the Baduy are still reluctant to send their children to school. They responded to the government appeal to join the development programme by saying that what they need of rice has been fulfilled by their *ladang* and they do not need the help and the introduction of knowledge by outsiders. The Baduy refuse to send their children to school, because according to them the more educated a person, the more treacherous he will be. The local knowledge that their ancestor passed down to them is sufficient to make them happy.

The prohibition of modifying the soil surface seems to be quite beneficial for the conservation of the soil, because any effort at modification with either hoes or ploughs would facilitate soil erosion.

These Baduy people are composed of two distinct clusters: the outside clusters, whose members wear black clothes, and the inner clusters, whose members are white-clothed. Both live in simple houses made of local materials and based on traditional technology. They eat uniformly cooked rice with salted fish, local vegetables, and local fruits, and use almost similar house utilities.

The two groups do not intermarry; they are quite endogamous. The outer clusters, who have direct contact with outsiders, are supposed to be the buffer community for the inner-circle Baduy.

The Baduy obediently accept and preserve all forms of taboo, which are considered the holy teaching of their ancestors, and practise an almost identical way of life. They refuse the influence of the outside world by avoiding much contact with outsiders and show an attitude which might be classified almost as xenophobia. The members of the society do not practise any form of individual ritualistic prayers the way Christians or Moslems do. The relation between man and god(s) is fully delegated to the *puun*, the politico-religious leader of the society.

All regulations and norms related to the Baduy's resource exploitative activities and the control of their communal life are institutionalized as life guidance for the community members and based on the belief in the superbeings as taught by their religion, Sunda wiwitan.

Most of the regulations and norms are based on prohibitions or taboos, *pamali* in the local term. All these taboos are inherited from generation to generation and are considered a sacred heritage.

Emile Durkheim (***see*** Morris 1988:115) defined religion as a unified set of beliefs and practices relative to sacred things, that is to say, things set apart from forbidden beliefs and practices, which unite one single moral community — all those who adhere to them.

Members of the society regularly and happily participate in the seasonal collective feasts as part of their religious ceremonies, which are performed according to the rhythm of planting or harvesting the rice. The aim of the rites is to worship the rice goddess, the goddess of fertility.

The fact that they accept similarity in their clothes, way of life, form and size of houses, etc., and also delegate their contact with god (Bathara Tunggal) are only examples of the communal and collective life which is rooted in and reinforced by their religion or their system of beliefs.

Although they recognize the word 'bathara', which is adopted from Hinduism, at the same time they include Adam as one of the ancestral names of the human being. Such a practice is only possible because they have no written tradition (used as a strict reference) and is only an effort of the Baduy to justify that their system of belief supports open-mindedness and has a basic universal idea.

The *puun* as religio-political leader of the Baduy is by many citizens of West Java and Jakarta considered to be a sacred figure, unpolluted by the modern way of thinking. He is considered a holy personage who gets easier contact with the superbeing. The *puun* is accustomed to be visited by the surrounding rural people and even members of the upper class of urban society, because he is supposed to be able to cure, to ask for mercy from the superbeing, to plant protective charms, to give protective amulets or invulnerability against black magic, etc. He accepts visitors for only a limited time, service offered and incantation performed lasting not more than 10-15 minutes. In return visitors present various articles such as knives, salted fish, resins, a white cloth, etc.

Although the Baduy include wild pig meat as their protein resource, the practice of raising cattle (or any quadruped) is prohibited. The government regulation to oblige people to adopt a legal religion (Islam, Christianity, Hinduism or Buddhism) has caused difficulty for many of the indigenous people, who do not understand the teachings of the imported religions. Therefore it is not surprising that members of the Suku Laut living on small islands between Malaya, Sumatra and Kalimantan have adopted Taoism, because it has no conflicting regulations to their own and there are no fixed regulations related to prayer. The Sakai of east Sumatra, who are accustomed to eat pork and to practise cock-fighting as part of their cultural rituals and feasts, will certainly suffer because of the introduction of imported religions.

The prohibition on raising cattle is a means of preventing cultivated plants in their *ladang* from being ravaged by browsers.

The Baduy people practise a communistic life in the strictest sense, in which no individual land ownership as their basic need resources is permitted.

The efforts of outsiders to convert their religion will practically change their body of knowledge, belief and customs. A most significant consequence of a change in their religion will be primarily on their traditional collective land ownership. Land will be divided into small plots owned by individuals. Facts indicate that the individual land presented by the government to the converted Baduy were manipulated by outsiders. The author is afraid that the converted Baduy will start to sell their land to fulfil religious rituals.

Converted Baduy have lost the charm of being exotic people, less polluted by imported (deviant) behaviour. Only recently the Baduy claimed their 2,500 hectares (half of their reserved forest) occupied by the outsiders.

The opinion that it is not worth it to visit and to present gifts to the outer or converted Baduy basically comes from the fact that the culture of the converted Baduy does not differ from that of the Moslem community in the surrounding area. The converted Baduy will certainly become more dependent on the introduced system, they will leave their traditional knowledge for newly adopted values, and start to be a part of the new system.

With religious conversion, the Baduy and many other societies will start to neglect their own traditional cultures and certainly it will be a total loss for many, because we have not fully documented their traditional knowledge, values, norms, and practices which might prove to be useful in the future, and which up to the present have maintained harmonious relations between the population and the environment.

Despite the refusal of the inner Baduy to accept any form of help offered or any change introduced by the government, at least local varieties of dry rice are still preserved and have not been replaced by the government's high-yield or pest-resistant varieties. There is a tendency among many communities to abandon their traditional local varieties of rice (*Oryza sativa var. Indicus*) in favour of the government's genetically manipulated varieties.

2. A second problem which is of great importance to the effort of preserving the MANS is probably related to the consequences of the introduction of new medical practices.

The government's efforts to better the welfare of the citizens (include MANS) include the establishment of the Public Health Services in various parts of the country.

To some extent the effort of lowering the infant mortality rate throughout the country has been successful, but modern medicine is still far beyond the reach of the common people. There are so many factors that do not support government efforts to provide people with an adequate and proper health service.

The limited number of health providers willing to work in remote areas, the inadequacy of health facilities provided by the government, the appreciation by MANS of modern medicine are still limited to curative efforts. Their economic status and the MANS' knowledge of hygiene and sanitation in particular are becoming main obstacles for the government to achieve success in promoting people's health.

There are reasons why local people visit or do not visit a clinic or consult or do not consult medical doctors. Medical doctors are not part of the society, most of them are outsiders who have become doctors through an expensive process of formal education. The practice of a medical doctor is a professional occupation which differs from the practice of a medicine man, who provides service to the members of the community merely as an expression of his solidarity mission.

Medical doctors wish to be materially well rewarded and run expensive and prestigious private clinics. Though many of them are obliged to serve the people (include MANS) in the Public Health Clinics, because of the small salary and the lack of facilities they do not provide proper service.

Although the cost of a visit to a Public health Clinic is undoubtedly quite low, the service provided is not always adequate and it is not rare for the civil servants of the clinic to be quite rude.

Secondly, there is no assurance that Western medicine guarantees a cure.

Thirdly, medical doctors offer cures for physical illnesses than for psychological problems.

How the members of the MANS perceive or interpret the problem they are facing, whether it is an illness, a disease, a psychological problem or human interrelation problem, is not well defined. Traditional healers offer solutions for all problems.

It is not surprising that in many areas, traditional healing is one of the choices, to which people in rural areas are still accustomed (***see*** Helman 1984).

Different ethnic groups and MANS practise different herbal medicine and traditional healing. Differences in practices are to some degree determined by persistent endemic diseases or traditionally recognized illnesses (Helman 1984:65-105) and locally recognized possibilities.

It should be noted that the practice of traditional medicine is transferred from generation to generation as part of traditional knowledge, which in many cases cannot be separated from the transferred system of belief or inherited religion. Local traditional medicine has been developed as a consequence of the environmental problems faced by the MANS over generations. Traditional medicine is becoming a body of knowledge and practices which form an element of the culture developed by MANS to adapt themselves to the environment. It is true that in Bali, for instance, the practice of traditional healing has been transferred from generation to generation based on written tradition (the use of *lontar*), even though many of the traditional healers acquired their ability to cure through the practice of asceticism.

Some of the Balinese or the Kalimantan *belian* believe that the choice of the herb utilized in curing a disease is obtained by inspiration, and such inspiration can only be obtained because the *belian* has passed a certain period of asceticism or because he is believed to have a certain mercy (*wahyu*) from the superbeing.

The traditional healing practitioner within a certain MANS is usually a middle-aged or old man, .who also becomes a central figure within the society beside the socio-political leader. If the socio-political leader is familiar only with each adult male of each household, the traditional healer recognizes almost all members of the existing households.

The traditional healer plays a role of great importance to the MANS. In many minority ethnic groups, the traditional healers attract foreigners and outsiders. The Banuaq healers who perform ritual dances and music as part of the treatment have attracted tourists to east Kalimantan. Those facts seems to have a positive effect on the confidence of the members of the ethnic group. But some outsiders who are followers of imported religions are quite cynical about these practices.

The Banuaq (one of the Dayak tribes in east Kalimantan) healers are supposed to use black magic and worship and utilize Satan or evil to cure people. Some young medical doctors oppose the practice, which is supposed to be only superstitious, hocus-pocus and relying on the pagan system of belief. Some of the incoming migrant followers of a certain imported religion comment that the ritual is too noisy and disturbing to the neighbourhood, although each year at the end of a particular month they practise a quite noisy activity.

Many members of the Banuaq consider that the existence of the *belian* (traditional healers of the Dayak) is still important, because not all problems can be solved by the institutions provided by the government. The practice of traditional healing by the Banuaq is encouraged by the local authority, because of its ritual attractiveness to foreigners. It is a pity that the rituals do not take place everyday.

Medical doctors are against the MANS traditional curing not because of the rational differences between modern medical concepts and traditional ones, but more due to the sentimentality and the differences in the system of belief of the medical doctors and members of MANS.

Fortunately, not all converted MANS such as the ones in Irian (West Papua) have lost their traditional healers. The Komoro on the southern coast of Irian still preserve traditional healing practices.

It is a pity that many tribes such as the Amomay are undergoing a degradation of their traditional practices because of intense contact with outsiders.

The introduction of clinics does not seem to improve the quality of life. Curative efforts and casual prevention of endemic diseases do not change the health status of the MANS. Facts indicate that these efforts only increase the dependency of the MANS on industrial products (drugs or chemicals).

The usual Western medical treatment depends on either injections or tablets. An injection can be directly offered to the patient during the visit. But take-home oral therapy, in the form of a capsule, tablet, pulverized drug or syrup, which should be taken three times a day, is not easily executable. There are not enough personnel to monitor whether patient really takes the tablet three time a day. The MANS are not accustomed yet to take medicaments three time a day. Only a few of the Amomay can even count to more than five. Better planned education (health education, particularly) seem necessary to really improve MANS life quality.

Comments and Conclusions

The contact between the MANS and outsiders (transmigrants, labourers engaged in mines, plantations or timber exploitation for instance) has different effects on different MANS. The xenophobic attitude of the Baduy in west Java prevents them from being disintegrated by modernization. They still preserve their identity, and outsiders respect their culture. But many MANS have problems because of contact with outsiders because of the incompatibility of the MANS' traditional values with those of the outsiders, or because of the cultural gaps existing between the MANS and the incoming community.

The involvement of many MANS in different exploitative activities has introduced monetization and a new value orientation. If conversion itself has already a disadvantageous and disintegrating effect on the MANS, the following monetization process seems to be even more damaging. Many of the MANS are not really conscious about the meaning of money as a means of exchange and saving. They are not accustomed yet to invest their savings; instead they spend all their money on alcohol or industrial toys. Therefore monetization is only helping the outsiders (the capital owners particularly) to get the natural resources of the MANS.

The effort to improve the health status of the MANS is only creating more dependence on Western pharmaceutical products. MANS are obliged to obtain money and spend it on something new that they do not really need. On the other hand, they will lose their traditional knowledge because of this supposed development.

The MANS have been totally changed from being dependent on nature to being dependent on technological or industrial products.

Traditional medicine is one of the practical aspects of traditional knowledge, and traditional knowledge is part of the basic teaching in MANS' traditional religion. Conversion will not only change their traditional life-style but may also cause the loss of traditional healing knowledge.

References

Bodley, J.H., 1982, *Victims of Progress*. Palo Alto: Mayfield

Boedhihartono, 1982, 'Current State and Future Prospects of Traditional Healers in Indonesia'. In David Mitchel, ed., *Indonesia Medical Traditions*. Melbourne: Monash University

——, 1993, 'Settlement Pattern in Jakarta'. In *Masyarakat Journal of Sociology*, 2:15-25

——, Boedhisantosa and Mary Hawkins, 1994, 'Thee Baduy'. In American Museum of Natural History, In *Traditional People of Today*. San Francisco: Harper

Deihl C. and R. Gordon, 1987, 'The Forgotten Refugees: The West Papuans of Irian Jaya'. In 'South east Asian Tribal Groups and Ethnic Minorities'. Cambridge: Cultural Survey, Inc.

Evans-Pritchard, E.E., 1952, *Primitive Religion*. London: Oxford

Helman, Cecile, 1984, *Culture, Health and Illness*. Bristol: Wright, PSG

Morris, Brian, 1988, *Anthropological Studies of Religion*. Cambridge: Cambridge University Press

Penz, P.G., 1993, 'Colonization of Tribal Lands in Bangladesh and Indonesia: State Rationales, Rights to Land, and Environmental Justice'. In M.C. Howard, ed., *Asia's Environmental Crisis*. San Francisco: Westview Press

6

Culture and Development

A Japanese Observation and Reflection

Minoru Kasai

The atomic bomb in Hiroshima was a decisive moment in history which indicated that man could finally destroy the whole world. Destruction of the whole world is no longer a daydream. It is not an abstract question which has nothing to do with the meaning of life, but raises questions of despair, endurance, hope and prayers for the wounded survivors caused by the destructive power of the atomic bomb.

My friend, a Zen master, has to live with this problem because his wife had to go through the hell-like experience of Hiroshima. She manages daily tasks as a wife and a mother, but she continuously suffers from pains and anxieties for children who may be hereditarily and socially affected. Ibuse Masuji, a famous Japanese novelist who died a few years back, left a touching story, *Black Rains*. It is a story of a young girl who suffered in Hiroshima and died in spite of all possible efforts by her family. The basic tone of the story is implicitly prayers. One of the specific features of this story is that nature is a part of suffering reality as if every stone and leaf has a hidden message.

MINAMATA

Death and life are a part of the Great Nature.

Being aware of this, my heart is serene and filled with joy.

This is one of the last poems of Miss Tatsuko Sasaki, who died at the age of 29 because of the world-famous Minamata disaster of industrial pollution. She was ill in bed for 15 years. It was a vegetative life because she could not move by herself without others' help. She left many poems, though she had barely finished her junior high school. Recently a collection of her poems was published with a note by the editor, sharing her reflections on Sasaki's poems in which her compassionate gentleness and consideration to others are revealed: father, mother, brothers, sisters, neighbours, children, cats, insects, moon, stars. She is touched by the irreplaceable meaning and value of life in all these in spite of the pain of her illness. Strangely, she does not complain about her destiny. Because of this, probably, there is transparency in her poems so that the deep peace of the running stream, the quiet earth, the glowing air, the shining stars, the songs of the birds and the standing trees is echoing in and through her poems. Yet the scars of Minamata pollution still remain because of the ceaseless sufferings of the patients and the earth affected by industrial pollution.

JAPAN, THE BEAUTIFUL AND MYSELF

This is the title of Kawabata Yasunari's Nobel Prize Speech (1968). Sasaki's poems remind one of Kawabata's speech and especially the poems quoted in it. The following is one of them:

What shall be my legacy?

The blossoms of spring

The cuckoo in the hills

The leaves of autumn.

This is the deathbed poem of the monk Ryokan (1758-1831). According to Kawabata, this poem conveys the essence of Japan and Japanese culture. The following poem, by the monk Dogen, the founder of Soto Zen in Japan (1200-1253) with the title 'Innate Spirit', echoes also the essence of Japan according to Kawabata:

In the spring, cherry blossoms,

In the summer the cuckoo,

In the autumn the moon, and in winter

the snow, clear, cold.

What is the essence of Japan? According to Kawabata, it is the emotion of old Japan, the heart of a religious faith in which there are hidden remarkable gentleness and compassion. It is strong fellow feelings.

The following poems of the monk Myoe (1173-1232) express fellow feeling and comradeship:

My heart shines, a pure expanse of light;

And no doubt the moon will think the light its own.

Opening my eyes from my meditation, I saw the moon in the dawn, lighting the window. In a dark place myself. I felt as if my own heart were glowing with light which seemed to be that of the moon.

This explains the occasion of the poem and at the same time it reveals deep communion and intimacy with the moon in silence. Myoe can never be lost in the darkness, for wherever he goes there will be light for one step more from within and without in his mystical experience.

Kawabata ended his life by committing suicide.

JAPAN, THE AMBIGUOUS AND MYSELF

This is the title of Oe Kenzaburo's Nobel Prize Speech (1994). He thinks Japan, the beautiful, no longer exists in contemporary Japan. He finds himself alienated from the mystical experiences of the Buddhist monks and their sense of beauty and cannot identify himself with it because Kawabata's *Japan, the Beautiful and Myself* isolates itself from the reality of Japan.

Then, what is the reality of Japan? Oe introduces Natsume Soseki, the greatest novelist in modern Japan, as the one who has observed the reality of modern Japan. Natsume speaks his view through Daisuke, the main figure of *And Then (Sorekara)*, published in 1909. Daisuke was quite blunt in expressing his criticism of Japanese society.

> The point is, Japan can't get along without borrowing from the West . . . . But it poses as a first-class power. And it's straining to join the ranks of the first-class powers. That's why, in every direction, it puts up the facade of a first class power . . . . And see, the consequences are reflected in each of us as individuals. A people so oppressed by the West have no mental leisure, they can't do anything worthwhile.

> They get an education that's stripped to the bare bones, and they're driven with their noses to the grindstone until they're dizzy — that's why they all end up with nervous breakdowns . . . . Unfortunately, exhaustion of the spirit and deterioration of the body come hand-in-hand. And that's not all. The decline of morality has set in too. Look where you will in this country, you won't find one square inch of brightness. It's all pitch black.

> Contemporary society, in which no human being could have contact with another without feeling contemptuous, constituted what Daisuke called the decadence of the twentieth century. The life appetites, which had suddenly swollen of late, exerted extreme pressure on the instinct for morality and threatened its collapse . . . . And finally, he understood that the striking growth of the life appetites was, in effect, a tidal wave that had swept from European shores.

Natsume was prophetic in his judgement of Japan past and present. Oe identifies his understanding of the reality of Japan with Natsume's critical understanding of Japan:

> Still, modernization continued with the post-war reconstruction and the subsequent period of rapid economic growth; but these have, in effect, led to a deeper kind of decline, a state of outright spiritual poverty. In this sense, Soseki was correct, frighteningly correct.

Now, what is the way out of this reality for Japan? Oe's view, identical with that of Natsume, is the following:

> If Japan is to find a way out of its current predicament — by which I mean its lack of any moral direction — then it must do so by establishing a sense of morality that can be shared with [the world community] but that, for its own purposes, is founded firmly on the traditions of Japan's premodern period.

But how is it possible? Natsume was pessimistic and fatalistic if Daisuke represents Natsume as indicated in the quoted statement.

> Look where you will in the country, you won't find one square inch of brightness. It's all pitch black. So what difference would it make, what

I said or what I did, me standing all alone in the middle of it?

In this regard, Oe is different from Natsume because he is much more destiny-oriented than Natsume. Oe's basic position is prayer. He has learnt this from the people of Okinawa, one of the bitterest battlefields in World War II, Hiroshima, and Hikari, his handicapped son. Oe learnt from them not only the reality of suffering but also silence and prayer. Hikari (which means light) spoke intelligible words for the first time at the age of 6 in the forest while Oe was walking with him. He particularly learnt symbiosis with the least and with nature from Hikari. Oe's prayer is that this coming 21st century will be the century in which Hikari may be able to live as a member of society. But the question still remains, is it possible?

Reflections on Culture and Development

It is certainly a central problem for Japan to reconcile tradition as culture and development as the above observation indicates.

Tradition as culture has been used frequently as a simple contrast to development and as such has taken on almost a pejorative meaning. Traditionalism refers to a situation where one takes the past uncritically as a model for imitation. Thus, nothing new arises from tradition identified with traditionalism. This is a narrow and unhelpful understanding of tradition. Tradition in terms of cultural identity indicates the capacity of a society to maintain continuity, coherence and integrity inspired and sustained by meaning. Tradition certainly involves memory of the past which can make sense of the present and provide a direction for the future. If this understanding of tradition is intelligible, then the picture of a society which has lost tradition being a society left adrift without direction or purpose becomes visible, as Natsume was confronted with.

Development being defined as a response is not a substitute for tradition as the end. It is one of the major functions of tradition to insist on the importance of the ends that are genuinely good in themselves, with which all the great religions and philosophies have been concerned. The slogan 'Wakon-yosai' (Japanese spirit and Western science), which seems to show a right relationship between tradition and development and has inspired development in Japan, reveals a problematic and fatal condition of the modern world. In pre-war Japan development began under traditional auspices. It was possible and effective because of a deep respect for tradition among the Japanese. But, in connection with militaristic nationalism, tradition was exploited with the motive of building a nation-state. Subordination, manipulation and exploitation of tradition by excessive nationalism led to policies oppressive within and expansive without and to the tragic ruins of Hiroshima and Nagasaki. If tradition is used for ulterior ends as the means, it is deformed and destroyed, as Oe's 'Japan, the Ambiguous' implies.

In post-war Japan, tradition freed from direct state manipulation has surprisingly maintained vitality in spite of loss of state support and has provided some of the moral stimulus to economic development. The spirit of the people, their work ethic, their social discipline, their ability to cooperate, all necessary to economic rationalisation, are rooted in one or another aspect of tradition. However, a crucial problem still remains: Is continuous economic growth compatible with traditional understanding of the ends of life? More precisely, it may be raised as the question: If tradition is being used as the means to economic ends, does the rapidly accelerating economic development undermine the tradition that has provided moral and religious motivation for its success? This is a famous question posed years ago by Max Weber about the Protestant Ethic; the very success of the Protestant Ethic destroys genuine Protestant religiosity. Family life, which cultivated the Japanese spirit, is an obvious casualty. With the trend of losing traditional family life, one wonders how long the work ethic and the social discipline which played such a significant role in Japanese development will be maintained.

Japanese tradition as a part of Asian and world tradition is very old and deep. It contains some of the profoundest reflections on the human condition known to men. It still has much to say about the ends of life. Both the success and the failure of development raise a fundamental question about the meaning of life. This question is not confined to the Japanese but is a universal problem, because the success or failure of development have given man the power to destroy all life on earth. This reminds one of the letter of the Chief of the Dwarmish tribe of 1854 in Seattle to the President of the USA. According to Professor A.K. Saran's exposition of this letter, the abolition of the sacred reality will inevitably bring the following consequences:

1. ceaseless expansion of commercialisation
2. destruction of nature and man
3. forgotten past and irresponsibility for the future
4. instrumentalisation of religions such as God as a means of success.

The Chief's prediction is unfortunately and undeniably true of modern life. Self-destruction of the whole world is not simply a daydream.

In this context, it is urgently necessary to hear the voice of tradition. But this is not easy as we have lost sensitivity to its reality because of our development. Tradition in the contemporary situation is simply a residue of the past like museum items and will be erased from the actual scene of life by progress as a historical necessity. This has been demonstrated historically. American native people (red people) are a tragic reminder of the violence of development. It cannot tolerate diversities of unity, but enforces the unity of diversities. However, today, success ideology of development cannot be accepted uncritically unless one is totally uprooted.

Restoration of the sacred reality is Oe's prayer. This is his shared prayer with the silent victims of Hiroshima through mythical encounters with them. The cries and prayers of the silent victims of Hiroshima, Nagasaki and Minamata, the victims of the self-destruction of modernisation, invite us to see the restoration of the sacred reality as the central issue of our day. If their cries and prayers reach us as a call to be sane and be one to participate in the shared history of mankind toward authentic and humane cultures, it will be difficult to erase them. We see this in the midst of the Hiroshima destruction. For the silent victims of Hiroshima, the call to sanity is nothing else but a plea for the establishment of the sacred reality as culture.

References

Kawabata, Y., 1969, *Japan, the Beautiful, and Myself*, Tokyo: Kodansha

Miyamoto, K, ed., 1994, *Minamata Requiem*, Tokyo: Iwanami

Oe, K., 1995, *Japan, the Ambiguous, and Myself*. Tokyo: Kodansha

7

The Role of Endogenous Culture in Socio-Economic Development of Korea

Sang-Bok Han

As Yogesh Atal (1980:1) pointed out fifteen years ago, development strategists and social scientists of the developing world have been finding fault with the Western paradigm of development and have been sloganizing the need for endogenous development. In defining the concept of endogenous development Alechina (1982:19-21), Loubser (1982:115-62) and the Korean Social Science Research Council (1984:33-5, 145-9) indicated the goals of development based on the basic continuity of the people's cultural traditions and the formation of endogenous innovative groups as the basic elements or components to be included in it.

When I discuss Korean culture or Korean endogenous culture in this paper, it does not imply only the unique and specific culture generated in Korea but includes also the exogenous foreign culture in its origin if it were indigenized and Koreanized by the Korean people in the course of acculturation. In this paper I will try to examine the traditional sources of Korean culture, and then to present three empirical cases of Korean socio-economic development based on endogenous culture: (a) biogas innovation as a simple appropriate technological development in rural Korea; (b) *saemaul undong* (New Community Movement); and (c) the Korean experience of economic development.

Traditional sources of Korean culture

Confucianism must be mentioned as one of the most important traditional sources of Korean culture and personality. The predominant ideology of the traditional society used to be what is known as the Neo-Confucianism of Ch'eng Yi and specially Chu Hsi (Kim 1988:202-3). As adopted and practised in Korea, it had become a very rigid ideology governing statecraft, principles of social organization and human relations, and behavioural norms on the one hand, and a very abstract system of metaphysical ideas on the other. Its application, however, was largely confined to the *yangban* ruling literary class except to exert harsh authoritarian control over the *sangmin* peasant commoner class and to justify the legitimacy of such control.

If Confucianism was the predominant and almost sole ideology of the *yangban* ruling elite, a mixture of three sets of religious beliefs and practices governed the life of the *sangmin* peasant class in traditional society. The oldest indigenous belief system was Shamanism, the next prevalent one was Buddhism, and the third was Taoism, not as a folk religion but as a system of philosophy. These three played the role of subordinating the masses to the authoritarian rule of aristocratic governance, while providing an outlet for the commoners to release the tensions and grievances caused by severe and rigid imposition of order and discipline, exploitation and repression on the part of the ruling class. Buddhism was the dominant and even state religion for almost a thousand years before the Choson dynasty. Shamanism and, to some extent, Taoism, through their rituals, helped maintain community identity and peace of mind for the suppressed peasant commoners.

From this cultural, ideological and religious backgrounds we may draw some items denoting the personality traits of the Korean people, including their typical behavioural orientations, principles of social organization, world-views, and other basic values. Authoritarianism, placing strong emphasis on hierarchical relationships and order in terms of parent-child, elder-youth, male-female, superior-subordinate status positions, and so forth, is a typical behavioural orientation of the Koreans. The traditional legacy of collectivism (the group over individual), connectionism (the tendency to build one's social network on the basis of certain particularistic relationships), and personalism (emphasizing close personalties) are the major traditional principles of Korean social organization. Secularism, supremacy of worldly accomplishments, and blessings in this world form the prevalent world-view. Irrational tendencies, formalistic ritualism, strong aspiration for education, and conformity to group norms and sanctions are the basic traditional values in Korean culture.

Whereas the authoritarian and formalistic elements presented above must have their origin mostly in the Koreanized Neo-Confucianism, the non-rational and humanistic parts may have emanated from Shamanism, Taoism and Buddhism. One very significant element common to all four religions is their secularism. No religion including Christianity, whether Catholic or Protestant, has escaped this secular tendency in Korean life. While Protestant denominations have contributed somewhat to the diminution of authoritarianism by bringing in democratic church organization and management, Catholicism does not seem to have ameliorated the authoritarian tendency in Korean culture and personality.

Japanese colonialism in a way reinforced the strong authoritarian mentalities and principles through its own militaristic Confucian statism. This was done by means of education, indoctrination and a whole variety of everyday practices. Secularism was also encouraged not only by the introduction of modern culture from the West but also by the very nature of Japanese culture itself. Even though exposure to modern science and capitalistic economic institutions through the modern educational system and economic policies of the colonial authorities may have modernized and somehow 'rationalized' the thought patterns and ways of life of the Korean people, this was not sufficient to change the tenacious emotional and personalistic inclinations. Rather, under the extremely distorted circumstances of colonial rule, such tendencies may have been reinforced. To release tensions and stress the Koreans sought comfort in more sorcerous Buddhism, Taoism, or even very fundamentalist Christianity, let alone indigenous Shamanism.

It is true that liberation from Japanese colonial rule and occupation by U.S. forces brought in many cultural elements and traits that may represent the exact opposite of the traditional characteristics enumerated earlier, and which are probably epitomized in Western democratic, rational, scientific, industrial values and model personality stereotypes appropriate to them. Such influences from the West have continued and increased over the years, particularly during the Korean War in which a large number of international armed forces participated, and during the rehabilitation efforts in its aftermath. Nevertheless, the basic traditional elements have lingered on, though perhaps a bit weakened and subdued. Korean society is organized basically on the principle of personalistic interpersonal relations, the intricate network of connections of a non-universalistic tint, quite individualized yet still very collectivistic in orientation and authoritarian-hierarchical in organization, putting on the ritualistic facade for face-saving, and strongly status and mobility oriented and meritocratic. The major religions have had little to do with rationalization of the people and society.

In spite of all this, Korea has made outstanding progress in the economic realm, creating an interesting case of an industrial capitalist society still compounded by all sorts of traditional traits which in general are considered inimical or at most not terribly conducive to such a development. We take it to be our task to unravel the distinctive features of Korea's development from the twisted point of departure.

The biogas innovation as a simple appropriate technological development

Biogas as an alternative energy source has been experimented with and promoted for Korean rural development since 1972. The Korean government has considered biogas from cowdung and its dissemination as an important part of *saemaul undong* to improve villagers' life-styles as well as to find a replacement for traditional energy sources including wood and grass.

According to an anthropologist's case study (Chun 1984), there were some endogenous innovative ideas for biogas development generated by the village on Cheju island. After using biogas for four months, one family had to restock cowdung as raw material for producing it. At that time they had a shortage of cow dung from their own cattle barn, so they collected horse dung from the hills and mountains to replace cowdung for filling the tank. Traditionally this area raised horses, and villagers used dried horse dung as their main source of fuel. The biogas from this restocking lasted a record time — up to 214 days — because of the use of horse dung. Because of this incident, the local office of the ORD is now experimenting with the use of horse dung as the main source of biogas raw material. Some villagers and officials like to think that horse dung needs more time to dissolve than cowdung because it contains more celluloid, which is a major component of vegetables and grass.

One family uses waste from the pigsty instead of cowdung as raw material to make biogas. The head of the household installed the tank beside the pigsty. There is another pigsty which is also a human toilet. The farmer gathers wastes from the first pigsty and puts them in the toilet mixed with straw and grass. Then the pig which lives under the toilet treads on the dung and agricultural wastes and finally the whole waste turns into good raw material, ready for being put into the tank of the biogas plant. This innovative idea is an especially good one because every individual household in this area raises at least one or two pigs under its toilet. The wastes from the pigsty are used as agricultural fertilizer. The main food for the pig population is without doubt human excreta. In this process of using the human toilet and pigsty refuse as agricultural fertilizer, there exists the danger of parasites. It has been a well-known fact that most serious health problems for Cheju islanders are caused by the pork tapeworm. Experience of the Chinese with biogas in relation to the parasite is relevant to this case. According to a Chinese report, developing a biogas programme is also an effective way to deal with excreta and improve the hygiene and standard of health in the countryside. In the fermentation of excreta the number of flatworm and tapeworm eggs and larvae detected was reduced by 99 per cent after 70 days of fermenting (Crook 1979:18).

One small-scale blacksmith who is a resident of the village carefully looked at and thought about the use of biogas. He suggested the use of biogas for welding. According to him, one could use a fan to increase the temperature. If one installed a fan next to the main gas pipe to blow and provide additional oxygen, the fan would function as a good bellows.

Even though there are some difficult technological problems to be solved, it will be necessary in the future to diversify sources of energy in Korea. Petroleum should not be the only modern energy source. It is a centralized source that is easily vulnerable to economic and political changes. Even further, economically speaking, we have learned that 'biogas plants can produce both fertilizers and energy cheaper than the conventional modern technology-based projects' (Bhatt 1980:169). The government is developing programmes for decentralizing energy sources and finding alternative energy. Government and people are still working to improve the technology of biogas plants. In this process, it is very important to note that 'in determining the viability of a biogas programme, it can be argued that the major factors in feasibility are more social than technical' (Crook 1979:12). Biogas offers a good possibility for developing a 'soft energy path'. After ideologically establishing the importance of recyclable resources for future energy use, it is possible to develop culturally acceptable and environmentally sound appropriate technology.

Saemaul undong (New Community Movement)

Saemaul undong is a comprehensive rural development programme that government and non-government organizations have implemented since 1970 to raise the standards of living. This programme adopted 'diligence, self-help, and cooperation' as its motto and stressed an extension of the idea of the community to encompass the entire nation. The programme was designed to increase farm household income by improving the agricultural infrastructure and seed varieties and by the application of new farming techniques. Also, it promoted cooperative production among households to increase farm output.

The ideology of the *saemaul undong* originated in traditional community life. Korean villages have a long tradition of self-government (cf. Han 1980). While major decisions were made informally in the past by a small group of influential men, meetings open to all males were also held periodically at which anyone could freely express his ideas. The result was a form of consensus politics controlled and directed by a small elite. *Saemaul undong* utilized this tradition, not to propagate general political skills but specifically in an attempt to involve the entire population emotionally as well as physically in selecting, planning and carrying out development projects.

Local officials encouraged farmers to hold frequent meetings with regard to the planning and carrying out of *saemaul* projects. In actual fact, however, the meetings were held mainly to mobilize enthusiastic participation in the movement and to organize the actual details of cooperative self-help projects.

The goals of *saemaul undong*, based on community needs and aspirations, are (a) to increase production from a limited area of arable land, (b) to earn more income, (c) to seek better security for community life, and (d) to look for opportunities in off-farm activities to improve social and financial status.

To implement these integrated goals of the movement, government, community leaders and people have striven according to overall rational plans and principles in the following ways:

1. The movement must be undertaken with integrated participation by the whole nation. Everyone in the villages should be able to participate. Plans and programmes have to be selected and exercised by the aggregate will of community members.
2. The *saemaul* spirit has to be instilled in the hearts of the people and practised in their everyday life.
3. All activities must be undertaken for the interest and benefit of the community and participants, and should be directly or indirectly linked to

an increase in production and income.

4. The government must assist and support exemplary villages which have successful results so that the people may be well armed with the *saemaul* spirit leading to cooperative work. This will stimulate lagging villages.
5. *Saemaul undong* is a long-term plan with scientific approaches and methods. The plan must continue forever to bring about steady improvement in people's lives.

The achievement of *saemaul undong* has been enormous. Numerous projects and programmes have been completed. The major ones include construction of physical facilities, environment, educational programmes and income increasing programmes. The dominant part of the *saemaul* projects consists of broadly defined rural infrastructure. The establishment of local community organizations and increased efficiency in the operation of the organizations such as community development committees and women's clubs could also be perceived as rural infrastructure. Therefore it can be concluded that the main emphasis in *saemaul undong* was placed on the construction of rural infrastructure by the utilization of available resources.

The basic orientation of *saemaul undong* for rural development, however, has changed since 1980. After the regime of President Park was over, the new regime of President Chun changed the orientation of *saemaul undong* from a government-directed system to a non-governmental autonomous one (Shin 1984:490-504). Under the umbrella of the *saemaul undong* headquarters at the top, many organizations including *saemaul* leaders' association and so forth were overlapped without systematic co-ordination. Thus *saemaul undong* was activated superficially without substantial effects until 1988, when the regime of President Chun ended. Now the *saemaul undong* Central Council (1990:98-120) makes an effort to revitalize and strengthen the movement of rural development.

According to a foreigner's observation (Aqua 1981:412), there is hardly an aspect of a Korean farmer's life that has not been marked by state intervention. Credit, education, ritual, transportation, and even recreation have all come to be regarded as objects subject to state control and supervision. Given the widespread intrusion of the state into virtually all aspects of rural life, it is noteworthy that *saemaul undong* seems to have had the effect of forecasting a positive image of the state among farmers, at least in the broadest terms. There were, to be sure, setbacks and failures, especially in the earliest stages of implementation, but over the course of ten years the steady and reliable supply of public goods and services to farmers helped to establish a new feeling of mutual support and even grudging respect among farmers and local officials.

The state's successful penetration of traditional rural power structures and communal networks is particularly noteworthy in the modern setting. Intense pressure has been exerted on local administrators by the central government to ensure the achievement of *saemaul undong* goals. The result is the transition of the local bureaucracy from a *status quo* and control-oriented institution to an action-oriented instrument of developmental change (Brandt and Lee 1981:90-91). The work-load of local officials is now much heavier than before, and they are preoccupied with encouraging, cajoling or bullying farmers into greater cooperative self-help efforts, rather than, as in the past, enforcing bureaucratic regulations and promoting their own interests. Most local officials now spend half or more of their time away from their desks talking to villagers and guiding or inspecting projects.

Along with this change in function and perspective there has been a more subtle shift in officials' attitudes towards the rural population. Since energetic participation by farmers is necessary for compliance with the insistent directives from the central government, their status relative to that of officials appears to have improved considerably. While there is no question of the superior authority and prestige of, for example, the sub-county head, his traditional attitude of arrogant condescension towards villagers is giving way, particularly among younger officials, to a relationship based more on interdependence and mutuality. Well-to-do farmers are now likely to have as much or more property and income as the higher ranking local officials. Also, their sons have usually graduated from high school, so that the great economic and educational gap that used to exist between farmers and officials has been significantly reduced.

The village meetings, it seems clear, do not merely rubber-stamp decisions previously made by the local government bureaucracy. In all the villages I visited, leaders insisted that the ideas for projects came from within the village — whether from the *saemaul* leader, the community development committee, or ordinary residents. These claims should be viewed cautiously, for administrators are the source of broad guidelines. But the villagers themselves must agree to particular projects and fill the myriad relevant details that are necessary for carrying them out.

The national leadership, for instance, may indicate it wants to concentrate on feeder roads, or water supplies, or whatever. This information is sent down the chain of command, but the operational decisions about where, how, when, and in some cases, whether, to start a project rest with the villagers. Because recommended projects often have a clear and immediate payoff, and because the government provides in many instances the materials for the projects, people appear generally willing to follow government suggestions.

Farm productivity change has served as the main engine for rural progress. The productivity growth resulted, in part, from government interventions such as agricultural research, extension services, and various development projects involving the creation of agricultural infrastructure. No less important were the unintended spillover effects from the rapidly growing industrial and urban sectors. From the industrial sector came high technologies and sophisticated farm machinery. Rapid urbanization has created increased demands for farm products, adding new incentives for farm households to attain a higher yield.

The Korean experience of economic development

Endowed with very little usable natural resources, either for domestic consumption or export, equipped with high density population, and having been unable to accumulate capital throughout the turbulent years since the late 19th century, the options left for the policy makers before the 1960s were quite limited. After liberation in 1945, Korea was almost a desert, with little industrial base, lacking well-trained managerial and engineering-technical manpower, and divided into North and South. Following political struggles, two separate governments were created, one each in the North and the South, by 1948. Three years of the Korean War since 1950 devastated the country not only economically but in terms of the national sense of unity that Korea had enjoyed for over a thousand years. Even more tragic was that merely a truce, not a peace treaty or peaceful unification, ended the battle, leaving the two parts of the divided nation suffering from tension.

It was the military regime that initiated the implementation of the first Five-Year Economic Development Plan beginning in 1962. The basic idea was to bring in foreign capital with attendant technology to build manufacturing industries which, in turn, would produce goods for export to earn foreign exchange needed to pay the foreign debt and help raise the living standards of the people. Thus, full-scale industrialization was pursued, beginning with light consumer goods, to be replaced by import substitute industries for a brief interval of time, and then eventually to build heavy chemical and capital goods industries for export, moving in the process from the labour-intensive to more capital-intensive high-tech industry (Kim 1986:9-11).

Since the launching of the first Five-Year Economic Development Plan, Korea has achieved rapid and sustained economic growth. Viewed from the supply side, Korea's development strategy pursued extensive growth on the strength of its abundant labour force and allowed expansion of foreign capital investment. On the demand side, increased exports emerged as the most important factor in economic growth.

Thus, it should now be easier to understand the role of endogenous culture in achieving rapid economic growth in the past three decades (cf. Han 1991). There is no doubt that government has played a key role in planning, implementing and evaluating economic development programmes, but we have to realize that the general attitudes and values of people also have an important bearing in this connection. Fortunately, we have some data which can shed light on the attitudes and values of the Korean people which contributed to the development of the Korean economy (Hong 1980:290-99). The economic achievement of the past three decades in Korea was favourably viewed by intellectuals. And people in all sectors, regions, and walks of life responded positively to the government's call for economic development. To organize the society for this job, the government decided to maintain a guiding hand in the affairs of the economy by pronouncing the policy of 'guided capitalism'.

Considering the dearth of resources and the shortage of capital required to take off, the government assumed the primary responsibility of capital formation, resource allocation, project selection, and a whole array of other activities for the sake of efficiency. The voluntary sector was not to be an equal partner but was a target for mobilization. In this respect, the Korean people got used to the idea of government mobilization, such as the traditional conscription system, and other programmes of mobilization regularly employed by the military regime. Thus, in a way, the entire country was organized on the principle of a centralized authoritarian structure.

One should also note that the traditional authoritarian, hierarchical and collectivistic orientations had their own share in this area. Nevertheless, close analysis should reveal that the stereotypical conception of the role of the traditional element may need modification. It may be true that loyalty or commitment on the part of select managerial and supervisory personnel with distinct family or other more personalistic connections was generated by such orientations. Under the circumstances, the source of commitment and loyalty must be found in immediate and concrete incentives. However, because they were short of such resources, Korean organizations had to opt for a more authoritarian principle of mobilization than either the traditional familistic one or the modern rational one. No doubt, besides the nationalistic cause, some concrete incentives were offered, chiefly in the form of status attainment, if not of the plush material kind. Despite their poor salaries, civil servants were able to enjoy power and authority. Despite their low wages, managers and workers could now enjoy a new status of prestige and pride. Nonetheless, the fundamental principle of organization had to be that of centralized authoritarianism. The need for such a centralized authoritarian organizational principle may also be understood in light of the urgency of rapid growth, which in turn required social and political stability more than anything else.

Neither the rationality of Confucianism nor that of Christianity, but rather very unusual non-rational forces have provided the impetus for the development Korea has accomplished thus far. The kind of rationality basically needed for technological production, management, and all the other know-how, attitudes, and behavioural patterns have been acquired through acculturation processes, mainly by means of education, mass communication, and other channels of information.

Strong adaptability is one of the behavioural features of the Korean people. Among other things, religious syncretism — specially noted for Korean society — must have helped instill this tendency of adaptability. Syncretic orientation in adopting and indigenizing alien religions has been remarkable throughout the history of this country. It was true even during the Choson dynasty which, of course, was an extremely rigid regime in an ideological, religious respect, when persecution of other religions and ideas was often severe. This syncretism is one of the central elements of shamanistic indigenous folk religion in Korea.

The basic reasoning behind this contention would be that syncretism, being an open orientation by implication, could encourage attitudes that are open-minded about adopting certain new patterns. No doubt, the this-worldliness of the Korean people and their religious inclinations also might have had their own role in enhancing their adaptability, including syncretism. Now, however, even this adaptability in itself may or may not breed the kind of 'rationality' Weber noticed in the spirit of Western capitalism of modern times. Whether that particular type of rationality is a requisite for capitalist development may be debatable. But if it is, then the future of Korea's capitalist development will largely depend on how successfully Koreans can utilize their adaptability to acquire that rationality to the extent that it is minimally required for that purpose. Our emphasis here has been that the major impetus thus far has been something non-rational rather than rational.

Conclusion

The socio-economic development of Korea certainly did not follow the development course of the West in many respects. Korea did not have what the West had, such as usable natural resources, capital accumulation, technological superiority, industrial base, the Western rationality, and so forth. But Korea had what the West did not have, such as its own development ethics, its use of human resources, its collaboration of government with business, etc. Certain unique Korean cultural values were utilized in the process of mobilization and organization needed to pursue the goal of socio-economic development in the context of a dialectical change consisting of twin processes of indigenous adaptive change and acculturation.

Thus Korea's socio-economic development may be regarded, on the one hand, as a consequence of the combination of certain traditional cultural values, modern science and technology, and on the other as a consequence of the combination of non-rationality and rationality in terms of Western usage.

Some distinctive traits of non-rationality including authoritarianism, hierarchical orientation, formalistic ritualism, collectivism, connectionism, personalism, secularism, and this-worldliness have their roots in such traditional belief systems as Confucianism, Buddhism, Taoism, Shamanism, and Christianity as well. These non-rational traits have played an unusually significant part in helping the country make good socio-economically. But these traditional belief systems are not the direct contributory factors in the effort to achieve socio-economic development in Korea. Rather, they have exerted a fundamental influence on the Koreans' ideologies, values, world-view, personality, and principles of social organization, which in turn has contributed to the development of Korea.

References

Alechina, Iraida, 1982, 'The Contribution of the United Nations System to Formulating

Development Concepts'. In Unesco, *Different Theories and Practices of Development.* Paris: Unesco

Aqua, Ronald, 1981, 'The Role of Government in the *Saemaul* Movement'. In Man-Gap Lee, ed., *Toward a New Community Life.* Seoul: National University Press

Atal, Yogesh, 1980, 'The Call for Indigenization'. In Jan J. Loubser, ed., *The Indigenization of the Social Sciences in Asia.* Copenhagen: IFSSO

Bhatt, V.V, 1980 'The Development Problem, Strategy, and Technology Choice: Sarvodaya and Socialist Approaches in India'. In Franklin Long and Alexandra Oleson, eds., *Community Development.* Paris: Unesco

Brandt, Vincent and Man-Gap Lee, 1981, 'Community Development in the Republic of Korea'. In Ronald Dore and Zoe Mars, eds., *Community Development.* Paris: Unesco

Chun, Kyung-Soo, 1981, 'Reluctant and Selective Acceptance: The Korean Case'. In *Biogas: Social Response to a Technological Innovation.* Jakarta: Unesco

Crook, Michael, 1979, *A Chinese Biogas Manual.* London: Intermediate Technology Publications

Han, Sang-Bok, 1980, 'A Study of Community Consciousness of the Korean People'. In *Korean Society and Culture*, Vol.3

——, 1991, 'Cultural Perspectives on Economic Development in the Republic of Korea'. In Yogesh Atal, ed., *Culture-Development Interface.* New Delhi: Vikas Publishing House

Hong, Sung-Chick, 1980, 'Values and Economic Development'. In Sung-Jo Park, Taiwhan Shin and Ki-Zun Zo, eds., *Economic Development and Social Change in Korea.* Frankfurt: Campus Verlag

Kim, Kyong-Dong, 1986, 'The Issues of Modernization Revisited: An East Asian View' Unpublished conference paper.

——, 1988, 'The Distinctive Features of South Korea's Development'. In Peter Berger and Hsin-Huang Micael Hsiao, eds., *In Search of An East Asian Development Model.* Oxford: Transaction Books

Korean Social Science Research Council, 1984, *Endogenous Development of the Korean Society.* Seoul: KOSSREC

Lubser, Jan J., 1982, 'Development Centered on Man: Some Relevant Concepts from Canada'. In *Different Theories and Practices of Development.* Paris: Unesco

Saemaul Undong Central Council, 1990, *Koreans and Saemaul Undong.* Seoul: SUCC

Shin, Yun-Pyo, 1984, 'A Study of the Development Strategy of the Non-Government Oriented *Saemaul Undong*'. *The Journal of Saemaul Undong Studies*, Vol.1

8

Sri Lanka and the Sarvodaya Model

P.D. Premasiri

The nature of the relationship between culture and development raises many interesting and important issues. Contemporary man appears to be heading towards the creation of a global culture, as a consequence of the universal influence of the knowledge base of the positivistic sciences, the associated technology and the closeness that has been produced by the development of modern means of communication and travel. The dominant development model that appears to be gradually conditioning a new global culture is the Western one, which is founded on materialistic ideology, secularism, consumerism, individualism and modern science and technology. In the context of this change certain questions of an evaluative kind seem to be raised in the minds of those who are given to critical and reflective thinking. Are any aspects of endogenous culture worth preserving or should all mankind uncritically and passively submit itself to the overwhelming influence of the growing global culture?

On the one hand it is argued that the attempt to impose alien models of development on traditional communities is detrimental to the preservation of their own cultures, which have traditionally maintained the cohesion and harmony of these communities. The consequence of the importation of an alien model of development is considered to be the impoverishment of the moral and spiritual basis of these societies. Despite the superficial appearance of affluence that the implementation of alien models of development produce, these societies are believed to lose their original stability as a consequence and ultimately become worse off than they were earlier. A monistic approach in the determination of development policy is therefore seen as ill-conceived by some critics on the grounds that adequate attention should be paid to cultural identity for a development process to ultimately bring about beneficial consequences to the community for whose sake it is implemented.

On the other hand, the Western experience of some of the consequences of the implementation of the Western model of development has resulted in scepticism about its validity even for Western man, not to speak of its universal validity. Such scepticism has made development theorists look for alternative models which may be derived from either some aspects of classical Western culture or from the Eastern cultures which are being undermined by the influence of Western ways of thinking. That everything is not well with the dominant concept of development today seems a reasonable opinion to hold.

The significance of the Sarvodaya movement in Sri Lanka may be recognized from both standpoints outlined above. Sarvodaya claims to offer an alternative development model which is rooted in Sri Lankan culture. It is therefore claimed to be more suited in the Sri Lankan situation to fulfil the aspirations of the Sri Lankan people in their development effort. According to the exponents of the Sri Lankan Sarvodaya ideology, development in Sri Lanka should be viewed primarily as a return to the conditions of the glorious past in Sri Lankan culture, not the creation of a new socio-cultural order through the implementation of alien models of development. Sarvodaya makes the further claim that it offers an alternative model of development which has a universal moral appeal and invites the serious attention of development theorists in search of alternative models of sustainable development. The objective of the present inquiry is (a) to explain the ideological and cultural roots from which the Sarvodaya model of development is derived and clarify the basic principles underlying the Sarvodaya philosophy of development with reference to its implications for contemporary society, (b) to present the practical methods and devices adopted by Sarvodaya for the achievement of its development goals, and (c) to evaluate the importance of the Sarvodaya development model in terms of its practical achievement in the Sri Lankan context.

'Sarvodaya' means the upliftment of all or the welfare of all. The origin of the concept of Sarvodaya can be traced to Mahatma Gandhi's thoughts on *svaraj* or self-government at the time India was struggling to gain independence from colonial rule. Gandhi gave a spiritual and moral interpretation to the concept of *svaraj*. The Gandhian social philosophy of non-violent means of social transformation was the central philosophy of the Indian concept of Sarvodaya. The Gandhian concept of Sarvodaya advocated true self-realization of the individual through dedicated service to the community, especially its weaker sections. Gandhi's Sarvodaya concept was a social ethic for the welfare of all. It was developed into a movement to promote spiritual socialism by Gandhi and other spiritually inclined Indian figures like Vinoba Bhave and Jayaprakash Narayan.

The idea of a new social order ensuring independence, self-reliance, and self-realization by following the non-materialistic, spiritual path of non-violence, sharing and truth emerged with the Gandhian Sarvodaya movement in India. The concept of Sarvodaya as well as the basic elements of the Gandhian philosophy of development inspired A.T. Ariyaratne of Sri Lanka to provide leadership to a parallel movement in Sri Lanka. Ariyaratne saw important socio-economic principles in the Buddhist heritage of Sri Lanka which could be utilized to evolve a development model which in his view was much more desirable in the Sri Lankan context than those policies which Western-trained planners attempted to impose.

Buddhism was the principal cultural influence on Sri Lankan society before the imposition of Western values. Mahatma Gandhi himself admitted the influence of the Buddha, in addition to a few other spiritual persons who influenced his philosophy of non-violent social change. In keeping with the Buddhist tradition, the Sri Lankan Sarvodaya movement interpreted the term Sarvodaya as the awakening of all. For the goal of Buddhism is liberation of man from the miseries of existence through spiritual awakening and the overcoming of the veil of ignorance. While admitting his indebtedness to the Sarvodaya ideal of Mahatma Gandhi and the *Bhudan-Gramdan* action of Acarya Vinoba Bhave, Ariyaratne, the leader of the Sarvodaya movement in Sri Lanka, maintained that the interpretation of the deep meaning of Sarvodaya was 'relevant to our own Sinhala Buddhist culture', and that 'the philosophy that influenced us most in evolving our Sarvodaya concept in Sri Lanka is Lord Buddha's teachings'.

The goal of Buddhism is liberation from suffering in a very deep spiritual sense. The central problem of life according to the teaching of the Buddha is suffering. Its causes are craving and ignorance. The awakening of man to the noble truths of suffering, its cause, its cessation and the path leading to its cessation, ensures liberation and happiness. The awakening of the individual to the truths of existence is the only means of eliminating suffering. Ignorance and craving are not only at the root of the suffering of the individual but also of the suffering that mankind produces in social interaction. Buddhism rejects the view that man can overcome suffering merely by changing the order of things outside of oneself. Whether it is the suffering of the individual or the suffering of the society, an inner transformation of the individual is considered to be the effective means of overcoming it. As long as one's action is rooted in greed, hatred and ignorance it creates suffering for oneself as well as for others.

The enlightenment the Buddha is supposed to have attained consisted of insight into the dependent co-origination of things, the three characteristics of being, namely impermanence, unsatisfactoriness and soullessness, or the absence of any essence or substance to be grasped as one's own true self. There is nothing, according to this kind of spiritual awakening, to be grasped either in the outside world or within one's inner self. The awakening to these truths ensures the resolution of all mental conflicts of the individual. Such a transformation of the individual, involving the eradication of greed, hatred and delusion, results in complete freedom from all impurities and fetters of the mind. Persons who have attained such freedom are considered the most suitable to render the greatest service to mankind. The path to be followed to achieve this goal is characterized by the avoidance of the two extreme life-styles of sensuous indulgence and self-mortifying asceticism. The foundation for the Middle Way is an ideology which avoids a materialistic world-view. The Middle Way emphasizes the cultivation of wholesome thought, speech and action, a right means of livelihood and the development of right effort, mindfulness and concentration. The essence of the Buddha's teaching is that human beings can be freed from unhappiness only by cultivating non-greed, non-hatred and non-delusion. Happiness cannot be attained by increasing one's wants but by spiritual discipline.

Although the teaching of the Buddha asserted that happiness could be attained only by cultivating an attitude of detachment and non-craving towards all empirical things, he did not ignore the material aspect of human living. Man is a combination of mind and matter. An individual is a psychophysical unit who constantly interacts with the mental and physical environment. Therefore, the human being has to satisfy certain material needs. However, the satisfaction of material needs may become an end in itself, resulting in limitless desires and craving, greedy competition and acquisitive tendencies, producing numerous psychological tensions and social conflicts. Buddhism therefore emphasizes righteous living (*samma ajiva*) according to which the economic life of man is required to be based on a moral and spiritual foundation. The supreme goal of Buddhism is *nibbana*, the absolute peace and tranquillity which is essentially spiritual in nature. Buddhism is not opposed to material progress so long as it is achieved without dehumanizing man. Material progress that conduces to the increase of craving, mutual enmity and hatred, lack of contentment and peace of mind, is progress achieved through unrighteousness. Such progress is self-defeating in that its outcome is suffering, both in this world and the next (Buddhism believes in the continuity of life after death). Lack of concern for the well-being of others, miserliness and selfishness are considered manifestations of man's ignorance. The sharing of benefits is the foremost virtue. Non-injury and compassion towards all sentient existence are considered the inviolable foundation for spiritual progress. Man is viewed in Buddhism not merely as a biological phenomenon but as a *samsaric* being. There is a concept of *summum bonum* to be achieved, and all aspects of life should be ordered in conformity to the noble way which is conducive to the attainment of this goal. Economic well-being is subservient to man's moral and spiritual well-being. Buddhism considers contentment as the greatest wealth that a man can acquire. It does not measure human progress purely in terms of economic growth. It is not difficult to see that the adoption of alien models of development inevitably results in direct conflict with the cultural values and life-styles to which the Sri Lankan people have been accustomed for many centuries through the influence of Buddhism. According to Buddhism development signifies the growth of humanity in terms of virtue and wisdom. This is why the concept of *bhavana* occupies such a pre-eminent position in a Buddhist culture. The three fundamental virtues of Buddhist living are sharing (*dana*), moral living (*sila*) and development of mind and character (*bhavana*). Buddhist teachings consist of a number of tenets which could be used to formulate an effective critique of contemporary development policy.

The most serious attempt to formulate a development policy based on the Buddhist ideology and value system in contemporary Sri Lanka has been made by the Sarvodaya movement. The movement has rejected both the capitalist model of development, which encourages individualism, competition, consumerism and affluence, as well as the communist model of development through violent revolution and state-imposed institutional socio-economic structures. It conceives of man's participation in the process of socio-economic development as a vehicle for the ultimate spiritual perfection of man. From the point of view of Sarvodaya, 'Development is ideally and essentially the process of awakening of individuals, families, rural communities, urban groups, the nation and the world at large. This awakening has six major dimensions, namely: Spiritual, Moral, Cultural, Social, Economic and Political. There should be balanced progress along all these dimensions occurring simultaneously, although, at a particular point of time, one or more of the dimensions may receive greater emphasis'.[1]

The Sarvodaya movement of Sri Lanka had its beginnings in 1958, when A.T. Ariyaratne, who was then a teacher at a leading Buddhist school in Colombo, organized some teachers and students of the school to work as volunteers in a backward village called Kanatoluwa.[2] Ariyaratne describes the first experiment of the gift of labour or the sharing of labour, which became a key concept and practical device in the Sarvodaya scheme of development as follows:

> They sank wells, dug latrine pits, cleared home gardens and planted various crops, inaugurated a formal educational programme, organized literacy classes for adults, conducted health lessons and demonstrations, child and maternity care work, singing and dancing classes, and they even established a place for religious worship for the people.[3]

Ever since this initial venture into a programme of community service, the Sarvodaya movement evolved as the most influential non-governmental organization in Sri Lanka with a development strategy and programme of its own.

Speaking at the ninth Niwano Peace Prize award ceremony in Tokyo in his commemorative lecture, A.T. Ariyaratne outlined the Sarvodaya philosophy of Development in the following terms: 'Society is composed of individuals, families, village communities, urban groups, national populations and humanity as a whole. We are all living on one planet and are commonly subjected to the limitations imposed by non-renewable resources, ecological balances, climatic and temperature changes, environmental factors, psychological and social dependencies, physical survival, existence, and the awakening of every one of us is dependent on all other living and non-living entities of our planet. For the sake of building a practical programme we formulated the Sarvodaya Goal of the awakening of all in terms of six objectives, which are: '*Purna Paurusodaya* or "Personality Awakening"; *Kutumbodaya* or "Family Awakening"; *Gramodaya* or "Village Community Awakening"; *Nagarodaya* or "Urban Community Awakening"; *Desodaya* or "National Community Awakening"; *Vishvodaya* or "World Community Awakening".'[4]

The Sarvodaya development concept starts with the individual. This is one of the fundamental premises in the Buddhist concept of development. The Sarvodaya philosophy seeks to achieve a two-fold liberation in every individual: 'First, within one's own mind or thinking process there are certain defilements one has to recognize and strive to cleanse. Second, one has to recognize that there are unjust and immoral socio-economic chains which keep the vast majority of people enslaved. Thus, a dual revolution pertaining to an individual's mental make-up and to the social environment in which he lives is kept foremost in the Sarvodaya Shramadana worker's mind and behaviour'. Sarvodaya conforms to the Buddhist principle that one who cares for one's spiritual well-being cares for others and one who cares for others cares for one's spiritual well-being.

Sramadana is the chief instrument through which Sarvodaya attempts to achieve its development goal. Sarvodaya recognizes four principles of personality development as the very foundation of Sri Lanka's Buddhist rural culture. They are the four positive Buddhist virtues of loving kindness (*metta*), compassion (*karuna*), sympathetic joy (*mudita*), and equanimity (*upekkha*). Sarvodaya considers the *sramadana* camp which it organizes in the village as providing the occasion to cultivate these virtues. In addition, it also provides the opportunity to practise the four cardinal virtues recognized in the social ethics of Buddhism, namely *dana*, the sharing of labour and skills for the benefit of others, *piyavacana*, pleasant language which creates wholesome social relationship, *atthcariya*, constructive activity; and *samanattata*, equal treatment of all involving a non-discriminatory social attitude characterized by a sensitivity to the other person's feelings and interests. In a *sramadana* camp, volunteers who share the Sarvodaya ideology and the people of the village community of all ages join together to undertake some task such as building a road, repairing a village tank or constructing houses or a school building. A *sramadana* camp is an educative experience from which three major benefits are expected: (a) provision of a first-hand opportunity for rural and urban groups to meet in a beneficial manner, thus bringing about mutual understanding and confidence in the achievement of common goals; (b) after generations of inaction and dependence the rural communities are stimulated into a new life of self-reliance and self-help; and (c) the emergence of a new rural leadership which is not split by caste, religion or political commitments, but which has been trained for a new development.[5]

Sarvodaya's avowed aim is to develop the 23,000 villages of Sri Lanka in which almost 90 per cent of the Sri Lankan people live. It believes that a prosperous society can be achieved when villages are developed and village autonomy is established. *Gramodaya* or awakening of the village is one of the most important aspects of the Sarvodaya programme. At an annual conference of the movement held in 1966 a resolution to launch a Hundred Villages Development Scheme was adopted. Instead of development planning and policy being determined by a central authority, Sarvodaya believes that the people themselves at the grassroots level should do the planning. People in the village should be made to understand their own problems and to find their own solutions. They should be made self-reliant in all aspects of their lives. With the process originating from the *sramadana* camp, Sarvodaya seeks the participation of every villager in the solution of the day-to-day problems in the immediate local environment. Sarvodaya has introduced in the villages various organized groups under the name of *haulas* — the pre-school group, the children's group, the youth group, the mothers' group and the fathers' group — for this purpose.

The movement, which started with a simple community service project in 1958, had by 1978 matured into a massive organization. In 1972 the Sarvodaya Shramadana Movement was incorporated in Sri Lanka by an Act of Parliament. The movement attracted the attention of Western donor organizations and monetary and other forms of assistance began to come in on a fairly large scale. The movement claimed to have some form of influence over 2,000 villages by 1978. The latest claim of the movement is that over 2,000 villages out of a total of over 8,000 villages which have had *sramadana* experience, have registered societies and democratically elected office-bearers carrying out the Sarvodaya development programme. It claims that the rest of the Sarvodaya villages are also on their way to such registration.[6]

Some idea of the extent to which Sarvodaya has grown can be gathered from the following:

1. *Poverty Eradication and Empowerment of Poor*: This programme is operated in 25 districts by 245 regional centres located in 2273 villages.
2. *Early Child Development Programme*: This programme operates in all districts. The special nutritional programme financed by the donor organization NOVIB operates in 7 selected districts.
3. *Sarvodaya Rural Technical Services*: For the last 16 years it has devoted its energies and resources towards provision of sanitation, housing and gravity water supply.

4. *Rural Enterprises Programme*: The objective of this programme is to provide financial assistance to rural folk in order to develop self-employment enterprises such as trade, agriculture and small industries.
5. *Elders' Action Committee*: The activities of this section are confined to performance of *sramadana* work with local and international groups. The promotion of peaceful coexistence among different ethnic communities has been given priority. Youth programmes and cultural activities at the rural level have been carried out by this section. The number of villages involved is 2,035.
6. *Sarvodaya suwasetha Programme*: The activities of this section are centred around 8 children's homes, 4 community-based rehabilitation centres, 2 elders' homes and 4 schools for disabled and handicapped children. It also offers a variety of other services to needy persons affected by calamities. The Savansahana, which is one of the most modern schools for the rehabilitation of deaf children, has residential accommodation for 100.
7. *Sarvodaya Samodaya Services*: The work of this programme is connected with the rehabilitation of drug addicts and other minor offenders referred to it by the law enforcement authorities.
8. *Shanthi Sena*: This section is organized for the development of youth with a view to enlisting their services towards participation in national development. It has 4,980 units with a participation of 54,499 youths nation-wide. They are concerned with the building of ethnic unity and the organization of cultural activities and activities connected with environmental preservation.
9. *Sarvodaya Savings Scheme*: Sarvodaya inaugurated in 1980 at the Kegalle Centre a Savings and Credit Society. Later on the programme was extended to 14 other districts, and it is operated from the headquarters in these districts. The Kegalle Society continues to operate as an independent unit. The number of accounts in the Kegalle society rose from 2,100 in 1980 to 17,736 in 1994 and the value of deposits from Rs.185,000 in 1980 to Rs.2,463,355 in 1994.
10. *Income Generation Projects*: Some of the projects run by Sarvodaya under this scheme are the Sarvodaya Vishva Lekha Printing Press and the Sarvodaya wheelchair project. The former is one of the most efficiently run income-generating projects of Sarvodaya.[7]

A study of the Sarvodaya movement in Sri Lanka reveals that it has been admirably creative, innovative and imaginative in evolving a philosophy of development which is truly indigenous. True to the spirit of Buddhist doctrine, from which it derives its inspiration, Sarvodaya gives priority to the spiritual and moral foundations of development activity rather than to economic growth and technological advancement. It emphasizes sharing and community and gives priority to the fulfilment of primary human needs. Although it solicits the assistance and guidance of experts and the educated elite, it recognizes the importance of decision-making from below. Sarvodaya advocates an intermediate technology, and environmental ethics consisting of reverence for life and nature. It seeks to achieve the right balance between material and spiritual well-being and conceives of the right type of development as leading to the establishment of a no-poverty and no-affluence society. It believes that these values that it seeks to promote are not alien to the rural culture of the Sri Lankan people. Sarvodaya adopts work-styles and methods of community organization which have an emotional appeal to the Sri Lankan villager. The village temple and the participation and leadership given by Buddhist monks figure prominently in all development activities organized by Sarvodaya.

The impact of Sarvodaya has undoubtedly been felt in rural Sri Lanka. The service it has already rendered towards the improvement of village life is commendable. Some of its concepts have had an influence at the national level as well. The *gamudawa* concept of former President Premadasa can be said to be a case in point. The practice of *sramadana*, the gifting of voluntary labour and skills for the upliftment of deprived communities, was introduced and popularized by Sarvodaya, and it is now commonly adopted by other organizations too as an effective mode of community service. The poverty alleviation programme of the previous government can be said to have been both conceptually and practically influenced by the Sarvodaya ideology. The Sarvodaya emphasis on *janasakti* (people's strength) may have influenced the *janasakti* concept of President Premadasa. Sarvodaya has also been successful in mobilizing the *bhikkhu* community, whose traditional role of giving moral direction to the lay community was gradually diminishing, to actively participate in the national development effort. Joanna Macy, who as a foreign observer studied various aspects of Sarvodaya activity in Sri Lanka, says: 'Interviewing scores of monks on the village scene, and observing these and many more of them at work, I was able to conclude that the role of the Sangha in Sarvodaya's grassroots development activities is extensive and significant'.[8]

The founder of the movement, A.T. Ariyaratne, holds that Sarvodaya has a universal message. The movement has established grassroots contacts with various villages abroad, particularly in Holland and Belgium. It is observed that there are striking parallels between the Sarvodaya concept of world awakening and recent developments in the West.[9] Kantowsky points out the potential of Sarvodaya Development philosophy to have a universal influence as a result of changing perceptions about development among the people of the Western world:

> In contrast to the late sixties, when redress of all societal evil was sought in a total revolution of the whole system, what we now see is the rediscovery of the individual. 'Voluntary simplicity', the power inherent in each of us to reject the persuasive message of the mass media, has become a force that is backed by a major shift in public opinion. A Harris survey of a cross section of 1,502 adults revealed in 1977 that the American people have begun to show a deep skepticism about the nation's capacity for economic growth, and that they are wary of the benefits that growth is supposed to bring. Significant majorities place a high priority on improving human and social relationships and the quality of American life than on simply raising the standards of living.[10]

Critics of Sarvodaya have raised certain issues regarding its possible impact at the international level. The problem of the Sarvodaya philosophy of development being eclipsed by the overwhelming influence of the national policies pursued by governments, backed financially and even dictated by powerful organizations such as the International Monetary Fund, is a reality to be faced. Such policies lead to the creation of the very features that the Sarvodaya philosophy of development has rejected. They promote the values of an acquisitive society, driven by material incentives and alien life-styles. The effectiveness of Sarvodaya in challenging the new knowledge base of the positivistic science and secular systems of thought which seek to displace the structures of knowledge and wisdom of traditional societies is called into question. The younger generation is being exposed to the scientific and technological knowledge of the new industrial civilization. Sarvodaya's capability of having a significant impact on educated youth exposed to such modern knowledge, who consequently develop a sceptical attitude towards the holistic modes of thinking of the traditional culture, can be open to doubt. Sarvodaya has also been open to criticism on the ground that while advocating self-reliance it has been operating largely on the basis of foreign aid. The danger of the emergence of a bureaucracy maintained by the foreign funds received by the movement, resulting in the establishment of the very social relationships against which Sarvodaya was originally canvassing, has been a disturbing thought even to some sympathizers. The importance of building a self-reliant economic base for the implementation of Sarvodaya development policy has become a matter of the foremost importance.

The fact that Sarvodaya offers an alternative theory of sustainable development which has a special relevance to the endogenous Sri Lankan culture cannot be doubted. One may also maintain that if one objectively assesses its importance with enough insight and foresight, it is by far the most preferable alternative to promote in the Sri Lankan context. But the day when such a philosophy and practical programme of development will win wide acceptance in Sri Lanka, to the extent of moving political forces to adopt it through constraints imposed by popular will and making a real impact at the national level, does not appear to be near. One can only hope that the contradictions inherent in the current models of development practised in Sri Lanka and abroad will eventually bring about this result.

Notes

1. *The Future Directions of Sarvodaya*, Sarvodaya Shramadan Movement, Moratuwa, Sri Lanka, 1994, p.2.
2. *Sarvodaya*, Detlef Kantowsky, Vikas Publishing House Private Limited, New Delhi, 1980, p.40f.
3. *The Sarvodaya Shramadana Movement*, Hundred Villages Development Schemes, paper read at a regional seminar on the role of youth in development, Bangkok, 1971.
4. *Ibid.*, p.4.
5. *Sarvodaya*, Kantowsky, p.48.
6. *The Future Directions of Sarvodaya*, Sarvodaya Shramadana Movement, Moratuwa, Sri Lanka, 1994 p.4.
7. Annual Report of Sarvodaya 01.04.93-31.03.94.
8. *Dharma and Development*, Kumarian Press, Connecticut, 1983, p.66.
9. *Sarvodaya*, Kantowsky, p.157.
10. *Ibid.*, pp.158-59.

9

A Cultural Policy for Thailand's National Development

Amara Raksasataya

The development of a cultural policy for any country is an extremely complicated task. There are many obstacles. First of all, culture is an abstract concept, thus elusive to define, to limit its parameters and scope. Everybody defines culture to suit himself. When a more comprehensive sophisticated definition is attempted, it becomes more difficult to explain. Secondly, the formulation of a cultural policy raises a set of complicated problems — what to include, how far, how much it will cost, how can it be implemented, how effective it will be and for how long, how to evaluate, how it can be made self-sustaining, who should administer it, what will be the returns on the investment. Thirdly, how much of its resources can a country commit to cultural preservation, promotion and development.

Despite all these difficulties, this paper is attempting to address these problems with the conviction that a more concrete policy could be developed for Thailand and other countries.

Meaning of culture

While 'culture' in many languages is a common word that conveys some acceptable meanings, it is also an elusive term when we want to know its exact meaning and scope, especially how to promote it, or how to make use of it in any particular way.

It Hindi, the word *sanskrti* means a conglomeration of values, beliefs, traditions born out of heritage. In Chinese, *wen-hua* literally means sentence-making, connoting respect for the written word. In many Western countries the term derives from the Latin *cultura*, which means a set of knowledge. In Thailand, a relatively new word, *wattana-dharm* has been coined. It means development, growth or evolution from an original state of nature (Raksasataya 1994:3-4).

When one wants to systematize its meanings it becomes officialise, with an accompanying complexity that most people will have difficulty understanding. In Unesco's definition, culture includes 'the whole complex of distinctive spiritual, material, intellectual and emotional features that characterize a society or social group. It includes not only arts and letters, but also modes of life, the fundamental rights of the human being, value systems, traditions and beliefs' (Unesco 1982:41).

The Royal Institute of Thailand defines *wattana-dharm* as 'things that make a group grow, a group's way of life. In the Culture Act of 1942, it means characteristics that show growth, order, harmonious progress of the country, and good moral standard of the people. Academically, it means behaviour and things that people in the group have produced or created from learning from each other and things that people make common use of within that group' (The Royal Institute 1983:734).

Even the office of the National Culture Commission of the Ministry of Education could not offer an official definition of the term. In many of its publications, the term is defined differently by various authorities, professors and learned men (Office of National Culture Commission 1994). In its most recent publication it gives two meanings. First, as a general meaning, 'culture is a way of life of people in the society, the pattern of behaviour and the manifestation of feeling and thought in various situations which other members of the same society can understand, appreciate, recognize and use together, which will lead to development of quality of life of the people in that particular society'.

Second, as an operational definition, 'culture means growth which is the result of relationship system between human beings themselves, human beings and societies, and human beings and nature. It can be classified into 3 aspects, namely spiritual, societal and material. Culture can be accumulated and transmitted from one generation to the next one, from one society to another until it becomes a pattern that people can learn and use to produce products and goods, both abstract and material. They are worthy of research, conservation, rehabilitation, development, transmission, promotion, creation of expertise, and exchange in order to create things which will help human beings to live in peace, happiness and freedom which are the base of human civilization' (Office of the National Culture Commission, 1992:6).

With such vagueness, it has been very difficult for the government of Thailand to develop its cultural policies and implement them effectively.

Attempts at cultural promotion in Thailand

Before 1932, Thailand was governed under an absolute monarchy. The monarchs were the patrons of all arts and cultural activities, especially at the national level. Palaces, public edifices, temples were places where all cultural activities took place and artists and learned men met. Several kings were themselves great artists and poets.

After the change to a constitutional monarchy or parliamentary system on 24 June 1932, successive governments, 51 cabinets altogether, paid different degrees of attention to national and endogenous culture. In 1943 the government created the Cultural Council. In 1953 it was enlarged and became the Ministry of Culture. Twelve national preferences were announced, covering various aspects of national culture — patriotism, new name of the country (Thailand instead of Siam), honouring the national banner, consumption manners, nation-building effort, national anthem for the king, language and literature, national dress, daily chores, assistance to children, the elderly and the disabled. Several other cultural aspects were strongly promoted.

After 1958 a new authoritarian group came to power. Its government wanted to expedite economic development. The First Five-year Economic Development Plan was announced in 1961 with no mention of cultural promotion. The Ministry of Culture was abandoned. A small division in the Ministry of Education was allowed. Though the successive five-year plans brought in a social component, cultural aspects remained ignored.

Economic development in Thailand has been regarded as highly successful. Material development does bring in many undesirable side-effects resulting in massive inequality and deterioration of the environment and cultural life. In 1979, the government decided to enlarge the Cultural Division by making it the office of the National Culture Commission with departmental status within the Ministry of Education.

In 1981, the government issued an announcement of the Office of the Prime Minister on a national cultural policy. Later the government announced detailed guideline, which provided an impetus to the cultural promotion effort (Office of National Culture Commission 1986). The Seventh National Economic and Social Development Plan (1992-93) has included the Framework and Direction of National Cultural Plan, which was adopted by the Cabinet on 27 December 1989 (Office of National Culture Commission 1994b:1-2).

At the moment the Eighth National Economic and Social Development Plan is being prepared for 1997-2001. It is expected that the cultural dimension will receive greater attention.

In addition to the Seventh Plan, which provided general direction and resources to implement regular plans, the present government has included culture in its Policy Statement to Parliament on 21 October 1992. The government will 'campaign to engage people, organizations, institutions and communities in activities relating to conserve, promote and propagate Thai arts and culture more actively' (Council of Ministers 1992:37).

In order to implement this policy the government has proclaimed the following programmes:

1. *Campaign for Thai Culture Year in 1994*: It provided special funds. Several public organizations and business firms provided funds to promote cultural understanding through television, radio and press.

2. *Thai Cultural Heritage Programme*: This is a Cabinet decision to extend the Campaign Year 1994 for 3 more years with different special emphases. For 1995 the Program emphasizes 'Culture and Development', for 1996 'Culture and Tourism', and for 1997 'Culture and Mass Media'.

Current cultural promotion activities

A. OFFICE OF THE NATIONAL CULTURE COMMISSION

Under the Thai Cultural Heritage Program (1994-97), the Office of National Culture Commission developed six main programmes, each with several projects, namely:

1. Public Relations Programme with 3 projects
2. Cultural Activities Promotion Programme with 11 projects

3. Books and Manuals on Culture Learning Programme with 3 projects
4. Public Sector Implementation Coordination Programme with 4 projects
5. Private Sector Implementation Coordination Programme with 7 projects
6. Programme Evaluation Programme with 3 projects (Office of NCC, 1994b: 10-19).

While it is not practical to go into the details of all of these programmes and projects, it would be useful to see the 11 projects in the Cultural Activities Promotion Programme. They are:

1. Project to promote loyalty to key institutions: the country, religions, and the monarch.
2. Project to promote family and communal life of the Thai people.
3. Project to promote Thai tradition, both national and local.
4. Project to promote the proper use of Thai language including speech, reading, writing and poetry.
5. Project to promote order, discipline, and values.
6. Project to promote virtues and ethics.
7. Project to promote the Thai way of life and folk wisdom.
8. Project to promote the Thai way of dressing.
9. Project to promote Thai arts.
10. Project to promote culture and tourism to ensure that tourists understand and appreciate Thai culture.
11. Project to promote culture and development in order to apply cultural dimensions to develop quality of life and society along with economic development with emphasis on sustainable development which balances man, society and environment (see details in Office of National Culture Commission, 1994c).

B. OTHER GOVERNMENT AGENCIES

In Thailand there are other public agencies that are related to cultural conservation, promotion and development, namely:

1. Department of Religious Affairs, Ministry of Education. This department takes care of all religions which have followers in Thailand. Since 95 per cent of Thai people are Buddhists, there are over 300,000 priests, 30,000 temples. The department has to look after temple property and assist the council of Senior Priests in their governance.
2. Department of Fine Arts, Ministry of Education, deals with all aspect of fine arts including restoration of archaeological sites, maintaining historical sites, buildings and parks, as well as national library and museum systems. It also runs schools for classical artists and national theatres.
3. National Identity Board, Office of the Prime Minister, deals with unique aspects of Thai national characteristics, mainly the promotion of the institution of the King.
4. Universities and educational institutions. All educational institutions have as a main function the promotion of cultural heritage. However, Silpakorn (Finer Arts) University is the one with special emphasis on arts and culture. It has the only School of Thai Architecture, and strong departments of archaeology and history.

C. EVALUATION

Despite a lot of effort on the part of the public and private sectors, the Thai cultural heritage is in danger of being inundated by materialism, monetary domination, American and European culture, and to a certain extent Chinese, Indian and Japanese culture. The government's efforts are usually intermittent and inadequate to sustain continuing involvement and appreciation among the younger generation. Fewer people go to temples, attending religious and cultural activities. Many traditional arts have no inheritors and subscribers.

An alternative cultural policy

As a matter of fact the cultural policy is inadequate, not comprehensive, and resource poor. To implement such a policy effectively is an impossible task. Even to evaluate the state of the cultural condition of the country to establish a benchmark is not simple. No one has systematically attempted to do so.

This author would like to suggest an alternative policy for the promotion of Thai culture which would include cultural dimension in the national development mainstream. In order to do so, it is necessary to ponder the following stages:

1. To define the term culture clearly, and simply.
2. To define the scope and activities of culture more clearly, in order to render them amenable to policy formulation.
3. To develop a strategy that will make culture pay for itself, economically and socially, to ensure sustainable viability.

CULTURE REDEFINED

Culture should be defined as 'anything that man has developed, improved, grown, altered from an original state of nature basically to improve the quality of life of man'.

Whatever retains its original state of nature is natural, unadulterated, unaltered, therefore primitive. When a man uses his hands to catch a fish and eats it raw it is uncultured. The culture related to fishing begins as soon as man begins to use tools to catch fish, and uses fire and utensils to cook and eat it. Therefore the stone age, copper age, iron age, up to the nuclear age, are major steps of human cultural upgrading.

Men improve things normally with the intention that they will make life easier, more satisfactory, more secure, more happy. Culture therefore often denotes better things in life. Though in fact in some cases, culture may bring more suffering — such as the cultivation of the poppy and turning it into opium and heroin, or sexual permissiveness leading to AIDS and death.

Culture can be transmitted from one generation to the next, from one locality to another, etc., often with some modifications.

Culture has different stages of development. It usually starts with a few men and their families. As human beings are social animal who live in groups, the individual's culture spread to group and then to commune. As a commune grows larger or communicates with other communes, communal culture would spread to a region or larger societies or other ethnic groups, eventually to the national level.

Of course one may subdivide culture physically into as many levels as one wishes; but here four levels seem adequate for policy-making (***see*** fig. 1).

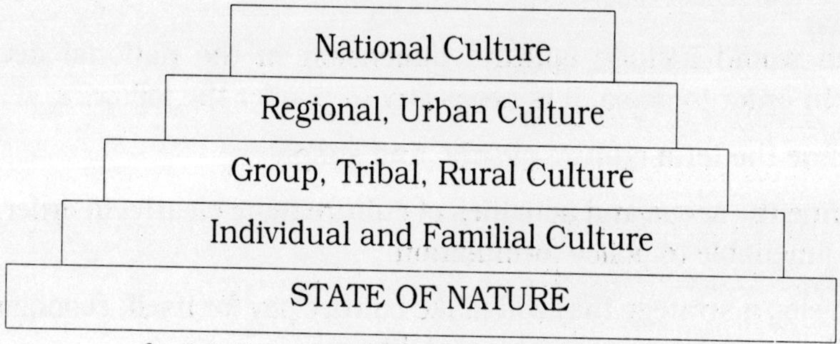

fig. 9.1 State of Nature and Cultural Development

Table 9.1

Some Cultural Activities at Different Levels

Individual and Family Level	*Groups, Tribes, Local Level*	*Region, Urban Level*	*National Level*
Life			
Family tie, marriage	do.	do.	Civil Law
Child rearing	do.	do.	do.
Caring of elderly	do.	do.	Social Welfare
Family rites	do.	do.	Ceremonies
Communication, Language	Vebal, Written	Literature	National Language
Learning	Education	do., Training	Education Systems
Faith, Value, Ethics	Folk Belief,	Religions	do.
Family authority, Creed	Tribal governance	Government	Government, Politics, Idiologies
Food			
Food Production	do.	do.	do
Agriculture, Gardening	do.	do.	do

	Individual and Family Level	*Groups, Tribes, Local Level*	*Region, Urban Level*	*National Level*
	Animal Husbandry	do.	do.	do.
	Fishing	do.	do.	Fishery
	Food Preparation,	do.	do.	Culinary arts
	Eating Manner	do.	do.	Social etiquette
Clothing				
	Clothing Preparation Dressing	Folk costume	Regional Costume	do.
Shelter				
	Building, House	Communal Site	Public Buildings	Architectural Style
	Furniture	do.	do.	do.
Health				
	Health Care	do.	do.	do.
	Medicine	Herbal, Acupuncture Massage	do.	Pharmacy, Medicine
Others				
	Household Utensils	do.	do.	do.
	Working Tools, Crafts	do.	do.	do.
	Games	do., material arts	do., local army, competition	Sports, games Military training
	Song and Dance Music, Plays	Folk arts	do.	do.
	Painting	do.	do.	do.
	Sculpture	do.	do.	do., Monuments

SCOPE AND ACTIVITIES OF CULTURE

While nobody can develop a comprehensive list of cultural activities, aspects, elements, etc., a suggested list on Table 1 below is merely an attempt to provide a basis for the development of a cultural policy.

From the list one can see that there are a lot of items that man has developed from a state of nature — things and non-material abstractions that he needs to survive. Once his life and his family are secure, several things will be developed for the use of his group, his society, and finally his country.

STRATEGY FOR CULTURAL DEVELOPMENT

Since cultural policies in the past failed because of complication, lack of resources, lack of implementation methods and lack of sustained interest, the new strategy will address these inadequacies:

1. The concept must be redefined and simplified.
2. Resources should be drawn principally from individuals voluntarily, smaller communities, groups, non-governmental organizations, religious and philanthropic organizations, educational institutions, etc., because there are so many things with cultural components spreading throughout the country that a government cannot look after all of them.
3. The resources from the government should be considered as secondary or supportive. Government should stimulate, co-ordinate, motivate and legislate private activities. It may support research and subsidize such activities. It should operate and control very few activities such as archaeological and historical sites, national treasures, protected areas. It may have to try to protect endangered cultural heritages such as wall painting, ancient vernacular languages and literature, palaces, public edifices. The national government should encourage local governments to support more cultural programmes.
4. Government should motivate, educate, demonstrate that material development at the expense of spiritual development or environmental degradation would not bring happiness, harmony, integrity, pride and honour and other elements of quality of life to most people, while culture can enrich the life of the people.

5 Government should emphasize that culture is worthy of conservation, promotion and development. Culture would pay back in terms of happiness and higher quality of life. Better still, it would give financial returns to those engaged in cultural activities.

The following occupations and undertakings can be promoted:

1. All folk arts and crafts, village traditions and rites. They can be a great attraction.
2. All performing and visual arts, music, dance, plays (including puppet-shadow), and boxing.
3. Personal museums for painting, artifacts, Buddha images, houses, socio-cultural museums, horticultural gardens.
4. Tourism, especially to historical, religious and cultural sites.
5. Hotels, resorts and recreational sites should be arranged in Thai styles. Meals and drinks, games, orchestras and performance, dresses, etc., can be offered in Thai style.
6. Temples can be used as places for education, training, continuing education, games and recreation other than for religious purposes, both for their own sake and for inducing people to get closer to religious training.
7. Basic needs of life such as food, clothing, shelter, even medicine should be added to cultural amenities.
8. Some old towns with traditional culture should restore their walls, palaces, temples, public places, traditional houses, dress, arts and crafts. This will help revive cultural activities as well as local economies.

In this way, cultural activities are compatible and complementary to economic development. It is well understood that in the next century — a few years from now — traditional economic activities such as agriculture and manufacturing will need only about 20 per cent of employable manpower. The rest will have to be channelled to service industries. Much of these could be well in culture-related undertakings. Cultural development can become an integral component of economic and social development.

References

Council of Ministers, 1992, *Statement of Policy of the Council of Ministers* by Prime Minister Chuan Leekpai to the National Assembly, 21 October (in Thai)

Office of the National Culture Commission, 1986, *National Culture Policy and Guidelines on Protection, Promotion and Development of Culture*. Bangkok: Kurusapa (in Thai)

———, 1992, Ministry of Education, *Meaning and Scope of Cultural Activities*. Bangkok: Kurusapa (in Thai)

———, 1994a, *Culture and Development*. Bangkok: Kurusapa (in Thai)

———, 1994b, *Main Plan of Thai Cultural Heritage Project 1995-1997*. Bangkok (in Thai)

———, 1994c, *Guidelines for the Promotion of 11 Thai Cultural Activities*. Bangkok: Kurusapa (in Thai)

Raksasataya, Amara, 1994, 'Cultural Dimension of Asian Paths to Development'. Keynote address for Regional Consultation for Asia and the Pacific of the World Commission on Culture and Development, Manila, 21-23 November 1994

The Royal Institute, 1983, *Dictionary*. Bangkok (in Thai)

Unesco, 1982, *Final Report of the World Conference on Cultural Policies'*. Cited in World Decade Secretariat, *Culture and Development: A Study*. Paris: Unesco

10

Local Knowledge and Development

Ngo Duc Thinh

Allow me to express my warm thanks to the Indira Gandhi National Centre for the Arts and to Unesco Professor Baidyanath Saraswati for their kind invitation to participate in this seminar. This is a happy opportunity for me to set foot on this wonderful land for the first time and to meet and learn from colleagues from India and other countries. On this occasion, originating from realities in Vietnam, I would like to share with our colleagues my thinking and experience related to the issues our seminar is interested in.

The peoples and nations in the orient

Although peoples in this region achieved high civilizations in ancient times, they engaged in industrialization and modernization later than Western countries. Only from the 20th century onwards, particularly in its latter half, did they begin to step on the path of industrialization and modernization. At present, there lies in front of them a Western model of development with its great achievement as well as its constraints and contradictions.

There was a long period when under the overwhelming influence of Western civilization, not a few people in Eastern countries got a complex of inferiority and even denied the values of traditional national cultures. On the plane of action, they adopted a stereotype of Western-type civilization for their own nations, the consequence of which appeared to be not much of a success. Although these countries made progress in terms of technology and economic growth, they are beset with many social upheavals, while their long-standing cultural identity could not be preserved nor developed further.

Facing such realities, in recent decades many people in the Orient have begun to review the path of development taken by their countries. Will countries in the East have to necessarily follow the Western model of development when engaged in industrialization and modernization? What development path is there which can ensure both economic growth and social stability and the preservation of national cultural identity? We believe that all development needs to ensure heredity and continuity. All communities need to move forward from their own existing traditions. That is the reason why elements of tradition must be considered as the basis of development. Traditional values encompass many aspects, including local knowledge.

Local knowledge is non-school knowledge. It is the experience accumulated by man through a long process of activity aimed at adaptation to and transformation of the natural and social environment, to meet material and spiritual needs. Such knowledge subsists and develops mainly not through studying and books but is usually disseminated and handed down, and enriched further through memory and oral diffusion by such media as proverbs, phrases, sayings, day-to-day professional practice performed by farmers, handicraft workers, fishermen and stockbreeders.

Categories of local knowledge

1. Knowledge of nature and environment
2. Knowledge of human beings
3. Knowledge of production
4. Knowledge of management of society and community

All nations on our planet accumulate extremely rich knowledge of their own environments. It is the knowledge of weather, land, rivers and seas, of various breeds of animals and plants. In ethnology, there have taken shape such disciplines as ethnobotany, ethnozoology, ethno-meteorology. For instance, we have inherited things that have been handed down to us since time immemorial, such as ballads on the various rainy seasons in the year and on other meteorological phenomena.

The Mang ethnic group has inherited in the same way a type of agricultural calendar, under which each sequential farming operation such as cutting trees, slashing and burning, sowing, weeding, harvesting, is closely linked with the appearance of various wild flowers in the forests. The Viet and Mong (Meo) ethnic groups have ballads handed down from generation to generation verbally which carry wisdom on how to select varieties of buffalo, horse, pig, chicken. Those ethnic groups engaged in slash-and-burn farming have a similar heritage of knowledge of classification of types of forests and strains of plants, and this knowledge helps them to select appropriate plots of land for growing rice or some subsidiary crop.

Like many other Asian countries, we have since long accumulated local knowledge of the human system, of keeping fit methods and curing diseases. However, since the Westerners penetrated our country and disseminated Western medicine, folk medicine was neglected and underestimated. Only in the last few decades, at a time the world followed a tendency to discover and develop the Oriental world, has this traditional medicine been given due consideration. At present, besides Western medicine hospitals, hospitals of Eastern medicine or of combined Western and Eastern medicine exist.

We also have a separate tradition of keeping fit and medical treatment based on the fundamental Oriental concept of the universe, to the effect that there is an interaction between yin and yan, mutual support between them, that the human system is a small universe and that diseases affecting it are a sign of loss of balance. Therefore, it is necessary though alimentation, medication including creating mental effects, to re-establish the yin-yan balance in order to regain good health. A dozen years ago, the Eastern physician Do Tat Loi managed to collect and classify some 1,500 medicinal plants. As early as in the 18th century, the eminent physician Le Huu Trac, in his work entitled *Nu Cong Thang Lam*, collected and analysed the curing effects of more than 200 different types of food and foodstuffs.

The knowledge of production is even more abundant and varied. For ethnic groups in Vietnam, the main production is rice farming, therefore the richest knowledge is also to be found in this area. The Viets living in the lowlands have reviewed all of their knowledge of farming and expressed it in crystallized form in the four words 'water, fertilizer, assiduity and seeds' (in Vietnamese: *nuoc, phan, can, giong*). As knowledge comes from experience, the more you are advanced in age, the more you are experienced in farming, and the Vietnamese phrase 'Lao Nong Tri Dien', which conveys that idea, serves as evidence.

Let us take the example of the slash-and-burn agriculture practised by the minorities living in mountainous areas or on the high plateau. In order to adapt themselves to and preserve the forest environment, and achieve productivity in growing rice and subsidiary crops, this population has created a system of cultivation with such techniques as rotation of crops, laying land fallow and inter-cropping. That is a 'self-support' technique (neither improving land by means of adding fertilizer, nor causing soil improvement), and also a technique that helps to maintain balance in one's favour (a balance between man and the environment). This is really an achievement of the traditional slash-and-burn farming highly appreciated by the agronomists working with the International Rice Institute. The question is how to assimilate and upgrade this knowledge of traditional farming techniques to serve modern agricultural production in the tropical and sub-tropical countries.

Knowledge of society and of community plays a very important role; it ensures the stability and invulnerability of traditional social relations. This is no longer pure knowledge but on its basis, there come into being rules that all must comply with.

With the Viet people, who have a relatively high level of development, each village has its regulations (village management rules). At present we have collected and kept in the archives some thousands of such documents.

With the Thai ethnic group, each of their Muongs (the Thai minority is divided into 16 Muongs) has a different custom (in their own language: *Hit Khong ban Muong*) which is recorded in the ancient Thai script. With these they have established rules governing relations of ownership, marriage and family as well as rituals and customs.

For those minorities without a written language, customary laws exist in the form of oral rhymes which establish rules of material and moral life and of social relations. We have so far collected dozens of such customary laws, each consisting of tens of thousands of verses. This is cultural heritage which is at the same time material that gives insights into the traditional society, and also serves as a standard for social administration by the ethnic minorities.

What was mentioned above is just a small part in comparison to the intellectual heritage handed down by our forefathers. Increasingly conscious of its great value, Vietnamese scientists have availed themselves of the encouragement and financial support of the State and over the past many years they have conducted programmes of research on and application of local knowledge to serve the livelihood of man in modern society. They have collected traditional knowledge on folk medicine, encouraged and promoted a combination of Western and Eastern medicine, the growing of herbs in family gardens and on the community's land, organized health clubs for elderly people.

Efforts are being made to initiate the studying of old village regulations for developing new self-management rules for villages, towns and cities. Our Institute has got an assignment from the State to conduct a study and collect village regulations of traditional villages of various ethnic groups living in Vietnam. In the initial stage, we have collected some thousands of these regulations and dozens of oral laws. They are the scientific basis for us to make our own contribution to the management of rural areas and to administrative reform in those areas.

In the agricultural aspect, we have studied folk experience of those farming systems which are appropriate to the various ecosystems in Vietnam, particularly the slash-and-burn farming system on steep hillsides, trying to introduce elements of modern techniques to update the traditional ones, in order to ensure both farming productivity and the preservation of the natural environment as well.

Local knowledge and social development

Local knowledge is the knowledge that has not gone beyond the level of experience, institutions and impressions, drawn from actual activities of man himself, and exactly for this reason it is of practical value.

To a modern society, in my opinion, this local knowledge does not lose any of its scientific and practical value. More than that, this people's knowledge which is perpetuated among the people, put into practice by the people in daily life, unlike modern knowledge which originates from inventions and discoveries by individuals or collectives, and only through experimentation, education and diffusion, can they reach the masses. These are two types of knowledge, two forms of information with different features, but are mutually supportive and complementary.

In order to preserve and bring into play local knowledge so that it becomes a factor in the development of modern society, we would like to recommend sponsorship by Unesco of the following activities:

Through varied forms, to educate people to overcome a complex of inferiority and the psychology of undervaluing traditional knowledge handed down by forefathers, merely tailing after Western knowledge and technology which is still rather widespread in Afro-Asian countries, in the Third World, to restore the value and pride of nations as regards their own intellectual heritage.

To encourage the collection, study and diffusion of local knowledge, to include such knowledge in the curriculum of schools, the greater part of which is actually based on Western knowledge. This is also a way of handing down the intellectual heritage from one generation to the next.

To encourage combination of Western and traditional knowledge, to use achievements of modern knowledge and technology to shed light on, elucidate and update the scientific and practical value of traditional knowledge. To create conditions for the people to inherit the intellectual heritage from their forefathers and at the same time continue to develop it creatively.

In short, local knowledge is an intellectual heritage and is national cultural identity as well. Only those nations that have learnt to prize it and bring it into play can take the path of industrialization and modernization while preserving their own identity, the original features of their nations.

11

Man in Relation to His Environment

Keshav Malik

Conditions influencing development or growth is how the dictionary defines the word environment. For the plant, as we know, sunlight, air and water are the environment. For insects and animals topography, climate, food resources as also the proximity of different animal species, or man, is the environment. Changes in the relationship or balance of any of these several factors determine the behaviour of the plant or the animal, although this becomes acutely evident only in the long run.

The real environment

Now the environments that influence or determine plants and animals also mould human nature. But for the purposes of this workshop, as indeed in any context, the generality of men are rather less concerned with these environments and more with the vital human forces or factors fatefully shaping man. If I may say so, man's real environment is men. It is social behaviour that conditions human development in any crucial sense of that term. And what is it that moulds social behaviour — ideas, beliefs, notions, biases, presuppositions? A child is born to all these and his unfolding character and physical nature reflect his mental inheritance. This is his real environment. All outwardly observable behaviour, all notable action could be traced to habits planted or shaped by belief.

The record of nations with vast differences in flora and fauna and in climate has shown us amazing similarity in outlook, temperament and attitude. Nations close in the first factors have shown an equal diversity in characteristics. History is replete with instances of the so-called national characteristics of a people, at once ranging from peaceable to warlike, from earthy to other-worldly, at different periods of their existence. These notable changes are due to a great many factors, but here, as I said, we must pay attention to those factors that, for our purpose, are the prime movers. Changes in dynasties, foreign conquests, floods, the havoc of drought, all these go to condition and influence man. And the aggregate of thus influenced men perpetuate the attitudes and the characteristics of the single individual. But many of the above-mentioned factors are only the outer determinants that passively shape man. The active element is the conscious shaping of the individual from man's own beliefs about himself, his nature, his destiny. It is these attitudes that determine man's relations to his time and life. When a man believes in predestination, his attitudes and behaviour are complementary. When a man believes that man makes history he assists at or is crucial to his own becoming. In other words, the state and nature of human awareness at a point of time in a cultural milieu are all important in the moulding or adapting of man to the total environment.

Two states

Now man's beliefs are expressed not always directly but through institutions, rituals, cults, ceremonials, and through the assertion of a host of group identities. These cultural or social artifices are almost of a hydraulic chemistry and of far-reaching effect on human conduct. As if in keeping with animal reflexes and instincts, they can through usage over time get to be solid, icy, inflexible, unpliable. In other words, they are not amenable to easy change or renovation. They perpetuate themselves because, in turn, human beings themselves are prone to act out of two different natures — the pre-rational and the rational, the one open to enquiry, prepared for adaptation. This second state, the fluid one, itself follows on a state of heightened awareness, of imaginative perception. It is to be in constant touch with essential human values, as also to be possessed of a realistic knowledge of the material means, in order so to effectuate those values. In the fluid state, as I term it, there is no sacrosanctity attached to means. Holiness inheres only in the essentials. On the other hand, in the 'iced state' of institutions the means themselves tend to become fixed, sacred; with the result that it becomes all but impossible to question them. Fresh adaptation, here, becomes quite improbable in relation to new environments. The truth of essential values is lost. Rigidity, inflexibility, conformity, these are the consequences.

Thus institutions, at once useful and inescapable in the pursuit of the necessary, the good or the truthful life, very often become ends in themselves. A great deal of human history is the chronicle of this predicament: that, on the one hand, without organizations and institution the fruits of human insight, ingenuity, intelligence cannot easily be handed down to the individual, and on the other, that once come into being the authority which organizations or those who hold power exert creates the logic of its own vested interest. But with luck, and given a degree of sophistication, these institutions remain what they are — means to serve the individual, materially or spiritually. At these moments in history civilization has a chance of being at its peak. The too anarchical individual tends to be asocial, whereas the individual well ensconced in the vestments of social organization tends to be authoritarian. Either way there is faulty adaptation in the essential growth and development of the human self. As one knows, the visions and insights of seers, saints, savants often get to be stratified in the narrow religious orders that follow them, so there is not too much room here for the mind, heart or spirit to move about. Similarly political or social organizations often frown on freedom of thought. It is solitary men really, therefore, who keep the ship of life on an even keel. Captains of state, kings, others, are good enough to guide the destiny of a nation in its race for survival. But from the long-term perspective they function within the confines of settled ideas and established, stratified power. No matter how civilized, the rulers are unable to break new ground. It is for this that men without organizational power but only with the power of their spirit, heart or mind chart the longer path. It is from these sources that better adaptations related to the deeper values are consummated.

Necessity and freedom

If necessity rules the choices of state, freedom does the movements of the men who bring about fresh adaptations to the environment. This freedom of the savant is not born of caprice but is subordinate to his adherence to certain self-transcending values. It is a question of opting for something which is not yet, for which the majority is not, to which the state is often opposed. Now to exist in such a condition of ostracism, aloneness or solitude and yet without any hatred or contempt for mankind is itself one of the supremely important factors in human evolution, in other words in the revolution of man's inner being. It needs moral courage. And indeed courage, on a lower plane, is itself the means for animal survival. But, as we know, man does not live by mere survival; even when in a depressed state mankind lives for and by spirit. For no man is so abject that he is unaware of his human self; his pride or his sense of integrity is born of some trace of awareness, of consciousness — that is, in his being able to reflect on lasting values in the context of time and death. Awareness of self stems from the human capacity to stand back from oneself and to imagine one's life as a non-person, and to imagine the other man as oneself. This is the inner situation that makes man human, above his normally animal, self-possessive nature. This it is, too, which ushers in the conflict of values in the human soul and a moral split between thought and act, between emotion and reason — which leads to a psychic sickness. But with self-discipline there may be a great inner joy, born of the conviction that goodness is its own reward, that to experience life intensely without possessing it is to live it richly enough. Now human history ever since settled society has been a saga of man attempting to transcend his narrower nature to attain the wider one. Since mankind at a certain stage of psychic development still does find life at the survival values good enough, but nevertheless comes to grief (meeting with the inevitable terrors of existence, destroyed in the endless conflicts of a divided mankind), the sensitive struggle to remind it either of a richer life as if offered by the arts and the life of the mind or of the religious one which helps draw men together. And it is in the light of this that new social orders are conceived. The fact is that the so-called self-surpassing values are far from practised. And yet, such is the logic of human evolution that they cannot be completely disowned, at least lip service needs to be paid to them. This is the reason for humans' lying to themselves and to others. But lying is a good adaptive device for the impersonal state or for the individual acting on behalf of state or party, though not for the individual who is a person, and moral. The individual's mortality, or rather his sensing of it, and a human organization's relative immortality, makes the individual the moral agent of possible social conscience and deeper sentience. It is this state of richer awareness, of a loftier, more delicate perception, that is in constant danger of being destroyed by the collectivity. But then awareness is the *sine qua non* of human existence as distinct from the indifferent brute one.

Mixture

A great many beliefs about nature, about man, about invisible phenomena are, with hindsight, seen as mixtures of pure truths and pitiable illusions, often providing hope and succour to mankind but without lifting it to the creative plane. Wherever the rational element is disallowed and knowledge becomes purely revelatory, to be dispensed by priests or spirituals, secular truth about man and nature cannot be further refined. In the end, the source of truth — or its explorer — is fallible man. A social order that realizes the importance of this fact ensures that the free process of truth recovery, or discovery, is continuous and that there is no monopoly on it. Now in human history several, if not most, political, social or religious orders have certainly not allowed this freedom with much pleasure. The result is that the individual, and with him the social order, often become hidebound. The overall environment and its relation to mankind then turns tyrannous, sterile.

But the baby should not be thrown out with the bathwater: there are those amongst us in today's world who, sensing the malignant element in religious orders have, at the same time, disowned all insight, all self-transcending values. But the moral and spiritual perceptions of humanity must be separated from the unfortunate doctrinaire theologies, moribund rituals and narrow confining loyalties. The essential illuminations of old still remain valid. Here, thus, is the crux of the matter, that a technically proficient mankind becomes the lord of the earth but not his own master. For him heaven and hell and God are dead. And yet, the fact remains that hell, heaven and the idea called God and so on, since they are metaphors for inner human experience rather than for outward reality located in some other time or place, cannot be dismissed. The terms define the qualities of life, and qualities of life cannot be brushed aside, they can only be refined of erroneous elements, pruned of extraneous unscientific implications. Thus the significance of convictions remains, orders of values remain and, so, prayer and penance remain, in order so to give form and direction to man's life. Man, after all, lives by meaning, his life is incomplete without it, that is, without his having told himself of the point or purpose of his life. Asceticism is not necessary to this quest, nor a resignation from life, nor a disjunction of the life of the body from that of the spirit. But a primacy of values is certainly called for. There is no democracy in the realm of values, only an aristocracy. Without such priority man's life, no matter how ample the means of physical survival or physical locomotion, remains not much removed from those of his earliest primitive forebears.

Mastery of the environment becomes more significant with man's acquisition of inner reason, as distinct from his understanding of the chain of cause and effect in objective phenomena. There need be no conflict between the two faculties. Able to cope ideally with his own reactions to human institutions, as with his own emotions, the possibility of real freedom arises; contrariwise, the outer freedom of movement and material control frees man from nature but not as far as his contradictory desires and promptings are concerned. With a balance struck in his affective and cognitive life, the relation to his environment is brought to a higher point of perfection. This process, though, can never be complete, because man is finite and the universe, infinite.

12

The Indian World-view and Environmental Crisis

R.P. Misra

The environmental crisis is no longer a danger still in the womb of time. It is already at our door. The people who feel concerned about the crisis ahead are ever growing in numbers, and they come from all walks of life: academics, intellectuals, scientists, technologists and artists. The search for a paradigm which can ensure economic development without jeopardising environmental quality is being intensified. This search is, however, still within the Western civilizational frame of reference. In fact, there is no serious attempt to look beyond the Cartesian world-view. We are not yet prepared to modify the development paradigm in vogue. We appear to be afraid of the future, not only the emerging future but also the alternative future.

The dominant groups in all societies still subscribe to the view that human ingenuity will triumph in the future as it has triumphed in the past. Science and technology will come to man's help and rescue him from ecological disaster. This group also believes that progress without tears is impossible. Humanity has always paid a price for development, and it will continue to pay it. The environmental crisis that looms large today is nothing but the price of progress.

This paper explores the potential of an alternative world-view in resolving the environmental crisis. It looks for avenues in Indian culture: its philosophy; its thinking; its life-style; and its approach to solving human problems.

The Indian world-view

India's written history goes back to over 5,000 years. Archaeological records take this culture further in the past. Its philosophy, thoughts, values and ethics have always had reverence for all that exists in nature, so much so that it evolved the concept of *vasudhaiva kutumbakam*, i.e. all that is alive, from plants to human species, belongs to a single family. They have originated from a common source and are interdependent. This cultural dictum was accepted not only by the people whom we now call Hindus, but also by other religions like Buddhists and Jains. Even religions like Christianity and Islam have been influenced by these values in India. The question is: Can the Indian world-view, as evident from its cultural heritage, be used as a paradigm for what Gandhi called a 'modern civilization', a civilization which treats nature not only as a source of livelihood but also as a source of life.

Indian culture is deeply rooted in two different but interacting traditions. The Aryans had their sway in the Indus and subsequently in the Ganga Valley: and the Dravidians to the south of the Vindhyas. The two interacted to produce not only the Vedic and post-Vedic cultures but also perhaps the Indus civilization. Many of statuettes and seals found in Mohenjo-Daro and Harappa, and later in part of Gujarat and Rajasthan, indicate that some of the concepts which now constitute the core of Indian culture were present in their incipient even then. For example, the statuette of the Mother found in Mohenjo-Daro points to what later gave rise to the concept of Mother Earth or Sakti.

ORIGIN OF LIFE

True, many schools of thought propounded by *rsis* like Carvak deny the existence of God or *paramatma*. What has, however, gripped the mind of India is not the deviations but a cross-current that 'there is One without a second', or "All this is Brahman'. Brahman is devoid of any attribute. Nothing can be positively postulated about him. He can be indicated only by 'not this, not this'.

This God without form is perceived by humans differently. These perceptions when generalized and collectivized give rise to various philosophies and religions. Religions are nothing but paths to one and the same reality. The concept of God unites all human beings into a single family. Nay, it unites all that exists in the universe — living and non-living — making them interdependent.

The Brahman reveals Himself in two ways: as unconscious or matter (*jada*) or conscious or live (*jiva*). It could also be called non-self (*acetana*) and self (*cetana*). While the non-self or unconscious is not eternal, the self or the conscious is eternal. The non-eternal ultimately ends as the atoms which went to create it. The *atman* is indestructible, it is part of *paramatman*. It cannot be reduced to atoms.

The concept of unity of life is not limited to the human species. It covers all forms of life which may be classified into:

1. *jarayuja* (viviparous)
2. *andaja* (oviparous)
3. *udbhija* (germinating)
4. *svedaja* (generated by heat and moisture)

The first are born of placenta, like human beings and animals; the second of eggs, like birds and reptiles; the third break through the earth, like plants; and the fourth are born of heat and moisture, like bacteria. Inorganic matter (*jada*) does not possess the above qualities even though the process of production of the two is the same.

Creation, according to Hindu thought, is not purposeless, nor it is random. Its goal is to move towards a perfect human being; towards *moksa* or bliss. Anything that endangers life on earth or which interferes with the processes to reach that goal, is undesirable. If there is anything that comes close to the Indian theory of evolution of life, it is the Gian theory.

CONCEPT OF PROGRESS

The Indian concept of progress is different from the one currently in vogue. Development, in the modern sense, essentially means economic development. It means higher GNP and per capita income and more consumption goods. A progressive society is one whose values do not clash with these developmental values. To receive development, people have to make certain sacrifices. They have to discard all those values which come in the way of development. To see divinity in nature is anti-developmental, for divinity is unintelligible. To think of unity of life is anti-developmental, for all other life forms are resources for the benefit of man. He can use them the way he wants.

Indian culture has a different concept of development called *mangalya*. It means a state in which man has no insurmountable problems and the natural, cultural and social environment in which he lives is conducive to his overall welfare. *Mangalya* is not limited to an individual; it covers all those humans and other lives in and around the individual. It is collective welfare. It carries man towards a blissful life. The collectivity includes all living and non-living entities the individual in question is linked to. Modern development can take place at the cost of other people and lives, and indeed at the cost of nature. But not *mangalya*.

There is another word that goes with *mangalya*: *kusala*. This conveys welfare in general, while *mangalya* conveys bliss. Indian culture has always aspired to achieve *kusala* and *mangala*. True, it has at times deviated from this path, but the goal was fixed, and society after brief interludes of deviations returned to the path of sanity, if we may say so.

Indian culture goes beyond human beings to take care of all that is living, from plants to elephants. It does not prohibit the use of nature. Rather, it encourages its use but only to the extent that its vitality is not adversely affected. One of the ways to maintain this vitality is to practise simple living and high thinking, and the other way is to insist on duties more than on rights of individuals. A farmer has the right to cut a tree, but only if he fulfils his duty to plant five other trees. The idea is that if everyone performs his duties honestly, the rights of all will be automatically preserved.

Ecological basis of Indian culture

It is for this reason that ever since the Indus valley civilization and more so from Vedic times, Indian culture has preached reverence for nature. It never thought nature to be a resource for exploitation. It always treated it as a source of not only sustenance, survival and happiness but also as a system of which humans are an inseparable part.

NATURE IS SACRED

All that exists in nature is essential for life. If nature were not evolved the way it has evolved, there would have been no life, or life would have taken a different form. Mountains, rivers, oceans, animals and plants are therefore sacred. They cannot be defiled. They should be used, but only with compassion and without jeopardizing their species. Beliefs that all that is valuable has come from the ocean, that the Himalayas are the abode of Siva, that the Ganga's water purifies everything, that the Ganga is a mother for the teeming millions even today, that the cow is sacred, all these have philosophical and scientific bases. God has come down to earth in animal forms too, like fish, boar, half-lion and half-human. Ganesa, who is worshiped all over India, is half elephant and half human. Almost all gods and goddesses have animals as their *vahan* (vehicles). Even the snake deserves our protection and reverence. Trees have received very special consideration, for they are the source of fruits, medicines and oxygen. Concepts of *kalpavrksa*, the tree which gives everything, and of *kamadhenu*, the cow which fulfils all desires, represent our values towards nature and life in general.

To say that all primitive societies had similar approaches to nature and that the modern scientific world cannot depend on such ideas for progress is to exhibit ignorance of what lies behind these traditions.

Modern man, proud as he is of his scientific and technological achievements, has been trying to develop methods and processes to uncover the mysteries of nature and use the knowledge so derived to control it and thus to induce higher productivity and secure a wide range of consumer goods which did not exist earlier. But any attempt to control nature can succeed only in the short run. In the long run nature appears to take revenge, because the natural system, including human beings, is governed by certain cosmic laws of integration and balance which the *Veda*s call *Rta*.

> The processes whose perpetual sameness or regular recurrence give rise to the representation of order obey *Rta* or their occurrence is R'ta, says Maurice Bloomfield. We read in the Vedas that 'The rivers flow R'ta. According to the R'ta the light of the heaven-born morning has come . . . . The year is the path of R'ta. The gods themselves are born of the R'ta or in the R'ta; they show by the acts that they know, observe and love the R'ta. In man's activity, the R'ta manifests itself as the moral law'.

To obtain nature's bounty, man must obey *Rta*: 'for one who lives according to Eternal Law, the winds are full of sweetness, the rivers pour sweet. So may the plants be full of sweetness for us'. The Vedic poet Atharva thus clearly reveals the human dependence on the order of the cosmos and the human role in maintaining it by observing the ancient law. He was perhaps the first deep ecologist of the world.

The same concept later finds a place in Buddha's *dharmacakra*. When a Buddhist lama turns his prayer wheel, he reminds us all of the *Rta*. As Jane Harrison notes, 'He finds himself in sympathetic touch with the Wheel of the

Universe when he performs the act Dharma-Chakra-Pravartana (justice wheel setting in motion). He dare not turn the Wheel contrariwise lest that were to upset the whole order of nature'.

The concept of *vasudhaiva kutumbakam* still prevails among the indigenous peoples in other parts of the world. It was also present in other great civilizations and cultures which gave rise to the great religions of the world. Raphael Patai in *Man and Temple in Ancient Jewish Myth and Ritual* says:

> The fact that primitive man draws no strict line of cleavage between the animal, vegetable, and mineral kingdom on the one hand, and human beings on the other, has been so often emphasized that it can be regarded as [an] anthropological commonplace'.

Jane Harrison in *Themis: A Study of the Social Origins of Greek Religion* says,

> To man, in the totemistic stage of thinking, Dike and Themis, natural order and social order, are not distinguished, not even distinguishable. Plants and animals are part of this group, a factor in his social structure. It is not that he takes them under his protection: they are his equals, his fellow-tribesmen; naturally they obey the same laws.

This integrated approach to life continued in India until modern times, because Indian culture never became a matter of history and museums. It has been alive and vibrant ever since it began. Indians, incidentally, believe that it had no origin, that it is *sanatana.*

CONCEPT OF PANCA BHUTA

According to the Indian cultural traditions, all that exists in the universe, whether organic and inorganic, has five constituent elements. These are:

Air

Water

Fire (heat/energy)

Earth (rock)

Space (ether)

Everything comes from varying combinations of these five elements and everything ultimately returns to them. These together create nature.

CONCEPT OF MOTHER EARTH

When the disciple asks Atharva Rsi about the nature of the relationship between man and Earth, the *rsi* says:

mata bhumi putro aham prthivya

Earth is the Mother; and we are her children.

When the pupil asks what is the nature of the Earth the *rsi* replies: 'The Earth has hills and snow-covered mountains; it has dense forests and soils of different colours; it is the mother of herbs, it has fire inside, and also gets energy from the sun; it produces a special odour which enriches all that exists and grows on it'.

The *rsi* adds, 'to protect us from all that is evil, the Earth contains pure water. It purifies all that is impure. It cleans everything that goes in it. Earth is a real purifier of all that is undesirable and unclean. Let us not hurt its vitals and its heart. Let us use it judiciously'. And he goes on:

jana vibrati bahudha vivacasam

nana dharmanam prthivi yathaukasam

sahasra dhara dravitasya ye duham

dhruvena dhamurenk pasphuranti

'The earth is full of variety; it contains people speaking different dialects and speech, of diverse religious customs, each living according to what they think is right. The earth contains innumerable valuable things. It bears trees and plants of great diversity. We should pay homage to that Earth'.

The *Prthivi Sukta* of the *Atharvaveda* represents the main currents of Indian thought insofar as man's relation to the Earth is concerned. The post-Vedic literature of Hindu, Buddhist and Jain thought is imbued with reverence, love, and compassion for nature and also with concepts of not only the unity of life but also the unity of what is *cetana* (living) and what is *acetana* (non-living). The *Svetasvatara Upanisad* captures the essence of this integration and unity when it describes nature in the following terms:

yo devo agro yo apsu yo visvam bhuvanamavivesa

yo osdhisu yo vanaspatisu tasme devaya namo namah

> The God who is in fire, who is in water, who pervades the whole universe, who is in medicines, who is in vegetation, we salute that God.

Indian culture paid special attention to land. Soil conservation methods developed in India are still unmatched. Green manuring, barn manure, crop rotation, intercropping, ploughing, irrigation and other agricultural methods and practices were designed to maintain and enhance the fertility of the soil. Soil erosion did occur on a minor scale, but the rainwater carrying the topsoil was never allowed to go down the streams. It was captured in ponds and tanks. These little water bodies of a few acres were excavated in summer and the soil removed was taken to the land again. It was also used for the construction or repair of houses. And thus the cycle continued.

WATER, THE PURIFIER

Pure and uncontaminated water commands a high value in Indian culture. No ceremony, from birth to death, is complete and perfect without *gangajal* (water of the river Ganga). The story of the descent of the Ganga has formed the subject-matter of many great books. In scientific terminology, it is a description of the hydrological cycle and of monsoon clouds bursting over the greater Himalayas. The water so released gets locked as snow. Snow flows through glaciers which ultimately form rivers like Ganga. But for the Ganga, the land between the Himalayas and the Vindhyas would have not nurtured such a great culture. The same applies to other Indian rivers, Sindhu, Brahmaputra, Mahanadi, Godavari, Krishna, Cauvery, Narmada and Tapti. Each one of them is sacred.

India has the distinction of developing unique irrigation systems as early as 3,000 years ago which conserved and replenished surface and ground water and improved the living environment. Those of us who are familiar with the Deccan plateau know that thousands of tanks which dot this region and around which villages are built provide an excellent example of how man can improve the environment. But for these artificial tanks, much of the plateau would have been barren and human existence precarious.

The annecuts that our forefathers built across rivers in South India point to what could be done to avoid the human tragedies of the Narmada project, for example. Wells of drinking water dotted the villages and towns of India. The water of these wells was kept clean by frequent withdrawal for irrigation. There was no chance of contamination.

One can give several examples of water management, particularly watershed planning and water harvesting. The choice of crops and trees depended on the climatic conditions, particularly rainfall. So even in the Rajasthan desert, people were able to maintain forests. Our forefathers knew the close relationship between trees, rainfall, water table and soil moisture. Cropping patterns were designed to conserve water and tanks were constructed to harvest it.

THE FOREST: THE ABODE OF THE GODS

Forests constitute a very important part of Indian culture. Most of the ancient books like the *Vedas*, *Puranas*, *Brahmanas* and *Aranyakas* were written by *rsis* living in forests, sometimes high up in the mountains. One finds references to three main types of forests *(vana)* in ancient times. These are:

1. *Mahavana*
2. *Tapovana*
3. *Srivana*

Mahavana was a dense, virgin and natural forest covering large mountainous, hilly and low-lying areas. Such forests were devoid of human habitation and human interference was therefore negligible. They were rich in biodiversity. They were the main sources of medicines. Lord Siva is the presiding deity of the *mahavanas*. No one dared to encroach upon them. They remained virgin and covered a large part of India.

The *tapovana*, as the very name, indicates was the forest where sages did *tapas* (penance and meditation). It had *asramas* where *gurus* taught their pupils. *Asramas* were away from human habitation and in the interior, but people had access to them for religious and educational purposes. They were full of plants and trees which gave edible and medicinal leaves, roots, fruits shade and soothing climate. It was in these forests that our *Upanisadas* and *Aranyakas* were written. There are still some *tapovanas* like the one near Haridvar.

Most of the *tapovanas* were destroyed during the last 500 years or so. And thus the tradition of *rsis* and *sadhus* living detached from the common people and engaging themselves in meditation, writing, and teaching died. It is pertinent to note that the *tapovanas* abounded in wildlife, but none was allowed to kill animals. Even princes were punished for killing animals as game. It was in these forests that training in the use of weapons was also imparted. It was part of the overall education of pupils. Thus matters pertaining to peace as well as war were really in the hands of saintly people. Trainees were prohibited from using arms for purposes which were outside *dharma* or moral duty. This is what ensured peace in society. People dejected with life went to the *tapovana* instead of committing suicide as happens today. Excommunicated criminals also went there for repentance and cleansing themselves under the feet of the *samnyasins*.

Srivanas were local (village or town) forests. They were not within human habitation; rather human habitation was within them. These forests were managed by village and town *pancayats*. People depended on them for fuel, medicines, fruits and other day-to-day domestic needs. While they had access to these forests, they also had the duty to conserve, protect, replenish and enrich them. Enriching was done through planting of trees in replacement of trees cut.

Srivanas had various kinds of trees, depending on soil, climate and other environmental conditions and local needs. *Tulsi* (basil) was found in abundance, for it was medicinal and at the same time improved the fertility of the soil. No *puja* of a Hindu god is complete even today without *tulsi* leaves. *Srivanas* abounded in fruit orchards. The concept of social forestry thus was known to Indians even in that deep past. We are now trying to import it from the World Bank.

Five species of trees were a must in the *Srivanas*. These were banyan, *peepal*, *asoka*, *bela* and *harada*. The banyan is a self-generating plant. It does not die. In fact it acquires the form of a grove in course of time. It is therefore associated with fertility and longevity. It is the abode of Lord Siva and Devi Parvati. It is shady, healthful and medicinal. The *peepal* (*ficus religiosa*) is perhaps the most sacred tree in India. It is the only tree that gives oxygen for more than 20 hours a day. It is on this tree that Hindus' ancestors reside. It is the incarnation of Lord Visnu. Every part of the *peepal* has medicinal value.

The *asoka* tree under which Sita, Lord Ram's consort, spent much time in Lanka, is a pain-killer, as the name indicates, apart from being shady. The *bela* (*aegle marmelos*) bears fruit of great curative value. It is useful in a large number of diseases. Its leaves are offered to Lord Siva. That is why wherever there is a Siva temple, there invariably are *bela* trees. The last of the five trees is the *harad* (*myrobalem terminalia shebual*). It is perhaps the most commonly used medicinal plant. It has great curative qualities and is relevant for practically all diseases.

The name *pancavati* is derived from these five trees. Every village had a *pancavati* even if it did not have a *srivana.* The trees were not necessarily the same as listed above, nor was the number of trees fixed. They differed from region to region and sometimes from place to place and people to people.

AIR CONTAINS PRANVAYU

Clear air was always cherished by Indians. They knew that trees gave oxygen, *pranvayu.* That is why breathing exercises were done in the forests or *pancavatis* and forests were given such prominence. And that is why every village had to have trees. Look at the old Indian architecture, the open spaces, the verandahs, the aspect of buildings, the windows, etc. All ensured the entry of fresh air. All religious ceremonies were performed in the open. People slept in the open except in winter. One has to go through the *slokas* of the *Rgveda*, the most ancient book of India, to realize the importance Indians gave to the natural environment and nature's laws. A glimpse at the miniatures of the Mughal period gives a clear indication of the importance that even the Muslim rulers of India gave to trees, foliage, plants and animals.

Indian and Western world-views compared

As Richard St. Barbe-baker says, 'this generation may either be the last to exist in any semblance of civilized world or it will be the last to have the vision, the bearing and the greatness to say "I will have nothing to do with this destruction of life; I will play no part in this devastation of land; I am determined to live and work for peaceful construction for I am morally responsible for the world of today and the generations of tomorrow".' He perhaps did not know that this is exactly what Indian sages said some 5,000 years ago and what many of the so-called primitive societies not only say but live even today.

Barbe-baker has in view the Western world-view and the man in the West who 'has lost his way in the jungle of chemistry and engineering and will have to retrace his steps, however painful this may be. He will have to discover where he went wrong and make his peace with nature. In so doing, perhaps he may be able to recapture the rhythm of life and the love of the simple things of life which will be an ever unfolding joy to him'.

Many others have expressed similar views. But those who still think that man will ultimately overcome all hurdles and that science and technology will resolve the environmental problems too, as they resolved other problems in the past, are not in a minority. In fact, the ruling elites all over the world subscribe to this view, and no amount of evidence that disapproves of their thinking can induce them to change their perspective. If they ultimately do accept a new world-view, it will be only because the ruling paradigms would have changed so much that facts no longer appeared credible. They flow with the current. When the current has changed, they will flow with the new current.

Thus the Indian world-view cannot stand the test of today's modernity, a product of the Western world-view. Within this paradigm, no argument in favour of an alternative paradigm will be accepted. The whole structure and superstructure of society today is built and sustained by the paradigm of modernism. A shift from this would be as painful as conversion to another religion. The whole pattern of life, mental constructs and images will have to change. As religious conversions have take place only under very special circumstances, the shift from the developmental paradigm to the ecological paradigm will also occur only under special circumstances of stresses and strains. It is the contention of this paper that such stresses and strains have already become visible. There are signs of a stir in the minds of people, elites as well as common people, which are portentous for the ruling paradigm.

What we see today in the world is an environment of crises. There is an ethical crisis leading to movements to reconstruct the polity. What happened in the USSR, Italy and Japan in recent months is a sign of the beginning of a new moral order. The environmental crisis has gripped the whole world — rich and poor alike. While the mainstream nations and people still pin their hopes on science and technology, strong voices calling for a new style of life and a new paradigm have now become audible. Grassroots level movements, small to start with, have begun networking themselves to have universal appeal and global impact.

Elsewhere there are revivalist movements, at times not very peaceful. They also are, in a way, voices of dissent, signs of frustration and attempts to get out of the Western bandwagon on which they were forced to travel. The revival of religiosity such as in Iran or Afghanistan should not be seen only as a craving for the dead past but also as a rebellion against the prevailing world order. Religion is only a rallying point. Attempts to crush such movements by force would make them more obscurantist. The unscrupulous will take advantage of the situation to divert the movement towards unintended goals.

In India too, rethinking has begun. More and more scientists, artists, scholars, men in public life, and people in general have started looking into their rich traditions which were lost as the Western paradigm superseded Indian values. In fact, the Hindu, Buddhist and Jain philosophies have started getting new adherents all over the world. Any attempt to delink Indian society from *dharma* or even religion in that sense is resisted. Even the modern Carvaks, for whom religion is the opium of the people, are changing. The citadel of communism has already fallen. Religion has come back in what was the USSR. It is now only a matter of years, not even of decades, for the Indian world-view to take root in India again.

Gandhi's contributions

We have had the great fortune of having persons like Mahatma Gandhi, Aurobindo and Vivekanand in the first half of this century, and saints like Acarya Tulsi, the Dalai Lama, Satya Sai Baba, the Paramacarya of Kanchi and many other *dharmacaryas* in the second half of this century to guide the destiny of India. Gandhi's greatest contribution was not the Independence of India, for India could not have remained in bondage longer than it was, but the framework of an alternative world-view and the methodology of achieving it. He gave the outline of an alternative civilization and a creative future for mankind. His genius encompassed all religious traditions of the world, for they were one and the same as far as the essentials were concerned. Rituals differ but the goals are the same, the methods are the same and the message is the same. They all are ecological and human. His often cited quotation that 'Earth has enough to meet everyone's need but not everyone's greed' is the centrepiece of the world-view of ecology and humanism that we are looking for. Let us not be carried away by the mesmerism of the Western world-view and heed the warning he gave to the world several decades before his assassination in 1948:

> God forbid that India should ever take to industrialism after the manner of the West. The economic imperialism of a single tiny island kingdom is today keeping the world in chains. If an entire nation of 300 million took to similar economic exploitation, it would strip the world bare like locusts.

Attempts at value education

Incorporation of the time-honoured Indian values discussed above in the educational system in India has been stressed from time to time. Mahatma Gandhi offered a new concept of education wherein head, heart and hand could be trained to work in unison and give rise to creative human beings. He termed it *nai talim* or New Education. It was new in the sense that it was completely different from the Western model of education in vogue. *Nai talim* laid great stress on pupils' contact with nature through manual work and on the concept of unity of life.

Somehow, the concept of Basic Education was completely rejected by India after Independence. The educational system which the British had created was not only retained but also strengthened. This was, however, not an isolated step. Other Gandhian concepts including that of development were also rejected. Now in the 1990, we hear more of Gandhi than we did in the 1960s through the 1980s.

As early as 1959, the Sri Prakasa Committee on Religious and Moral Education set up by the Ministry of Education stated,

> Many ills that our world of education and our society as a whole is suffering today resulting in widespread disturbance and dislocation of life are mainly due to the gradual disappearance of the hold of basic principles of religion on the hearts of the people . . . . The only cure, it seems to us, is in deliberate inculcation of moral and spiritual values from the earliest years of our lives.

Let us note here that in the Indian context, religious and moral education incorporate ecological and environmental education.

The Commission on Education (1964-66) chaired by the late Professor D.S. Kothari was more vocal on the issue of value education:

> Modernization did not mean, least of all in our national situation, a refusal to recognize the importance of or to inculcate necessary moral and spiritual values and self-discipline. While a combination of ignorance with goodness may be futile, that of knowledge with a lack of essential values may be dangerous.
>
> The weakening of social and moral values in the younger generation is creating many serious social and ethical conflicts in western societies and there is already a desire among great western thinkers to balance the knowledge and skills which science and technology bring with the values and insights associated with ethics and religion

> at its best, viz. a search for the knowledge of self, of the meaning of life, of the relationship of man to other human beings and the ultimate reality. In the situation that is developing, it is equally important for us to give a proper value orientation to our educational system.
>
> India has a unique advantage with her great tradition of duty without self-involvement, unacquisitive temperament, tolerance, and innate love of peace and reverence for all living things. Too often are these precious assets forgotten and we tend to relapse into moods of pessimism, fears and forebodings, discord and destructive criticism. A new pride and a deeper faith expressed in living for the noble ideals of peace and freedom, truth and compassion are now needed.

Several other committees, commissions, seminars, conferences and plan documents have since then repeated these views. Not much, however, happened in policy and programme terms, and the educational system of the country continued as usual. The call for a new education policy, however, became so persistent that Parliament, under the 42nd Amendment Act of 1976, inserted Fundamental Duties to match the Fundamental Rights guaranteed by the Constitution of India. Among these duties, at least five were pertinent to the environment. These are:

1. to promote harmony and the spirit of common brotherhood amongst all the people of India transcending religious, linguistic and regional or sectional diversities; to renounce practices derogatory to the dignity of women;
2. to value and preserve the rich heritage of our composite culture;
3. to protect and improve the natural environment including forests, lakes, rivers and wild life, and to have compassion for living creatures;
4. to develop scientific temper, humanism and the spirit of enquiry and reform; and
5. to safeguard public property and to abjure violence.

The incorporation of environmental protection among the statutory duties of Indian citizens was perhaps inspired by the Stockholm conference on the environment in which Mrs Indira Gandhi, the then Prime Minister of India, played a leading role.

The *National Education Policy Statement, 1986* included these points and suggested a national curricular framework which included:

> the history of India's freedom movement, the constitutional obligations and other contents essential to nurture national identity. These elements will cut across subject areas and will be designed to promote values such as India's common cultural heritage, egalitarianism, democracy and secularism, equality of sex, protection of environment, removal of social barriers, observance of small family norms and inculcation of scientific temper.

The Ramamurthy Committee, which reviewed this policy in 1990, had this to say:

> The hidden curriculum, as distinct from the explicit ones obtaining in the classroom situation, is much more important for the development of balanced personality amongst the students. It is also the role of value education to bring about integration of the hand, head and heart to ensure that education does not alienate the students from the family, community and life. One of the key roles of education should be creation of a work culture at all stages of education so that the individual develops into a socially and economically useful human being with respect for the welfare of all livings beings *(sarva bhoota hitha)*. Above all else, critical appreciation and concern for the cultural and artistic heritage of the country has to be instilled amongst the students. It is this package of values which will help the creation and sustenance of an enlightened and human society in the country.

The five-year plans of India have consistently upheld the need to promote value education. The Seventh Plan (1985-90) stated:

> Value orientation of education should constitute a special thrust in the Seventh Plan, teacher education particularly being oriented for this purpose.

Earlier, in 1981, a seminar on value education held at Shimla said:

> There should be an integrated approach in the value oriented education programme. Instead of tackling piecemeal with such areas as awareness of ecology, environmental protection, community

development, productivity, population stabilization, aesthetic education, national integration and international understanding, etc., they should be handled in a comprehensive manner under the broad spectrum of social responsibility and inner development of human personality.

Light in the darkness

Even though the educational system of the country has not yet responded favourably to the above recommendation and business of education is as usual, attempts at value education have not been lacking. A number of institutions have taken up this challenge with all earnestness and have shown quite encouraging results. Among these institutions, mention may be made of:

1. Institutions associated with Satya Sai Baba
2. Institutions associated with the Ramakrishna Mission
3. Institutions associated with the Aurobindo Ashram
4. Vanasthali Vidyapeeth, Rajasthan
5. Jain Vishva Bharati, Ladnun, and related institutions
6. The Saraswati Vidya Mandir System of Schools

A recent report on the work-load on pupils in primary and secondary education (Yash Pal Committee Report, 1993) strongly recommended the Gandhian approach to learning (without mentioning Gandhi's name).

There are many other institutions in different parts of the country. Those listed above use different approaches and methodologies with the same end results. What runs through them all is the thread of spirituality and ecological thinking. All these institutions instil value education through coursework as well as practice. The fact that their network is expanding, and they are being voluntarily accepted by parents as the right institutions for their children, is indicative of the wind of change.

In addition to these institutions, a large number of NGOs and voluntary agencies have now entered the field of value education in India. Some of them have evolved innovative programmes, particularly in the area of environmental education. Recent attempts to learn from the environmental values of tribal and village communities are indicative of the approaching scenario. The great religious traditions are being explored again to distili much of the environmental values which are now lost or getting lost, and which need to be revived, to bring about an eco-development process. We do thus see some light in the darkness.

Let us not be perplexed; let us follow the Upanisadic exhortation:

> *uttisthan jagrat prapya varan nibodhat*
> *dyurasya dhara nisita duretyaya*
> *durgam patham tat kavayo vadanti*
>
> Get up, wake up, and learn from the knowledgeable. As it is difficult to walk on the razor's edge, so it is difficult to walk on a right path.

That the right path of development is the ecological path is the message of Indian culture.

References

Archer, A.A., *et al.*, 1987, *Man's Dependence on the Earth: The Role of Geosciences in the Environment.* Nairobi: UNEP and Paris: Unesco

Banwari, 1992, *Pancavati: Indian Approach to Environment.* New Delhi: Sri Vinayak Publications

Swami Budhananda, 1980, *The Saving Challenge of Religion.* Madras: Ramakrishna Math

Ciriacy, S.V., *et al.*, 1967, *Natural Resources: Quality and Quantity.* Los Angeles: University of California Press

Eyre, S.R., 1978, *The Real Wealth of Nations.* London: Edward Arnold

Gandhi, M.K., *Hind Swaraj.* Ahmedabad: Navajivan Press

Goldsmith, Edward, 1992, *The Way: An Ecological World View.* London: Rider

Harrison, Jane, 1927, *Themis: A Study of the Social Origin of Greek Religion.* Cambridge: Cambridge University Press

Hira Lal, *Nature Cure.* Manuscript in press, 1993

Mehta, Rohit, 1982. *The Fullness of the Void.* New Delhi: Motilal Banarsidass

NASA, 1969, *Resources and Man.* San Francisco: W.H. Freeman & Co

Narang, Sudesh, 1993, *Atharva Vediya Prithivi Sukta.* New Delhi: Paridhi Prakashan (in Hindi)

Patai, Raphael, 1947, *Man and Temple in Ancient Jewish Myth and Ritual.* London:

Thomas Nelson

Ministry of Education, Government of India, 1959, *Report of Committee on Religious and Moral Education*

——, *Education and National Development: Report of Education Commission (1964-66)*

——, 1968, *National Policy on Education*

Ministry of Human Resource Development, Government of India, 1985, *Challenge of Education: A Policy Perspective*

——, 1986, *National Policy on Education*

——, 1993, *Towards an Enlightened and Humane Society: Report of Ramamurthy Committee*

...mmentation

Ministry of Education, Government of India, 19[illegible], Report of Committee on [illegible] and [illegible].

——, Education and National Development, Report of Education Commission 1964-66.

——, 1968, National Policy on Education.

Ministry of Human Resource Development, Government of India, 1985, Challenge of Education: A Policy Perspective.

——, 1986, National Policy on Education.

——, 1992, [illegible] Report of [illegible] Committee.

13

Cultural Heritage, Cultural Empowerment and Development

Ram Bapat

All over the world a sentiment and a concern for sustainable development is growing. Increasing numbers of individuals and organisations are becoming aware of the growing ecological and environmental crisis produced by the culture of hedonism and self-gratification built into present-day industrial, scientific and technological civilisation wedded to the pursuit of profit as an end in itself. Thinking people are getting perturbed by the manner in which a sense of history, tradition and purposive long-term action are being given up as of no use by those who occupy the citadels of global power and material riches. A longing for self-reliant, communitarian and spontaneous cultural development is being expressed by diverse sections of the world population. In the words of Saul Bellow,

> the old forms of existence have worn out, so to speak, and the new ones have not yet appeared and people are prospecting, as it were, in the desert for new forms (Bourne *et al.*, 1987:15).

And yet it would be worthwhile to acknowledge at the outset how difficult and complex a task it is to work out cohesive and practical policies and models to achieve holistic creative development. In the arena of culture and creativity in particular, the reasons do no lie so deep as to seem unfathomable.

I

In spite of very high GNPs, individuals in post-modern societies have come to realise that in everyday life, the bonds that build fellowship and reciprocity in family, work-place and community are getting attenuated. People do not feel confident that they can live in tune either with time or with place. This feeling has been caught well by a contemporary observer of the Western scene. Invoking the perceptions of modernity entertained by Marx, Nietzsche and Baudelaire, he says:

> They can illuminate the contradictory forces and needs that inspire and torment us. Our desire to be rooted in a stable and coherent personal and social past, and our unstable desire for growth — not merely for economic growth but for growth in experience, in pleasure, in knowledge in sensibility — growth that destroys both the physical and social landscapes of our past, and our emotional links with those lost worlds; our desperate allegiances to ethnic, national, class and sexual groups which we hope will give us a firm 'identity', and the internationalization of everyday life — of our clothes and household goods, our books and music, our ideas and fantasies — that spreads all our identities all over the map; our desire for clear and solid values to live by, and our desire to embrace the limitless possibilities of modern life and experience that obliterate all values . . . . Experiences like these unite us with the nineteenth century modern world: a world where, as Marx said, 'every thing is pregnant with its contrary' and 'all that is solid melts into air'; a world where as Nietzsche said, 'there is danger, the mother of morality — a great danger . . . displaced onto the individual, onto the nearest and dearest, onto the street, onto one's own child, one's own heart, one's own innermost secret recesses of wish and will' (quoted by O'Neill 1988:502-3).

II

But we begin to experience a sense of resignation and remoteness when we consult the metropolitan thinkers for solutions. In relating culture to whatever is named as modernisation or late capitalism or post-industrial society, or in relating culture to the social relations of production, power, and class, these thinkers get themselves polarised, although not for accidental reasons, into two warring camps. Contemporary German social theory, for example, represents the first camp. The erosion of the distinction between high culture and so-called mass or popular culture in today's consumer society disturbs it. It therefore produces massive critiques of the culture of industry and consumerism in the age of late capitalism and culminates in the theory of communicative action. And yet these massive works fail to provide any practical and political guide for action. As Rick Roderick puts it:

> The lessons the critical theorists drew from the history of marxism was that an inattention to philosophical and methodological questions had disastrous theoretical and practical effects. In this context, they argued for the relative autonomy of theory . . . . With the exception of Marcuse at certain points in his career and the early Horkheimer, the critical theorists rejected any direct links between the elaboration of theory and participation in political struggles (Roderick 1986:150).

Working in the hoary tradition set by Aristotle and refashioned by Kant, which associates melancholy and sympathy with moral freedom and sensitivity, critical theory in effect defends nostalgia (Stauth and Turner 1988:510-13). It is no wonder, then, that in spite of their stout defence of the philosophical discourses of modernity celebrating emancipatory reason, order, coherence, unity, and universality, both Marcuse and Habermas exclude Third World concerns from the ambit of their analyses and disown any responsibility towards it.

The new French social theory represents the other camp. In terms of its critical theory antagonists, it represents

> an emotional current of our time which has penetrated spheres of intellectual life. It has put on the agenda theories of postenlightenment, postmodernity, and even of posthistory (Habermas 1984:3-14).

Emphasising the new forms of technology and information, the computerisation of society, the increasing role of simulations and models, the superabundance of cultural goods, the effacement of the boundary between art and everyday life and so on, current French theory talks about the post-industrial age, the erasure of the distinction between the real and the appearance, and even the end of the social. To face this novel world, it wants to shape a matching radical stance which would go beyond the philosophers of modernity and Marx in particular (for example, ***see*** Derrida 1994:54-56). Most of these French thinkers want to radicalise the Hegel-Marx tradition by incorporating insights from Nietzsche, Heidegger, Freud and Saussure. Unlike their German counterparts excepting Marcuse, they want to adopt interventionist radical politics (***see*** Derrida 1986:168). More notably, they do not mind making some gestures towards the Third World (for example, Derrida 1985:290-99).

And yet the new French social theory culminates in the politics and aesthetics of desire, sensation and immediacy. In its practical effects it appears to be primarily negative. Catherine Zuckert has provided a good demonstration of this point while discussing the politics of Derridean deconstruction. She states:

> In arguing that there is no stable system of meaning or order — natural, logical, or historical — Derrida may free his readers from the spectre of 'totalization', but by virtue of the same argument, he deprives them of the capacity to think, much less to act on their own behalf. If all opposites are fundamentally and inseparably linked, as Derrida maintains, there are no alternatives, no 'either-or's between which to choose. We may be freed *from* complete domination, but we are not free *to do* much. Difference continues to operate whether we will it or no . . . .
>
> As Derrida himself observes, 'it is not certain that such thinking can bring together a community or found an institution in the traditional sense of these words'. According to Derrida, we do not completely and simply share anything with anyone — ourselves, much less our nation or species. There may be a good deal of historical overlap in language and customs, but there is no common room or ground. There are only and always differences and hence, opposition, division and strife (Zuckert 1991:354-55).

Thus the new French social theory's endeavours to keep alive 'historicity' in the face of a teleological history end in varieties of messianic messages which on examination are found unfortunately to be full of passivity. Its political and cultural implications are 'parochial, if not provincial'.

The current spectrum of theoretical dissent in the United States is also quite big. It spreads, say, from Frederic Jameson on the one hand to Richard Rorty on the other. But in reality these dissenting voices get totally smothered by the voices raising the cries of the end of history and so on, the triple-angled domination in the spheres of polity, economy and culture is so complete and so elemental.

III

Our voyage of discovery in the realm of current cultural discourses in the post-modern societies in search of guidelines for practical, transformative models for facing the desert-like cultural reality within our own country has thus been proved practically futile. Yet such journeys will be both unavoidable and desirable for the present and also for a long time to come for the following reasons.

Let us first note the compulsive element or elements. In the first instance, globalisation as it operates today is bound to threaten the plurality and diversity of all cultures. In the words of Panikkar:

> Today culture is an important component of domination, both of and within developing societies. The ideological apparatuses of state and of multinational agencies brought into being by [the] technological revolution have ushered in this possibility. During the last couple of decades, [the] culture industry in the capitalist west has undergone transformation beyond recognition. A very large volume of capital has gone into this industry . . . and that cultural capitalism has displaced manufacturing as a source of wealth and influence.

Panikkar also reminds us that

> what is happening, however, is not such an innocent process of acculturation, permitting the acceptance or rejection of cultural elements based on freedom of choice. On the contrary, the power differential inherent in economic relations determines cultural interaction . . . . The exogenous cultural presence is not only unsettling the indigenous but also trying to hegemonise it for legitimising a concept of social development modelled on the advanced capitalist societies (Panikkar 1955:374-77).

In the second instance, as M.P. Rege puts it so well:

> The concept of science as the only rational form of knowledge and that of civil society as the only rational form of society came to us as gifts of a colonial rule which disrupted the traditional forms of life in India. This certainly complicates our situation. But even if they had been presented to us in an altogether peaceful manner they would have posed a serious challenge, indeed a threat . . . (Rege 1994:271-73).

For diverse, and more often competing and even contradictory reasons, diverse sections of our society from the top to the bottom want to realise these two concepts in accordance with their requirements. We therefore are bound to follow the post-modern societies in the future as well.

In the third instance, we may have very cogent and legitimate reasons to question the extrapolation of these Western culture-bound rationalizations to encompass Third World situations (Daya Krishna 1995:93-96). And yet we find ourselves in a situation in which the question is not 'how to maintain and express their autonomy in the sphere of cognition but how to reclaim it' (Rege, 1994:272).

But there do exist superior and more dignified reasons for watching the advanced societies to better know how to link our own cognitive and cultural heritages for strategies for sustainable development.

Paulo Freire and Edward Said have identified one such factor well in understanding the relationship between home and homelessness, exile and critic, or another self and one's own identity. Border-crossing not only helps to break taken-for-granted barriers of thought and experience, but more importantly, saves intellectuals from the risk of

> being too remote in their work as intellectuals from the most real, most concrete experiences, and of being sometimes lost, and even somewhat contended, because they are lost in a game of words . . . 'specializing in the ballet of concepts' (Giroux 1994:146-48).

Paul Ricoeur has put this relationship still better. According to him, recognition of the error in identifying science and technology with 'the relationship of truth which we can have with all things' induces us 'to discover what, in the cultures of the past, is more than merely pre-scientific'. For the same reasons, receptiveness to other cultures prepares us 'to apply to ourselves the distinctive significance of a particular tradition' (Ricoeur 1976:13-33).

Mahatma Gandhi had taught these insights with a far sharper sense of reality and a clearer vision moulded by the various traditions within our country. Making a distinction between imitation and assimilation, he wanted us 'to build a new culture based on the traditions of the past, enriched with the experience of later times'. This was for the simple reason that his religion, 'whatever it may be called', demanded the fulfilment of all cultures (Gandhi 1930, 1940, 1944).

IV

The detour taken in the third section was necessary for a simple reason. Culture-wise, India nowadays is as much part of the kingdom of darkness as of the so-called post-modern world. Now if any flicker of hope and enlightenment is available, our refusal to accept it would offer another demonstration of the sunken state of our civilisation and culture by laying open our misplaced pride and smugness. But the problem is that as we have seen, even the most advanced consciousness and thought in the advanced capitalist world have nothing to offer in terms of a fresh utopia and praxis to their own and to the rest of the world. In the given situation, we are led to listen to the voices of our own tradition, and they are not that inaccessible if we care to follow them. Moreover, some of these voices possess a rare virtue — a practical ability to link stark realities with utopian norms and vision.

Listen to Ananda K. Coomarswamy, for instance. His following statements reveal a courage to grasp reality as it is:

> We have gone so far as to divorce work from culture and to think of culture as something to be acquired in hours of leisure; but there can be only a hothouse and unreal culture where work itself is not its means; if culture does not show itself in all we make we are not cultured.
>
> Culture originates in work and not in play.
>
> The artist is not a special kind of man, but every man who is not an artist in some field, every man without a vocation is an idler . . . . . No man has a right to any social status who is not an artist.
>
> To 'enjoy' what does not correspond to any vital needs of our own and what we have not verified in our life can only be described as an indulgence.
>
> The ideal of voluntary poverty, which rejects utilities, can be readily understood. It is easy to see that an indefinite multiplication of utilities, the means of life, may end in an identification of culture with comfort, and the substitution of means for ends (Coomarswamy 1956:15-16, 23-24, 25, 48-49).
>
> It was not indeed 'taste' that brought us to the use of homespun, nor,

> on the other hand, was this merely an outwardly imposed privation; . . . for the present we are assured that to be arrayed in glorious garments is not merely bad economy, but also bad taste (Coomarswamy 1977:98-99).

Mahatma Gandhi urged us to think about the following issues:

> Self-expression and self-government are not things which may be either taken from us by anybody or which can be given us by anybody. It is quite true that if those who happen to hold our destinies, or seem to hold our destinies in their hands, are favourably disposed, are sympathetic, understand our aspirations, no doubt it is easier for us to expand. But after all self-government depends entirely on our own internal strength, upon our ability to fight against [the] heaviest odds. Indeed, self-government which does not require that continuous striving to attain it and to sustain it is not worth the name (Gandhi 1927).
>
> The duty of renunciation differentiates mankind from the beast.
>
> Some object that life thus understood becomes dull and devoid of art, and leaves no room for the householder. But renunciation here does not mean abandoning the world and retiring into the forest . . . . Joy has no independent existence. It depends upon our attitude to life . . . . Joy, therefore, is a matter of individual and national education (Gandhi 1980:38-39).
>
> Our (basic) system of education . . . leads to the development of the mind, body and soul. The ordinary system cared only for the mind . . . . The function of Nai Talim is not merely to teach an occupation, but through it to develop the whole man (Gandhi 1962:117, 122).

Sankho Chaudhuri offered the following insights to us. While discussing a cultural policy for folk and tribal art he stated:

> It would be wrong to label their art with a capital 'A' in the contemporary sense of conscious self-expression. What they do is only an extension of their daily existence.

> We tend to associate the word 'encouragement' with the development of any form of art. This presupposes a lack of utility for the object, but if the latter is essential in a people's life it does not need this encouragement. In fact, if by encouragement we mean creating a large market, it is doubtful whether the creation of a market disproportionate to production capacity is at all beneficial. We have seen how this exaggerated demand at times completely debases taste and demoralises the artisans (Chaudhuri 1975:151, 154).

I think that the above insights provide practical guidelines for linking cultural heritage with strategies for sustainable development. In fact, there can be no better framework for policy in particular in a country where the majority of the people still suffer from poverty, want, malnutrition, dreariness and illiteracy. A set of such policies alone would nourish the self-confidence and creativity of the citizens, autonomy and experimentation of the community and a utopian and not creative memory of tradition).

V

The price which we have paid for deviating from the creative and critical tradition within our country is too well-known to demand repetition. The Government of India announcement of 7 May 1990 captures the depth of our failure so well. It says,

> Despite efforts at social and economic development since [the] attainment of independence, a majority of our people continue to remain deprived of education. It is also a matter of grave concern that our people comprise 50 per cent of the world's illiterate, and large sections of children have to go without [an] acceptable level of primary education (Ramamurthi Committee:iv).

Given this kind of performance of our elites, and, more pertinently, the poverty of ideas from which I suffer, I am offering the following proposals for your consideration. Though they may appear very mundane and perhaps somewhat removed from the thrust of my argument so far, I believe that somehow they do have a subterranean relation with what I have said earlier.

1. *An action plan for developing the public library service*

Until we develop an effective public library service for the first-generation literates who constitute the majority of our educated citizens, we will not be able to meet the real hunger of these citizens for more and better information and knowledge. Our formal educational system manufactures at the most practically semi-literate persons. We find time and again that they suffer from a lack of easy and cheap access to library facilities.

I endorse the observations made by Subhag C. Biswas in this connection:

> Had the public library service developed properly, alongside our educational programme, our *socio-economic condition* would have been more encouraging that what it is. The public library network requires heavy capital investment and the returns are only indirect. State Governments are reluctant to invest large amounts from their limited resources as they feel other priority areas can provide better results for economic growth. Lack of political will prevents us from a developing a nation-wide public library service on *modern* concepts [emphases mine] (Biswas 1992:273-75).

Please note that this is *not* a demand for a national library facility with huge libraries necessary for the higher echelons of the intelligentsia or policy-makers but a plea tor a national library network based on community-centred, community-managed medium-sized, good but non-elitist and yet modern library centres.

2. *A museum system for cultural empowerment*

If we give up traditional concepts of a museum, we will be able to dismantle the cultural barriers that prevent the participation of communities and the people as a whole in museum activity. In their new role museums can play 'an important part in shaping cultural perceptions within their communities, as people everywhere become more aware of themselves and their surroundings' (Pearce 1991:vii).

The premise of the new museum theory coming up in the post-modern world tells us that

> the past is something that belongs to all, irrespective of the circumstances of their birth and upbringing. Consequently everyone should have the right to gain access to their own history, even if they choose not to avail themselves of this opportunity. Museums and similar organisations are one of the principal means by which people can gain access to the past, and everyone should thus have the

> opportunity to visit them and feel at home in them (Merriman 1991:1).

The irony is that Coomarswamy would have accepted this position, although for very different reasons. In a well-known argument concerning the exhibition of works of art he had opposed their display on grounds of 'our fashion' or 'aesthetic motives'. Treating the museum as 'the sworn enemy of the methods of instruction currently in our Schools of Art', he wanted the museum exhibition to return to the 'savage levels of culture' where objects were custom made and made for use and not for profits or novelty (Coomarswamy 1956:7-22). The idea was to use the museum to oppose the present world based upon greed, commercialisation, and elitism. We can therefore understand the lament of Sankho Chaudhuri about the transfer of the Museum of Tribal Art from Chhindwara to Bhopal at an earlier seminar on cultural policy held by the Indian Institute of Advanced Study, Shimla. He had made a call 'to make small museums, not for the urbanite's amusement but to be used for reference and inspiration by young tribesmen' (Chaudhuri 1975:157).

The well-known artist K.G. Subramanyam offers us a similar insight in his very recent and contemporary comment. Acknowledging Ananda Coomarswamy's still compelling impact on thinking 'made more than 50 years ago' he feels disturbed by the implications of the country's new economic objectives on 'a variety of art practice, both professional and non-professional' within our country. Subramanyam is still a sober realist. He knows that we cannot keep tradition 'forcibly alive', that 'we cannot stem social change', and that 'no society exists today in isolation'. And yet knowing that 'what concerns them (the government and the trading community) most are export earnings, not human refinement', he states:

> In these circumstances the least we can do is to visually record the whole heritage, collect object specimens of the best kind, document methods of fabrication and use and house these objects and data in museums and archives region to region, speciality to speciality. These can recreate for the interested a picture of various art forms and educate them to value them. And provide, if an art form disappears, the wherewithal with which to recall it. This may motivate some to cultivate them in the new circumstances and use them for the new purposes. Even sow the seeds of tradition in a non-traditional world. And teach the future planners to be more sensitive and circumspect (Subramanyam 1995:14).

Sustainable development demands an urgent building up of such museums and archives for the future-oriented persistence of our culture and heritage in the world of post-modern technologies and capitalism.

3. *Handing back people's own ancient sites and monuments to local communities*

Given the current state of our polity and the mood of the country, I am not sure whether it would be prudent to offer the third proposal. Its rationale and scope as well as the manner and the timing of its application demand serious consideration. The proposal is about community participation in the preservation of ancient sites and monuments.

The Unesco document entitled *Cultural Policy: A Preliminary Study* (second revised edition of 1969) states:

> The aim in all countries is no longer merely to preserve ancient monuments and sites but, above all, to present them to the best advantage and give them place once more in the economic and social life of the community. They are no longer merely places to be studied by archaeologists and art historians, but *means of cultural action* which can be used to awaken people and make them appreciative of the culture and of the cultural heritage of mankind as a whole. The great archaeological treasures of some countries have led to the development of excavation sites as open-air museums, tourist attractions as well as relics of the past with much to teach . . . . Sites and monuments are also becoming a link in the cultural action chain [emphasis mine] (Unesco 1969:33).

The same document points out that preservation is now looked upon 'as a means of defence against an anonymous technological civilisation and of safeguarding folk values. It has, therefore, become a part of social and cultural development' (p.38). We know how due to lack of funds, trained manpower, and the lack of a truly post-colonial, people-oriented national policy on such matters, most of our pre-colonial sites and monuments, barring of course some well-known exceptions, are suffering from neglect, lack of immediate, living and creative contact with the surrounding community, and excessively narrow legalistic jealousies entertained by the government departments concerned. They appear so forlorn, so lifeless and so subject to the vagaries of nature and vandals.

Handing over these sites and monuments would no doubt demand some initial guidance and control for the sake of achieving authentic, form-faithful preservation and also the protection of the law of the land. But it is high time that we return this heritage of the people to their own custody. Let us free ourselves from the clutches of colonial and commercial concerns in such matters.

4. *Need for a national policy for securing beautiful and useful public buildings*

This final proposal does not involve a need for additional funds, manpower or big bureaucracy but only imagination and determination. We have spent crores of rupees on public buildings since Independence. Barring some rather rare exceptions, they do not serve the expectations of beauty and use in a fused manner or even separately or partially. They do not show a stamp or a style of any kind including even the bastard styles. They are as soulless, graceless and inelegant as most of our post-Independence development. Spending public funds for raising structures in tune with nature and the cultural heritage is as much a part of alternative development philosophy as anything else. Anything which falls short of these norms must be deemed from now onwards as a serious failure of public responsibilities and duties.

References

Bellow, Saul, 1987, 'The Moronic Inferno'. In Bill Bourne *et al.*, eds., *Modernity and Its Discontents*. Nottingham: Spokesman

Biswas, Subhag C., 1992, 'Wanted An Action Plan for Library Modernisation'. In the editor, *Hindu*, ed., *The Hindu Speaks On Libraries*. Madras: Kasturi and Sons

Chaudhuri, Sankho, 1975, 'Cultural Policy for Folk and Tribal Art'. In Satish Saberwal, ed., *Towards a Cultural Policy*. Delhi: Vikas

Coomarswamy, Ananda K., 1956, *Christian and Oriental Philosophy of Art*. New York: Dover

——, 1977, *Coomarswamy: Selected Papers I*, ed. Roger Lipsey. Princeton, N.J.: Princeton University Press

Daya Krishna, 1995, 'New World Order and Indian Intellectuals'. In *Economic and Political Weekly*, Vol.30, No.2., pp.93-96

Derrida, Jacques, 'Racism's Last World'. In *Critical Inquiry*, No.12, pp.290-99

——, 1986, 'Critical Response', trans. Peggy Kumuf. In *Critical Inquiry*, No.13

——, 1994, 'A Lecture on Marx'. *New Left Review*, No.205

Featherstone, Mike, 1991, *Consumer Culture and Postmodernism*. London: Sage

Gandhi, M.K., 1927, Untitled. *Young India*, December

——, 1930, 'The Loin Cloth'. *Young India*, 30 April 30

——, 1940, Untitled, *Harijan*, 30 April

——. 1944, quoted in *Gandhiji: 75th Birthday Volume*. Bombay: Karnatak Publishing House

——, 1962, *Basic Education*. Ahmedabad: Navajivan

——, 1980, *From Yeravda Mandir*. Ahmedabad: Navajivan

Giroux, Henry A., 1994, *Disturbing Pleasures: Learning Popular Culture*. New York: Routledge

Habermas, Jurgen, 1981, 'Modernity versus Postmodernity'. In *New German Critique*, No.22

Merriman, Nick, 1991, *Beyond The Glass Case: The Past, the Heritage and the Public in Britain*. Leicester: Leicester University Press

O'Neill, 1988, 'Religion and Postmodernism'. In *Theory, Culture and Society*, Vol.5, Nos.2-3

Panikkar, K.N., 1995, 'The Draft Programme of Action for the World Summit for Social Development, Copenhagen'. In *Economic and Political Weekly*, Vol.30, Nos. 7 & 8

Pearce, Susan M., 1991, 'General Preface to Series'. In Nick Merriman, *Beyond the Glass Case*. Leicester: Leicester University Press

Rege, M.P., 1994, 'Cultural and Political Autonomy in the Indian Context'. *New Quest*, No.107

Ricoeur, Paul, 1976. 'Introduction'. In *Culture and Time*. Paris: Unesco

Roderick, Rick, 1986, *Habermas and Foundations of Critical Theory*. London: Macmillan

Stauth, Georg and Bryan S. Turner, 1988, 'Nostalgia, Postmodernism and the Critique of Mass Culture'. In *Theory, Culture and Society*, Vol.5, Nos.2-3

Subramanyam, K.G., 1995, 'When Nations Grow Old Art Grows Cold". In The *Sunday Times of India*, 22 January

Unesco, 1969, *Cultural Policy: A Preliminary Study*, second revised edition. Paris: Unesco

Zuckert, Catherine, 1991, 'The Politics of Derridean Deconstruction'. In *Polity*, Vol.23, No.3

14

Population, Environment and Development

Socio-Cultural Pitfalls Planners must Avoid

Ashish Bose

In an era of economic liberalisation, privatisation and increasing globalisation, economics will dominate the scene unless vigorous efforts are made to safeguard the socio-cultural environment. In spite of the famous conferences at Stockholm (1972) and Rio (1992), and the increasing concern for the environment, there is a tendency to think of the *physical* environment alone. The socio-cultural environment gets a back seat. Therefore any attempt to relate culture with development is welcome.

There is considerable 'cultural illiteracy' among our policy-makers, planners, administrators and experts (Indian as well as foreign) which comes in the way of the success of many developmental projects launched with good intentions. By 'cultural illiteracy' we mean ignorance of socio-cultural factors affecting development, inadequate acquaintance with grassroots reality and a lack of comprehension of the vital role which culture plays in the development process.

During my field work in various parts of India over the last three decades, I have learnt the need for collecting data on socio-cultural factors in all benchmark surveys, resurveys, evaluation surveys, etc. I propose to discuss a few case studies on the intimate link between culture and development.

Case study 1: The buffalo meat processing plant in Punjab

The most recent example of the relevance of the cultural context in development plans in the post-economic liberalisation era that I have come across is in the prosperous state of Punjab. A private limited company wants to operate a 100 per cent export-oriented buffalo meat processing plant near Derabassi in Patiala District, on which it wants to invest Rs.480 million. The company has a valid licence from the Government of Punjab. The people in that area as well as a leading political party strongly protested against the functioning of this plant on religious grounds. This led to a confrontation between the Government of Punjab and the private company. The Chief Minister of Punjab finally made a statement in the state assembly (Vidhan Sabha) that the government had decided to close down the plant in deference to the wishes of the people. The Chief Minister said that there were three aspects of this factory, namely economic, medical and religious. While he had no quarrel with the economic aspect of the project, he had serious reservations about ignoring the religious aspect (*Tribune*, Chandigarh, 29 March 1995). The Chief Minister also asserted at a public meeting that 'the killing of animals to fill human stomachs was irreligious' and therefore his government would not allow the newly set up slaughter-house to function (*Hindu*, Delhi, 1 April 1995). There is no doubt that a 100 per cent export-oriented meat industry would have brought considerable money and foreign exchange to Punjab, but obviously neither the private company which decided to set up the factory nor the state government, which gave a licence for it, had given any thought to the socio-cultural and religious aspects of this plant. As a result, this company was put to a tremendous loss, which could have been avoided if a proper market survey had been conducted with imagination to include socio-cultural factors.

This reminds me of a very ambitious project to generate electricity through bullock power which was launched by an American philanthropist in an Indian village in the early 1960s. Among other things, the project wanted to improve the nutrition level of the rural people. The sponsors built a huge tank for fish culture with the aim of adding to the protein content in the diet of the villagers. As the whole project had an air of secrecy (because the sponsors were not sure whether they would ultimately succeed in generating electricity through bullock power) and the village people were not taken into confidence at any stage, when the tank was built and the villagers were told about the nutritional value of fish, they retorted: 'But we are Gujars and therefore vegetarian, we will not eat fish'. I had a close interaction with these village people as I was conducting a demographic survey with my research team from the Institute of Economic Growth in this very village. When I asked the villagers why on earth they did not tell the foreign experts that they were vegetarians, their reply was: 'Nobody asked us if we eat fish, and when we saw the tank being built we thought it was a *dhobi talao* (tank for washing clothes).' To my mind, this is a glaring example of cultural illiteracy. The project failed on economic grounds also because the cost of generating electricity through bullock power was found prohibitive. All that the foreign donor succeeded in demonstrating was that it was possible by an accelerated rotation of a specially designed machine to generate electricity through bullock power. But this could have been demonstrated anywhere in the world. There was no need for the sponsors to come to India. For the record, I may be permitted to state that as the then Prime Minister, Jawaharlal Nehru, was enthusiastic about this project since the sponsors had told him that this new technology would revolutionise Indian villages, as a young researcher I had managed to convey to Pandit Nehru that the project was a failure and there was no such revolution. I am sure that the Prime Minister must have got similar information from other sources also, and his enthusiasm for this project evaporated in no time. The foreign philanthropist had to hand over the project to a foreign foundation which, in turn, wanted to hand it over to the villagers: but there were no takers. When I asked the village leaders about this project they said: 'It is much better to buy a diesel generator and draw water from the well. Besides, our bullocks are not strong enough to generate so many rotations of the wheel at such a high speed. We will have to buy very sturdy bullocks and the cost of feeding them will be prohibitive. If the donors had told us what they were doing, we could have given them all this information; but nobody consulted us'.

Case study 2: People's participation in a health and family welfare project

The case study above shows a complete lack of people's participation in a project which was supposed to benefit them. I shall now give a case study where the donors insisted on people's participation right from the beginning. These projects are called 'area projects' and are funded by donor agencies like the World Bank, UNFPA, USAID, DANIDA, etc. These were well-meaning health and family planning projects aimed at ensuring that the para-medical personnel were within the reach of the people in order to improve the rural health delivery system. In those days, there was a Primary Health Centre (PHC) for every 100,000 people. Each PHC had several sub-centres and each sub-centre was meant for 5000 people. At the sub-centres there was provision for one male multi-purpose worker (MPW) and one female multi-purpose worker (called ANM — auxiliary nurse midwife).

The area projects stipulated that at each sub-centre a one-room residential unit would be built with an adjacent courtyard, and next to the courtyard there would be the sub-centre dispensary. It was felt that access to health care was limited as public health workers had no place to stay near the sub-centres. Further, as there was no proper building for the dispensary, the health service was poor. The investment on this physical infrastructure of a dispensary and residential unit for the ANM was intended to go a long way in strengthening the rural health delivery system. The foreign sponsors insisted that it should not be a giver approach and there must the fullest participation of the people. Under the area projects, the village councils or *pancayats* had to give land for the construction of the sub-centres and the nurse's quarters. Enormous funds were sanctioned to the government by the foreign donor agencies for creating this infrastructure.

At the request of the then Secretary in the Ministry of Health and Family Welfare, I had, along with my research team, tried to assess the working of these projects in several parts of India during 1983-85. In my judgement, most of the projects had failed. One important factor contributing to the failure was the giving of free land by the *pancayats* for this project. Theoretically it could be agreed that in a poor country villagers would not be able to contribute any money which could match the money put in by foreign donor agencies, and therefore the only thing that the villagers could collectively do to show their participation was to donate land. But what was not realised was that in an agricultural country the most precious asset is land. As a result, what actually happened was that the worst possible land on the outskirts of the village or some low-lying area or uninhabitable land was donated to the sub-centres. As a result, when the sub-centres were built, no nurse could stay in them because of sheer physical insecurity. As one of these nurses observed: 'Some mad dog must have bitten the experts in New Delhi. How can they think of locating sub-centres in such lonely places and ask an ANM to stay there? Even in the daytime we did not feel safe, let alone at night'. The ANMs never stayed at the newly-built sub-centres.

I asked one of the foreign sponsors why there was no provision for housing of the male multi-purpose workers. His reply was, 'We were told that in India it would be scandalous if we built two adjacent quarters, one for the male MPW and the other one for the female MPW'. Such reasoning assumes that nurses stay alone in India. The ground reality is that in this type of situation, there would always be a family with the ANM; and the same would be true of the male MPW. As a nurse explained to me, if at least there were two families staying side by side, the ANMs would have felt somewhat secure.

To me, the area projects are glaring examples of cultural illiteracy on the part of foreign experts and Indian bureaucrats and their near-complete ignorance of ground reality. Again for the sake of the record, I wish to state that my confidential report was so disturbing for the Ministry of Health & FW that a copy was sent to the then Prime Minister, Rajiv Gandhi. He acted quickly and a high-powered Steering Committee (as suggested by me) was appointed to look into the area projects. I was drafted as a member of this Committee, but to my surprise, instead of interaction with the foreign donor agencies, the same set of bureaucrats was brought together with one or two non-official members, to discuss the area projects. It was a futile exercise and nothing came of it. After Rajiv Gandhi, no Health Minister has bothered to look into the socio-cultural dimensions of the area projects, which is quite understandable as the only concern is for the foreign exchange component of these funds.

The donor agencies have also recognised that these projects did not quite succeed and the accent now is on training. While training and upgrading medical skills is important, the neglect of the socio-cultural environment may make such training ineffective. India's family planning programme is not sensitive to gender issues. One may ask: Why are 96 per cent of the sterilisations female sterilisations? Why have the men walked out of the programme? Can we succeed merely by giving more incentive money for male sterilisations compared to female sterilisations? Are there deep-rooted social and psychological factors conditioning Indian society? In short, contraceptive technology, no matter how good it is, will not succeed if we ignore the social and cultural context. What sort of training do the area projects give to take note of this vital cultural context? India's family planning programme will not succeed unless we get out of the sterilisation trap and look beyond contraceptive technology. Thanks to the increasing funds and the growing number of foreign donors and the mushrooming of foreign-funded NGOs, there is every possibility that NGOs will jump onto the international bandwagon and make a further mess of the family planning programme. We must beware of the *kubuddhi* (bad advice) of culturally illiterate experts, both Indian and foreign.

Case study 3: Overcoming the son-complex through IEC

Information, education and communication (IEC) is an international buzzword and all family planning programmes, whether funded by the Government of India or by foreign donor agencies, allocate large sums for it. Our field work experience is that much of this money is wasted. In fact, we have lampooned IEC as 'incompetence, extravagance and corruption'. Under conditions of mass illiteracy, what information do we give to our masses? Is it enough to devise a red triangle for family planning services? Will people make a beeline for contraceptives wherever they see a red triangle?

This reminds me of a hilarious episode. In the early 1960s a communication expert from the West came to advise the Government of India about propagating the small family norm among the rural masses. His strategy to overcome the constraint of illiteracy was to buy an elephant, put a red triangle on its decorative cloth and parade the animal from village to village to convince people about the 'elephantine' nature of India's population problem! This culturally illiterate expert did not know that an elephant in Indian mythology stands for prosperity — the elephant was born in the clouds, which bring rain and therefore prosperity in an agricultural country. Indian temples are full of the elephant motif and several Western scholars have worked on this symbolism in temple architecture. To cut a long story short, the elephant project was a disastrous failure and the elephant died of starvation.

A marked bias for sons is a cultural trait in India and many other Asian countries. Is the son-complex basically a religious phenomenon as most Western experts think? My field work convinces me that the son-complex is basically a strategy for survival and an economic phenomenon. The empirical evidence shows that most traditional families in India (except in Kerala and some communities in North-East India and a few other places) would like to have at least *two sons* before they think of family planning. To overcome this bias for sons, the Family Welfare Department spends a lot of money putting out posters and advertisements on radio and TV saying that 'son or daughter — it is all the same', 'a girl is as good as a boy', etc. Many posters show a couple with only one daughter with a beaming smile, with the red triangle in the background.

We were doing field work in Rajasthan. Our survey showed that every family gave more or less the same answer: 'We want two sons'. For a moment, I thought the investigators had filled up the schedules sitting in a coffee house! But I had full faith in their integrity. I went from village to village and got the same answer. Finally, I asked a village woman why she wanted to have two sons. She retorted quickly: 'Is this a question to ask? Why do you have two eyes?' I could not answer this question. The Rajasthani village woman put her hand on one eye and elaborated: 'If one eye is lost, the other eye will still remain'. This set me thinking and I coined the term 'demographic fundamentalism' to indicate the inherent desire for two sons, a phenomenon which cuts across socio-economic classes and is both rural and urban. It is broadly true of all religious communities also.

The question is: 'Can we overcome demographic fundamentalism by the IEC strategy and by saying that it makes no difference whether one's child is a boy or a girl?' When I discussed the government poster with villagers in different parts of India, I got responses like the following:'How can the government say such foolish things? The girl has to be married and we have to save money and pay a dowry. Will the government pay the dowry? When the girls are married away, where is my family? If we have no sons, who will look after us in old age? Will the government take care of us?' These are valid points. In a country where social security is confined to government employees and the organised sector, the rural masses are just left out. It is only family solidarity which sustains them. It is wrong to think that it is only in old age that one has to depend on sons. Throughout one's lifetime one has to depend on sons in an agricultural country. The land has to be protected from intruders, the property has to be saved from floods and other natural disasters, and so on. When the breadwinner falls ill, even minor sons step in and keep the family going. It is not religion *per se* and the thought of rituals after death which worry the average rural family but the fear of unemployment, sickness and economic insecurity. Thus parents feel secure if there are at least two sons.

Unless there is an objective change in the economic condition of the people and their basic needs are met, I do not see how any IEC strategy alone can lead to the acceptance of family planning. The successful demographic transition in Kerala and Tamil Nadu has many lessons for us, but given the demographic diversity of India it would be hazardous to make any generalisation. In fact, one should guard against demographic pitfalls which are largely statistical in nature. To give one example, when the 1991 census results were declared, there was a feeling of elation in some government circles that the literacy rate had risen to 52 per cent, i.e. the *majority* of Indians were literate for the first time. But this overall figure is highly misleading. The same census also revealed that only 39 per cent of females were literate; that is to say, the *majority* of girls and women in India were *illiterate*.

Or take the figure for the birth rate. According to the Registrar General's SRS figures for 1993, the overall birth rate in India was 28.5 per 1,000, but it was as high as 36 in UP and as low as 17 in Kerala. Or take the infant mortality rate (IMR). It was 74 in India as a whole but 110 in Orissa and 13 in Kerala. Such striking demographic diversity makes generalisations and models untenable in India.

Discussion

The three case studies we have presented raise important policy issues which deserve careful thought from our planners and policy-makers as well as from researchers. If we want to improve the quality of life, it is not enough to be guided by purely economic considerations and the profit motive or the prospect of earning foreign exchange. If the Punjab Government is forced to close down a buffalo meat exporting factory on religious grounds, it cannot be dubbed communal. As the Chief Minister rightly said: 'There are three aspects, economic, medical and religious'. If the social environment is polluted by such slaughter-houses, policy-makers must act. But the question is (and this was also raised by the Punjab Chief Minister): What happens to slaughter-houses all over India? Maneka Gandhi, an environmental activist and a former Minister for Environment, did succeed in getting a semblance of medical and environmental cleanliness in the slaughter-houses of Delhi by going to the court. Can we introduce environmentally safe and humane measures in all slaughter-houses or is there no such thing as a 'humane measure' when one takes to killing? Should the whole country opt for vegetarian food? What should be our development strategy for food and nutrition, keeping in mind the socio-cultural dimensions of non-vegetarian food?

Next we come to people's participation in health and family planning programmes. Insisting that villagers should give free land for building sub-centres is a misguided strategy and should be undone. After the passing of the 73rd amendment to the Constitution and the empowerment of *pancayats*, the people will have a greater say in implementing developmental programmes at the local level. Implementation of health and population control programmes has been included in the functions of the *pancayats*. The question of the insecurity of the nurses working in the sub-centres must be squarely tackled by the *pancayats*. If this problem is not solved, access to health care in rural areas will remain problematical. An alternative health development strategy which relies on the local people to deliver health services can be visualised, where the nurses will stay with their own families in their own houses and serve the local community. This calls for recruitment and training at the local level rather than a policy of recruiting nurses from outside who will face perpetually the problem of staying in secluded areas in houses built by the government on land donated by villagers. Is it possible to have hostels for nurses in selected rural areas and give them vehicles to go to their places of work and bring them back? Should we opt for husband and wife teams of multi-purpose workers?

A lot of thought must go into evolving a health delivery strategy at the grassroots level, keeping in mind India's demographic diversity. Socio-cultural factors and gender issues must not take a back seat in evolving such strategies.

Finally, on the difficult question of communicating effectively with the illiterate masses, a fundamental question to ask would be: Why keep the masses illiterate? On the question of the son-complex one would ask: Why deny social security to the rural masses?

The International Conference on Population and Development at Cairo (1994) formulated an elaborate programme of action and asked for more funds for expanding family planning programmes in the developing countries. The Swaminathan Committee on Population Policy (1994) asked for a paradigm shift in our plans and programmes for curbing population growth. The paradigm shift is to move away from the present sterilisation-centred family planning programme to an integrated programme which will take full note of the eco-system, gender issues, basic needs and democratic norms. The policy advocated is pro-nature, pro-women, pro-poor and pro-democracy. The policy (draft) links population to social development and urges the government to appoint an independent Population and Social Development Commission. The emphasis, however, is *not* on apex institutions but on effective participatory planning and implementation of programmes at the district level. It is proposed that each district should draw up its own *socio-demographic charter.*

Unity in diversity is a good national slogan, but when this diversity is reflected in demographic imbalance between states and regions and between socio-economic groups and communities within a region, it should cause concern. There should be effective developmental strategies aimed at reducing such imbalances and ensuring equity. Jumping onto the bandwagon of globalisation is not the answer to these problems. Our cultural values must counteract the mindless consumerism propagated through the electronic media. The population problem of India cannot be solved by gimmicks.

The current strategy of family planning, based on technology and monetary incentives and the use of the electronic media, may appeal to the West as a solution to India's population problem. But in our view, it will not succeed. In a lighter vein, we call this strategy COMIEC, where CO stands for contraceptive technology, M for monetary incentives and IEC for information, education and communication.

The strategy we are advocating can be summed up in the acronym BLISS, where B stands for basic needs, LI for literacy, S for secondary level schooling and the second S for skill formation.

Considering population size, per capita income and the level of poverty, South Asia is indeed the world's leading problem region. One does not have to argue much in favour of effective poverty alleviation programmes. In our scheme of things, family planning should be an integral part of all poverty alleviation programmes. This does not mean that ration cards should be denied to persons with more than two children and maternity leave should be denied to women with more than two children. India is proud of her democracy and there should be no aberration in our democratic norms of behaviour, including reproductive behaviour. In a people-oriented family planning programme, the government must apply its mind to fulfilling the basic needs of the people, which include primary health care. According to the philosophy of Jawaharlal Nehru, health includes family planning. Therefore, we challenge the school of thought which relies heavily on technology, money power, and media power to motivate poor, illiterate, malnourished Indian masses to take to family planning. Development is the best contraceptive and the vicious circle of poverty and population can be broken only if we give the same attention to poverty as we give to population.

15

Voluntary Action and Alternative Development in Tribal Areas

Sachchidananda

After attaining independence most Third World countries embarked on the path of modernisation to catch up with Western countries in the shortest possible time. The national elites in these countries bent their energy to accomplish this task. The experience gained during the first two development decades amply showed that the two concepts of modernisation and development were most inadequate to solve the problems facing the people in these countries. Although some economic growth was registered, the process brought in its train greater dependence on Western countries and widened the gulf between rich and poor in different countries. At some places this led to the emergence of powerful social movements. This invited a backlash from vested interests tending to promote parochial and obscurantist values which militated against the goals of modernity.

The development experience among the tribal communities is not very different from that of general society in India. In certain cases, tribals have been hurt rather than helped on account of the development effort. In most cases it resulted in development for the few and destitution for many. The experience of the pains of development is very poignant. Some of these are quite visible while others can be discovered after a deep probe into the social fabric.

In India the bulk of the tribal community is spread over middle India from

Gujarat to West Bengal and in the north-east. The tribals in the north-eastern states form a majority there. The tribals in middle India live interspersed with the dominant population. It is there that their deprivation and exploitation are the worst. Tribal policies in India suffer from a hangover of the colonial past. The British system of administration tended to impair their social solidarity and weakened the authority of their social heads and *pancayats*. Until recently, when rules against alienation of ancestral land were promulgated by the government, the ancient tribal customs against such alienation were disregarded. After Independence efforts were made to integrate the tribals into the mainstream of the Indian polity through elimination of exploitation and positive measures for raising their levels of living. But even forty years after Independence they are being deprived of command over the resources which they enjoyed in their respective areas. The opening up of inaccessible tribal areas has aided this process. The tribal people along the arteries of communication are being squeezed out of their land. The new enclaves of affluence in tribal areas have no place for tribals. They are losers on all counts and are victims of a system in which those responsible for policy-making suffer no embarrassment and qualms of conscience.

The problems of tribals coming under the sway of large industrial, mining and irrigation projects are most acute. It is a pity that the difficulties of the tribals were not perceived earlier. The issues are not just alternative use of resources or cost-benefit analysis of projects. They are deeper and involve human rights, civilisation's values and national obligations. The tribal people are faced with rapid change, which tends to create a crisis in their life. Displacement spells disorganisation and destitution. They lack skills for an alternative way of life. It is at this stage that the concept of sustainable development or alternative development has to be thought of. Unfortunately not much thinking in this regard has come from the government. It is on account of this that the role of voluntary agencies in this field becomes important.

I

The experiment in alternative development which is the theme of this paper has been carried out in the Santhal Parganas by the Badlao Foundation during the past ten years. The Santhal Parganas is the north-eastern extension of the Deccan plateau. The region is bounded on the west and south by a number of districts of Bihar and to the east by some districts of West Bengal. Ethnologically, it is the abode of two important tribes, the Santal and the Paharia. The activities of the Badlao Foundation are spread mainly among these tribes in the districts of Deoghar, Godda and Dumka.

The Santal are the largest tribe of eastern India. In Bihar alone they number more than two millions. The traditions of the Santal represent them as a group wandering from one land to another until they found their present home in Chhota Nagpur and the adjacent districts. On the basis of their traditions, several theories have been put forward to account for their origin. About the middle of the 18th century Chhota Nagpur was the chief habitat of the Santal. At the end of the century, as the jungles were being cleared and the pressure of population was keenly felt, they moved up towards the virgin forests in and around the Rajmahal hills. The Permanent Settlement of 1793 forced the landlords to pay more attention to land improvement and reclamation, for which the Santal were increasingly used. In 1832 the government set apart a large area in the Santhal Parganas for the settlement of the Santal. This region was known as Damin-i-Koh. The population in this tract increased from 3,000 in 1838 to 82,795 in 1851. Thus from the middle of the last century Damin-i-Koh became the main concentration of the Santal.

In reclaiming land and clearing jungle the Santal have few equals in India. They live in villages consisting of a long street with a single row of dwellings on either side. Santal houses are built of mud but roofed with country-made tiles. The houses are kept very neat and clean and the outside walls are painted with exquisite designs. The Santal are settled agriculturalists and use simple agricultural implements. However, they derive a part of their sustenance from the forest, since their agricultural field are monocropped. The Santal produce rice, maize, millets, beans, and vegetables. About 82 varieties of wild plants, 70 varieties of fruits, 7 varieties of resins, 31 varieties of mushrooms and several varieties of jungle millets are gathered at one time or other. Wild foods are collected by women who work together in groups. Santal men go on hunting expeditions.

The Santal live in nuclear families and are patrilineal in descent. Several kinds of marriage are prevalent, but the most prestigious one is that in which bride-price has been paid. A daughter does not have a share in her father's property but she can hold moveable property like money, goods and cattle. Women's status in society is high and in most cases they run the households. However, they do not have political or religious rights. They are not members of the village *pancayat*, although Santal society is highly democratic. Women work with men in fields, farms and forests. They go to the market and strike bargains for the surplus produce of the family. Santal society is marked by a spirit of cooperation and it is manifested not only on the occasion of festivals but also in all kinds of social and economic activities. Friends share wedding expenses with each other, help each other in cultivation, lend each other plough cattle and rally to each other's help at birth, sickness, or death and assist each other with loans that are free of interest. Santal religion is a potent force in strengthening the social solidarity of the people. The Santal concept of righteousness is bound up with its social or tribal consciousness. They have an excellent and well-ordered village organisation with a hierarchy of village officers and courts for dispensing their unwritten law. The unique form of punishment called *bitlaha* is used to bring to book persons guilty of transgressing the social code regarding sexual relations inside the clan and outside the tribe.

The Sauria Paharia, the largest Paharia group, accounted for 65,000 persons in 1988. The Sauria Paharia are basically shifting cultivators and live on mountain spurs in very small villages. They have a feeling of animosity toward the Santal who live largely on the plateau and use more sophisticated tools for agriculture. They speak a language which belongs to the intermediate Dravidian group so widely different from the Austric speech of the Santal.

Sauria Paharia settlements comprise ten to fifty houses. The houses are very small and rickety compared to Santal houses. Their main occupation is slash-and-burn cultivation, known locally as *kurwa*. They move from field to field after a few years. They use only the digging stick for putting in the seeds. They grow maize, millets, beans and pulses. Some of these tribesmen have picked up settled cultivation if they have some plain land. The Paharia as compared to Santal are more dependent on the forest. Earlier they used to make some money by cultivating *sabai* grass. But now they do not do so in a big way as its market has shrunk. The cutting down of forests and the restrictions placed on their exploitation led to a reduction of their resource base. Although the Sauria Paharia have cherished a healthy relationship between nature, man and the spirits for a long time, they are extremely frustrated as their gods have failed to protect them from the ravages of time. Abject poverty and disease have made them panic. The steps taken by government for their welfare have largely bypassed them, and they remain one of the most backward tribal groups in the state.

II

It is in this background that the Badlao Foundation is concentrating its effort. In recent years, voluntary initiatives have raised debates on new issues and concerns which have emerged from our development programme over the past four decades. The issues of deforestation, air and water pollution, ecology, rights of women and rural labour, rights of construction workers, occupational health and safety, land degradation and alienation, housing rights, right to information and work, adult literacy and education of women, etc., have been articulated by individuals and organisations involved in voluntary action. Although even earlier the role of voluntary agencies in bringing about development was recognised, it was only in the Seventh Plan document that the role of voluntary organisations was clearly set out. Voluntary agencies were not only to supplement government efforts but also to offer the rural poor choices and alternatives. Thus the voluntary agencies could experiment and innovate new schemes and programmes to bring development to the rural poor. Since they had close links with the grassroots, they were expected to elicit people's participation in a much larger measure than otherwise. The development package could differ from area to area and even from village to village. The voluntary agencies were not expected to supplant government efforts and replace dependence on the government by dependence on themselves, but in helping people help themselves. People have to be made aware of their own problems. They have to work out the priorities themselves in view of the limitation of resources.

The Badlao Foundation was established by certain activists who were inspired by the J.P. movement which took place in the mid-1970s. In the early 1980s there was no voluntary organisation in the pockets in which work was started. The area chosen was about eight kilometres from Mihijam on the Bihar-Bengal border. Long economic deprivation and the excesses perpetrated on them by the moneylenders had put the tribal population in a state of despondency. In such a situation an all-round effort had to be made to generate income for them through fresh schemes, i.e. sericulture, livestock, milch cattle, cottage industry, small trades, social forestry, spinning, weaving, etc. In addition to this, there was urgent need for educational and health programmes for the people. The Foundation set before itself the following tasks:

1. To develop skills and self-reliance in social, economic, cultural and political fields through raising social consciousness and sense of civic responsibility among the tribal and poor population for bringing about their socio-economic transformation
2. To initiate small economic programmes for women through the creation of

Mahila Sabhas

3. To mobilise different segments of the society, particularly the youth
4. To organise discussions, meetings, environmental festivals, exhibitions, cultural programmes, and to conduct tours for tribal people to acquaint them with successful development efforts
5. To conduct training in ecology and environment

The fast depletion of forest cover in the region affected the life of tribals very adversely. They depended for their livelihood, in large measure, on the forest. They took advantage of various kinds of timber and non-timber produce. In the lean months of the year, they could subsist on products like *mahua* and jackfruit. The cutting of forests was accelerated by the local contractors in collusion with the lower functionaries of the Forest Department. They cut more forest than they were permitted to. The Forest Department held that the illegal cutting was the work of tribals, and a large number of Santal and Paharia were sent to jail on this ground. The depletion of forest resources led to the disappearance of a large number of medicinal plants which were used for curing human and animal diseases. It also led to the disappearance of a large number of animal species. Valuable pasture land was also lost and it has become a problem for the grazing of domestic animals. In some areas where certain communities were dependent on pastoral activities, their source of income disappeared. The cottage industries in the village, which provided sustenance for certain communities, decayed in course of time due to lack of availability of raw materials which were derived from the forest. Prominent among them was the production of cotton, *taser* silk, the lac industry and the growing of *sabai* grass, which was used for the production of paper.

To add to this environmental degradation, the proliferation of stone quarries and stone crushers brought untold misery to the people. After the quarries were exhausted the entire landscape was marked by pits and nothing could be produced there. On account of strong winds stone dust coming from the stone crushing machines spread along the nearby fields and reduced their fertility. Not only this, the health of the people working in the quarries and living in nearby areas was also affected. They began to suffer from lung diseases such as silicosis and asthma. They also complained about skin diseases and deafness. Protests made by local people against the opening of stone crushers went unheeded on account of the influence of capitalist interests.

Another impact of the depletion of forests was the drying up of rivers and other sources of water. Many rivers which were earlier perennial changed their character and water was available in them only in the rainy season. The amount of precipitation was also reduced, resulting in scarcity of water. As a result, people have to drink stale and contaminated water. This has led to the appearance of many diseases.

The landscape changed a great deal on account of large-scale soil erosion. In many areas land was rendered uncultivable due to sand and the formation of gullies. All this led to reduction in the cultivable area. The process of desertification has set in and more and more land is turning barren.

Faced with this ecological problem the Badlao Foundation took steps to restore the ecological balance by arresting further degradation and conserving and regeneration of the existing natural resources. The steps taken were threefold: adoption of sericulture as a supplement to agriculture in a big way, ecological cultivation and afforestation. All this needed building of awareness about environmental degradation among the people by pointing out how it was affecting their life adversely and how it was going to affect future generations. Since the women suffered most on account of environmental degradation by way of loss of food resources, employment opportunities, and migration of the menfolk in search of employment away from home, an effort was made to carry on the awareness programmes most vigorously among them through village Mahila Sabhas.

It was seen that the area was ideally suited for the plantation of *arjun*, *asan* and mulberry trees on which silkworms could be reared. The Foundation started a training programme to impart knowledge to a group of women about the complete process of sericulture, from silkworm rearing to silk production. The men were left undisturbed to carry on their own activities. The training was divided into phases. Once the training in worm rearing was completed, the women were trained in reeling and spinning. Later on they were also trained in weaving on looms. Nowhere in these parts do we find women engaged in weaving, but here women have eagerly taken up this activity. Engagement in such activity gives them supplementary income. This was augmented by other income generation schemes like goat rearing, raising of fruit and vegetable seedlings, horticulture, etc. A number of case studies of women showed that family income went up with these activities. The example set by some of the beneficiaries were ample demonstration to their neighbours to follow suit.

The second activity of the Foundation to restore the ecological balance was ecological cultivation. On account of the decline in the productivity of land, government effort was directed towards the use of more and more chemical fertilisers. However, it was found that the excessive use of chemical fertilisers was extremely harmful to the land in the long run. It has been observed that a balanced integration between plants, animals and insects is essential for sustainable development. The tribals had a strong tradition of using green manure for better produce. The Paharia engaged in shifting cultivation, which was an appropriate technology designed to regenerate forest and restore soil fertility. The burning of the undergrowth provided ample fertiliser for the shifting cultivation plot. After a few years, the plot was left fallow, the forest regenerated and thus the shifting cultivation cycle was maintained. In the shifting cultivation field there has been a tradition of mixed cropping. If one crop fails, the other crop helps the people to tide over the crisis and there is never a total famine in such areas. However, with the conversion of many of these plots into settled cultivation fields, the regeneration process has stopped. Studies made by scientists have made it clear that this pattern of ecological degradation is marked in this area after it changed from a collectional economy to settled agriculture. Almost all the farmers of the region are small and marginal farmers with uneconomic holdings. They are now looking for opportunities other than agriculture to make a living. Large numbers of them have become daily wage earners and migrate to neighbouring areas in search of seasonal employment. The Badlao Foundation targeted this group for experimenting in ecological cultivation.

To start with, the Foundation introduced ecological cultivation in ten villages of Madhupur Block of Deoghar district in 1989 with the following objectives:

1. To raise awareness and knowledge about ecological cultivation among individuals and peasant groups
2. To train and mobilise peasants in the operational area for reducing the use of chemical fertilisers in order to retain and enhance the productive capacity of the land
3. To train the farmers about the need to preserve and increase environmental capital for future generations
4. To discuss with the beneficiaries some of the aspects of the traditional cultivation system in relation to ecological constraints
5. To increase among beneficiaries knowledge of the environment
6. To safeguard the environment for the present and achieve full harmony

with nature.

Thus the spectrum of ecological cultivation has four components: (a) awareness, (b) analysis of the situation, (c) conservation and (d) sustainable development. Awareness includes making individual farmers conscious of the physical, social and economic aspects of the environment.

The experiment in ecological cultivation started with four farmers, two using the present system and two the innovative method. Before launching the programme, comprehensive soil testing and crop-wise doses of green manuring required in the fields were done by the Foundation. When the final accounting was done, it was evident that ecological cultivation is a viable proposition. In the present system 35 per cent of the operational cost is incurred on chemical fertilisers and pesticides. In the experimental area green manuring and compost accounted for only 23.5 per cent of the cost. In addition to economy, ecological cultivation ensured the retention of soil fertility over a longer period of time. Later on the area of ecological cultivation was extended. Training was provided for this purpose to farmers in a number of villages. The popularity of green manure has gradually increased. Many farmers are now retaining *dhaicha* seed for use year after year. The main reason for the adoption of ecological cultivation is reduction in the cost of inputs. This is accompanied by water harvesting, which has reduced the cost of irrigation.

The environmental programme of the Foundation was also devoted to the regeneration of forests. In some areas where large chunks of land were available, the Foundation began afforestation work by planting trees yielding fruit, fodder and fuel. In some villages in the Jarmundi Block such plantations was done over 177 acres. Both grafted and local trees of different species were planted. Mango, guava, lemon, *amla* and coconut trees were most popular. The plantations were done in four villages. A total of 3,900 fruit trees wee planted, fodder and fuel species numbering more than 16,000. Irrigation was provided for the new plants. Grafts, seedlings, manure and agricultural implements were given to the farmers in these villages. In about three years the barren fields have turned green. Some of the quick-growing fuel and fodder trees are being used by the village people. The fruit trees will begin to give yields in a couple of years. The village people have realised the importance of these plantations. They take care of the plants and protect them from being destroyed by animals. They also look after the nurseries with loving care.

In all its activities the Foundation has involved the beneficiaries in the different programmes so that they do not regard the innovations as impositions from above. Participation of the people is coming in large measure because the Foundation is interested in their integrated or total development. The educational and health programmes have endeared this voluntary organisation to the people. Increasing awareness has made them conscious of their own ability to contribute to their well-being. They now take full advantage of governmental schemes and the credit facilities being extended by banks. Their concern for conservation of the environment is evident in their efforts to minimise the felling of existing forests and saving them from the depredations of unscrupulous elements. The apathy to their environment and development is no more evident in the operational area of the Foundation. With alternative avenues of income from agriculture, sericulture and other activities both men and women are keen to improve their quality of life. Their aspirations have gone up. Thus the Badlao Foundation has shown ways in which the tribals in the area and other people can help themselves. It has also set an example for other voluntary organisations to work for sustainable development in tribal areas.

16

Development Problems and Traditional Cultures

Reflections on the Management of the Aged in India

P.K. Misra

Humans are one. They belong to a single species. They have a long history. Even in prehistoric times there were migrations, near and distant, all over the world. Seas, rivers, lakes, mountains, deserts and forests have not been able to deter human beings moving from one place to another. Come to think of it, migrations of people like the Jarawa (a classic food-gathering and hunting Negrito group) to another island in Car Nicobar or of the Toda to the Nilgiris, or of the Ladakhi to the Ladakh region, speak about the immense capacities of human beings. Some such movements might have been prompted by compelling natural, social or economic circumstances, but many were not. Being mobile at one stage and sedentary at another is a part of human nature. It appears that human beings are restless in either state (Misra 1986). They are curious about themselves, about the things around and beyond them, and are ever eager to impose order on them. Apart from the immense capacity to endeavour, to learn, to innovate and to adapt to any ecological condition, they add to their cultural baggage by borrowing. Any attempt to characterise people in terms of indigenous and non-indigenous amounts to taking a very short perspective of history. Such categories, if anything, are basically political.

Dynamics of culture

If culture is 'the way society formulates and deals with the basic problems of human existence' (Heesterman 1972:97), people living in different environments are likely to develop different cultures. But the very fact that human beings have been restless and have been migrating should indicate that they have not been satisfied with either the way they had formulated the problem of existence or the way they dealt with it. Whatever may have been the reason, as a result of their migrations and through various means of communication people have been exposed to different cultures. Thus cultures have grown through a process of borrowing, retaining and inventing. The process is extremely complex, because even a thing like borrowing is not simple. The borrowed item goes through cultural processing and is only then adopted. The process is further complicated by the fact that human beings attach meaning to cultural items and meanings may be multiple depending upon the context. Culture is also not a loose assemblage of discrete items; there is some degree of integration in them. One can argue that perfect integration is never achieved, and if that should happen a culture would never change. But cultures do change, some change very rapidly and others slowly. It is possible to argue that change is to seek better integration in the culture. To achieve that, there has to be a scheme. This scheme has to be experimental, otherwise there would not be any necessity for borrowing or inventing. In a culture, what is seen is just like the tip of an iceberg, a lot in terms of ideas, values and morals remain submerged but directs actions. All cultural practices, beliefs, ideas, morals, values and the attempts to integrate them would be senseless if the culture does not have goals perceived and defined by it. There can be a debate about the goals, but to claim its non-existence would mean that each aspect of culture has its own autonomous and *ad hoc* existence. If that be so, all discourse about culture would be meaningless.

While working among the East Indian population in Trinidad, I noted that the Indians there have a separate identity of their own. The Indians there were an uprooted population — they were taken there as indentured labourers, separated from their people and villages. They were a subordinate people, coming as they did from a colonised country to another colonised country, and they had no voice. Their cultures, languages and religions were stigmatised. Those among them who changed their religion were the favoured lot. In spite of all these odds, they were able to reconstruct a culture of their own and establish their identity. This culture is certainly different from what they brought with them but very distinct from what the local culture is. Analysing these developments, I had written, 'in order to do what a culture does, it may adopt several strategies. It may allow individuals and some groups within to play intervening roles of bridge or buffer between the dominant groups in a multi-ethnic situation. Then there may be some issues which may cut across the individuals and groups. Such groups, individuals and issues to some extent are responsible for the large systems to function and at the same time allow the specific cultures to play the roles they have defined for themselves' (Misra 1994:11). Culture, in the long run, seems to be indestructible unless by some catastrophe. It has the capacity to regenerate itself around some ideas, some symbols, some institutions and activities. In the case of the Trinidad Indians I have shown that their population size, acquiring land, forming uni-ethnic villages, political actions to protect their interests, formation of the Indian association, struggling to get some of their rituals recognised, collecting contributions for the Bengal relief fund, arrival of Indian films and music, visitors from India, attempts at reviving rituals, performance of community worship, building temples and mosques, building networks through pandits and *tharia-lota*, were used to form a community of their own (*ibid*). Whatever they have constructed has to cope with external pressures and inner conflicts. It is not that culture resolves all conflicts. In fact, culture may regenerate itself, weaving its way through conflicts. In Trinidad, for example, the Indians have constructed a kind of duality of 'inner' and 'outer' lives to cope with the apparently contradictory Indian and Western values (Misra 1994:4).

A couple of decades ago Singer, in his study of the Indian joint family in modern industry, made a similar observation: 'Structural change and structural persistence are not mutually exclusive phenomena, they both are occurring simultaneously' (1968:438). In a detailed study of nineteen outstanding industrial families he found that there was a clear-cut separation of work and residence. The home becomes the sphere of religion and traditional values, while office and factory become the sphere of business and modern values. He calls this separation compartmentalisation. 'Compartmentalisation is an adaptive process which permits the incorporation of innovative patterns of thought and behaviour associated with modern industry without too direct a collision with traditional modes of thought and behaviour' (*ibid.*, p.439).

A study of development programmes initiated by the Government of India among five tribal groups in south India indicated that the response of each group was different (Misra 1982). In another study it was noted that of the two tribes inhabiting the same ecological region, one tribe totally rejected most of the development programmes while the other accepted them with some enthusiasm (Misra 1970). It was found that acceptance and rejection of specific development programmes were correlated to the social structure and values of the respective tribes. This was significant because both the groups were very poor and barely managed their existence by food gathering, some agriculture and extraction of minor forest products. Yet both the groups were very concerned about their cultures and retaining their respective identities.

Even in a situation where there were enormous existential difficulties, Thorbek, in her study of a slum in Sri Lanka, found that the slum dwellers there were more concerned with their relations with spouses, children, mothers, relatives, neighbours, performance of rituals and what was right and wrong, than with money alone, in short with their culture and values (1994).

Cultural variety

Elsewhere too, particularly in the emergence of ethnic conflict all over the world, it has been noted that cultures cannot be changed or preserved at will. The indirect evidence of the existence of the immense varieties of cultures all over the world in spite of powerful forces unleashed by modernisation supports the above hypothesis. Culture has its own internal dynamics. Each culture, in a way, is unique. In the process of its growth it develops its own emphasis. These emphases make each culture appear different. They allow people to feel 'good' and 'satisfied'.

Thinking of the varieties of culture and their interrelations, the image that comes to mind is that of an unspoiled tropical forest where there are immense trees, plants and creepers, growing in and out of each other, together providing shelter and nourishment to innumerable varieties of creatures. The whole is a system but each element in it has its own identity and function. For obvious reasons this imagery cannot be pushed too far in understanding human societies, yet keeping it in view I would like to make the following points.

The individual culture is part of a larger system. The relevance and meaning of the individual culture can be appreciated and fully understood only in the context of the larger system. Deviation from this perspective leads to distortion in understanding, though it is true that big and strong societies have grown at the expense of small and weak ones. It is difficult to conceive of a world which has a uniform culture. None can deny that despite pressures even the small and weak have been able to maintain their cultural identities. By this I do not mean that they have remained static. Far from it, they too have been adapting and changing, and also influencing the larger system through a complex process of inter-culturation. The very fact that cultural variety has existed both in time and space shows that there are innumerable ways to formulate and deal with the problem of human existence. The larger system, if it is a system, has to be connected with its constituent parts — howsoever remote and thin these connections may be. This way the distinctions between endogenous and exogenous models of development, tradition and modernity, become dim. It is true that cultures cannot be kept isolated. It was not possible in the past and is much less possible now in the wake of the communications revolution.

Culture and development

This is the era of development. The world has been divided into developed and developing. The developing are exhorted to hasten and catch up with the developed. All kinds of packages have been created so that the developing world is able to meet at least the basic needs of its people. Meanwhile, in spite of all pious thoughts and plans, the gap between developed and developing within and between states has widened. This has increased anxiety the world over, particularly on account of the realisation that the world is an integrated system. The problems of one region, whether they are ecological, social, economic or political, are bound to affect the other regions too. There is yet another realisation, that development without intense humanism is self-destructive — it is the Hiroshima path. The situation now is far more dangerous than it was fifty years ago. Several countries have developed perilous capacities. Now the crucial question is whether it is possible to break or change the direction of development. One of the ways that has been suggested is to bring the required thrust of humanism into the development process. In this volume Kasai writes that tradition should continue to guide individuals and societies in their search for a just order and society, and development should supply more effective means for their search. But in Japan, he writes, tradition was exploited for just the opposite ends. There is enough evidence from all over the world that culture has been used for economic development and hegemonic tendencies. Even Kasai, after expounding the profoundest thoughts of Japanese tradition, ends by saying that the events of the past are the reminders of the violence of the development.

Why does this happen? It is seen that in practice development means material advancement. All the great thoughts about developing the finer aspects of human beings do not get translated into reality. They remain in the books. Even if it was intended, no one would know how to go about it. Therefore a peculiar situation prevails: while human beings can boast of tremendous material development, the same cannot be said about their own quality. They remain the same while they are expected to help in establishing a just order. For the same reason the matter of establishing a just order cannot be left to culture or tradition, as the context has considerably changed. Both traditional thought and modern experience will have to be focused on human development.

Human heritage

Right from the time human beings became cultural beings, they have been exploring the external universe and making internal arrangements of living. Over time such discoveries and arrangements have become part of the human heritage. It will be futile to argue whether fire or the innumerable varieties of food that we consume, or the various tools that we use, or the idea of counting, or the families in which we live, were found in east, west, north or south. What was found suitable was adopted with appropriate modifications by different cultures. In the same way modern discoveries are becoming part of the cultures of big and small countries. While such developments have apparently made life easier, they have thrown up many new, serious and urgent challenges before mankind, such as the phenomenal rise of human population, environmental pollution, demographic transition, etc. In this paper I intend to focus on the problems caused by demographic transition, resulting in the rise of the population of the aged. I argue that the management of the aged raises the issue of human development.

Demographic transition

A significant change has been taking place in the demographic structure of various countries. Their populations have been ageing. It is a dynamic phenomenon. It means more rapid increase of the proportion of old people as compared to other age segments. Till recently it was thought to be a problem of the developed countries, but now it is becoming a problem of the developing countries also. 'In 1985, there had been 427 million elderly persons (aged 60 and above) accounting for 8.8 per cent of world population. In relative terms, demographic aging was most advanced in the more developed countries where the elderly accounted for 16 per cent of total population as opposed to 7 per cent in the less developed countries' (UN 1988:3). An international symposium on population structure and development recognised that population ageing was taking place in the context of a rapidly increasing total world population. 'Growing from an estimated 2.5 billion in 1950, it had reached 4.8 billion in 1985 and was projected to reach 8.2 billion in 2025' (*ibid.*, p.3). In India, the ageing process of the population is yet to set in full swing since fertility has not come down significantly; but that is no relief as in absolute terms there were more than 43 million people above the age of 60 in 1981 (Guha Roy 1987:61). The percentage of persons in the age group of 60+ in 1961 was 4.57, in 1981 it was 5.14, and in 2001 it is likely to be 7.11 (Chowdhary 1992:30). That is, the population of the aged in the country is already large and is going to be larger still, which is a consequence of development. What problems and issues does this demographic change bring forth?

Problems and issues

The rise in the number of those who are 'non-productive' and who do not generate any 'hope' immediately raises an economic problem. It is also a social problem: Who is going to provide support to them and how? Apart from food and shelter, the old need care and medicines. They also crave love and tender care. They would like to interact, be heard, be visible, and would like a bit of space of their own and have a constructive and creative role to play in society. Among the old, the problems of old women, single, divorced and widowed, are different from those of old men. In a column in a newspaper an elderly male wrote:

> I am 65 years old and I lost my wife about two years ago. But for the feeling of loneliness which has me in its grip every once in a while, I am happily placed in life. My children are happily married and settled. They look after me well but have their limitations. I am beginning to feel that it will become difficult to cope with life without a partner. Much of life's charm has indeed vanished ever since the death of my wife. I feel like I have everything and yet nothing. I agree with 'Mr K.', who felt that widowers and widows could lead a happier life if they have companions to avoid loneliness. And especially at a senior age, the need for a partner to share life with intensifies greatly. In today's social context, however, elderly widows and widowers have little choice but to suffer silently (*Times of India*, 30 March 1995).

In the same paper another old person wrote, 'I am a single senior citizen and I feel there are many facets to the problems of single elderly people in our society. It concerns widowers, widows as well as bachelors and single women in advanced age groups. Harking back to past traditions and past family systems cannot be solutions'. Apart from the problems of the reasonably healthy elderly, the problems of the disabled and senile are of a very special kind.

Ageing marginalised

There are not many studies focusing on these problems. A quick glance at the available literature indicates that Indian society does not even realise that a serious human, social and economic problem is at hand which needs immediate specialised attention.

The Western response to the problem has been liberating the old from various kinds of filial responsibilities, making them economically as viable as possible and handing over the problems of health and care to specialised institutions. In the United States of America, apart from schemes of pension, insurance and retirement benefits, the health care of the aged is linked with the social security system. Mobile home service for the aged has been devised in order to lessen the pressure on institutions and costly nursing homes. How exactly these institutions work and what problems the old people under these schemes face are a different matter. However, it is clear that while these institutions can meet the material needs of the aged, they cannot do much when it comes to love, warmth, and the desire to be heard and to be visible.

The Indian situation

In India the situation is far more complex. An overwhelming number of people live in rural areas but migration from rural to urban areas is substantial, which creates problems for the ageing at both ends. If children go to urban areas leaving behind the aged in the rural areas, that creates one set of problems, and if the old are taken along, it creates another set of problems. The growth of the urban population and urban centres have been haphazard, and there are acute shortages of housing and other facilities. The health care system is woefully inadequate and there is hardly any specialised agency focusing on the old. There are no programmes available to train people taking care of the aged. In other words, the entire responsibility of taking care of the old continues to be with the traditional institution of the family.

Biswas's study of 13 villages in Giridih district of Bihar conducted at two points in time shows that an overwhelming number of the aged lived with their sons —

90.32 per cent in 1960 and 88.36 per cent in 1982. There were very few who decided to live with their daughters. Biswas writes, 'In substance, therefore, sons were the first choice for old age care, and they were often referred to as old age insurance for which property was transferred to [them] as premium' (1987:46). In the same study it is pointed out that 14.29 per cent old men and 57.78 per cent old women were dissatisfied with the care and service they got. Of those in ill health, a third of the men and more than half the women felt that they were not properly cared for (*ibid.*, p.53). As regards the interpersonal relations of the ageing with the other members of their families, the study found that a majority of them were bound by bonds of reciprocal respect and love, irrespective of complaints about accommodation, food and care. Dissatisfaction was greater among those who were fully dependent on their supporters. It grew keener and more bitter with age. Ageing women as a rule were neglected (*ibid.*, p.57).

The study highlights that in the rural areas the families of male children provide care and support to the aged. They are bound by traditional norms of respect and love. But now they are getting increasingly marginalised.

Ageing in urban areas

In urban areas the problems get further accentuated. Community support is weak and the kin network is diffused over a large area and relatively ineffective. The entire responsibility of support and care of the ageing falls on the male children with whom the ageing live. The composition of the family in urban areas is becoming nuclear and smaller, as a result of which there are fewer people available in the house to provide care and comfort to the ageing. Those who are available are torn apart by the stresses of urban living. Women too in the urban areas are now working outside the family. They have fixed schedules of work and have other pressures on them. Children are loaded with their studies, competitive examinations and concerns for making their careers.

The authority that the ageing exercised on their children in the past as a result of greater experience has almost vanished, and the aged are now told, 'You don't know'. There are several reasons for this admonishment. First, the children of the ageing are not in the same profession. Second, the quantum of information which their children claim to have makes the ageing look almost primitive. Third, the whole techno-economic situation has now completely changed, which leaves the ageing bewildered and redundant. When paucity of accommodation, high cost of living, general stress and tensions at all levels are added to these, the problems of the aged are extremely serious.

Discussion

The ageing pose a serious human problem. Since they are considered 'non-productive' and as they also do not generate any hope, it is all the more necessary that serious attention be paid to them. They raise moral questions and direct our attention towards transcendental values. In the past, ageing was not a serious issue and societies did not give it priority. They dealt with it as a natural phenomenon. Family members were responsible for the care and management of the old. But now the situation is different. The size of the people in the ageing category is already bulging and it is growing very fast. The problems posed by ageing are by no means accidental and isolated. They have grown as a result of the development process itself. The entire emphasis of development is on individual success, career promotion, entrepreneurship, investment, capital building and profit. In such a scheme of things, there is hardly any scope for thoughts about human development. At family, community and government levels the problems of the ageing get no or very low priority. It is taken for granted that the problem will get solved on its own or that it is a problem of individual families, with communities and governments having nothing to do with it. The family, where the ageing are supposed to get care and comfort, is on the rocks and in any case shrinking. The members of the family are spread around in pursuit of their careers.

The old, on their part, are not getting detached either. They think that they are going to live for ever and that in any case this is not the time to quit. The ideas of *vanaprastha* and *samnyasa* are too remote and idealistic. They are bored looking after grandchildren, listening to religious discourses and devotional music, making rounds of holy places or just sitting before the small screen. They seek companionship, appropriate creative and constructive roles.

Modern societies are following an ostrich-like policy in this regard. The Western solution to the problem has been old age homes, pensions, social security and health care. No doubt these are important steps, but these programmes are caught up in the conceptual groove that the old have lived their lives and at best they need some material comforts. In any case the old are marginal, backyard people and come in the category of waste. This attitude is exactly what development has to avoid. Development that does not develop the sensitivities and quality of human beings is a potential monster, a Hiroshima. The management and care of the old illustrates this point very well. A concern for non-productive people, sparing a thought for those who have been consigned as waste, would resolve most doubts about development. Development in the last analysis should mean enhancing the capacity of people to establish a just society.

In India even systematic thinking as to what should be the policy towards the ageing has not begun. At this stage in history the country is caught up in the whirlpool of market forces and resultant consumerism. Consumerism thrives on waste and decay. Consumer as well as producer know very well that this kind of development is not sustainable. A shift from consumption to conservation, from individual to community, is bound to take place, which will be in keeping with the Indian ethos. It is possible to be modern with the emphasis on conservation and focus on the community. This point gets very well illustrated in the management of the ageing. Taking care of the aged means highlighting the importance of conservation and humanitarianism. It will also strengthen the community, for the aged can be best taken care of within the fold of the family, bound by filial rights, duties and obligations. There is no institution that can replace the family but there is room to build into it the ideas of equality, justice and freedom. All this will not happen automatically. The focus has to be human development. That will provide new strength to the family and further support from the community. The old and infirm may find loving care.

As far as the ageing of the disabled and senile is concerned, apart from giving them specialised attention through nursing homes and mobile health units, family members will have to be trained in their care. It is to be borne in mind that care cannot be given by mere emotions and a sense of obligation. There has to be proper understanding of the problem and of the remedial measures which can be provided by modern knowledge of health and medicine. Thus a combination of modern knowledge and intense feeling for those who are non-productive can provide physical and emotional comfort to the old.

References

Biswas, S.K. 1987, 'Dependency and Family Care of the Aged'. In S.K. Biswas, ed., *Aging in Contemporary India*. Calcutta: The Indian Anthropological Society

Chowdhary, D. Paul, 1992, *Aging and the Aged*. New Delhi: Inter-India Publications

Guha Roy, S, 1987, 'Demography of Aging: Indian Experience'. In S.K. Biswas, ed., *Aging in Contemporary India.* Calcutta: The Indian Anthropological Society

Heesterman, J.C., 1972, 'India and the Inner Conflict of Tradition'. In S.N. Eisenstadt, *Post-Traditional Societies.* New York: W. W. Norton & Co.

Misra, P. K., 1970, 'Economic Development among the Jenu Kuruba'. *Man in India*, Vol.50, No.1

——, 1982, 'Differential Response to Change: A Case Study of Economy, Society and Change among Five Tribal Groups in Southern Zone'. In K.S. Singh, ed., *Economies of the Tribes and Their Transformation.* New Delhi: Concept Publishing Company

——, 'Mobility Sedentary Opposition: A Case Study among the Nomadic Gadulia Lohars'. In Joseph Berland and Hatt T. Salo, eds *Peripatetic Peoples.* Special Issue of *Nomadic Peoples*, Nos. 21 and 22

——, 1994a, 'Cultural Design in Identity Formation in Trinidad'. Unpublished

——, 1994b, 'Reflections on Inner-Outer Duality in Gender Relations among the East Indians in Trinidad'. Unpublished

Singer, Milton, 1968, 'The Indian Joint Family in Modern Industry". In Milton Singer and Bernard S. Cohn, eds., *Structure and Change in Indian Society.* New York: Wenner-Gren Foundation for Anthropological Research

Thorbek, Susanne, 1994, *Gender and Slum Culture in Urban Asia.* New Delhi: Vistaar Publications

United Nations, 1988, *Economic and Social Implications of Population Aging.* New York: United Nations

17

The Barefoot College in Tilonia

Sanjit (Bunker) Roy

The Social Work and Research Centre (SWRC) started officially in the village of Tilonia on 5 February 1972. On that day the Government of Rajasthan agreed to hand over a 45-acre 21-building one-time TB sanatorium to the SWRC on a long-term lease for Re. 1 per month. But it was not until November 1972 that the SWRC managed to begin with a groundwater survey of the 110 villages of Silora Block for the Rural Electrification Corporation. This project took two years to complete but resulted in the electrification of almost all the villages in the block a decade later.

The Barefoot College (BC), as the SWRC is called (also identified as Tilonia by the name of the village), was the result of practical experience. It was not inspired by books or by the theories of academics or practitioners based in urban areas. It was the result of hours of work in the villages, weeks of meeting ordinary peasants and years of living in rural India. It was prompted by above-average individuals who wanted to get together and live and work in a village setting. Tilonia's beginnings were the preparation that usually goes with the establishment of a project. No ideological leanings of any kind, no costly survey to decide what to do, no assistance from the traditional, well-established voluntary movements of India, whether the Gandhian, the Sarvodaya, the Christian or the Ramakrishna Mission. In any case, at that time, the BC was too small to get their attention or interest.

The BC wanted to break away from the 'social work tradition', which in India had acquired an urban, middle-class, academic colour, and there could not have been a better way to do this than using a professional groundwater survey as an entry point.

Furthermore, in India, among groups oriented to social action, research had acquired a dirty name and the BC wanted to move away from the concepts and traditions of research prevailing among academic social and physical scientists; the purpose was to make research more pragmatic, of a 'dirty hands' type tied directly to action. In a modest way, the Barefoot College has proved its point.

Many people who had started projects earlier did not give this non-professional approach much of a chance. The BC was in fact taking calculated risks on a number of fronts:

1. It was advocating an integrated approach over a sectoral one because it believed that rural life could not be compartmentalised as experts had traditionally done.

   In a village, for instance, a shopkeeper is more than just an outlet for provisions: he keeps seeds and fertilisers for distribution, he sells contraceptives, he reads newspapers and disseminates information, and sometimes he is also a member of the village council. He in fact is the last word in integration. This applies also to the school teacher.

2. No project plan was designed in advance, no clear time schedule, no detailed programme activities, no organisational and administrative arrangements, project staff or physical inputs, etc. Tilonia let the organisation grow as a process where human beings and their development, their confidence and personal growth meant more and mattered more.

3. The investment was more in people than in projects. This has been the first priority. No recruitment through advertisement but by word of mouth, by trial and error.

   BC started with a groundwater survey and gradually built in a health and education programme (1974) when they managed to attract two well-trained and highly motivated women from the Tata Institute of Social Sciences. In 1975-76, when the BC managed to locate the right person, it started the Rural Industries Section and the Agricultural Extension Programme (1975). Other programmes followed until 1979, when the BC changed its way of functioning and decision-making. No longer did it depend on the director, but a group was formed which took all the major decisions. The BC could not possibly plan and implement programmes from Tilonia for a territory of 500 square miles; the block was sub-divided into field centres, each looking after 6-25 villages depending on the staff and their capacity.

The areas on which the Barefoot College concentrated were:

1. *Groundwater*: Survey, site selection, installation of hand pumps, repair and maintenance through community participation.
2. *Education*: Nursery schools, evening schools for dropouts, classes for women and girls.
3. *Medical care*: Preventive health programmes where a doctor is not needed, TB eradication, eye camps, immunisation camps, family planning camps, pre-natal and post-natal care, appliances for the handicapped, testing drinking water for contamination, decontamination of wells, homoeopathy.
4. *Women's programmes*: Training of traditional midwives, motivators in famine relief camps, nursery school teachers, awareness generation, work among rural women.
5. *Agricultural extension*: Development of unused and underutilised land allotted by government, soil and water testing, groundwater survey, engineering survey, seeds and fertiliser loans, credit, grain storage, marketing facilities, social forestry.
6. *Rural industry*: Working with leather workers, weavers and rural women in order to generate more income for their families; assistance with raw materials, marketing, design, and credit.
7. *Appropriate technology*: Use of biogas for generating power, photovoltaic cells for generating electricity in night schools, dispensaries.
8. *Animal husbandry*: Demonstrate how stall feeding of goats is useful for milk and meat but constitutes an ecological hazard; rearing of rabbits and sheep; the BC dealt only with the poor peasants' animals, not with buffaloes and cows.
9. *Communication*: Use of traditional media like puppetry to communicate with the rural poor; use of street plays and other media.

Goals of the barefoot college

A. PROBLEMS TO BE SOLVED

From the very beginning it was not BC's intention to solve problems. Much more important was the belief in starting processes that went in the right direction. Basically, the SWRC saw the following problems being faced in the rural areas:

1. *Lack of professionalisation*: Too many projects based in the rural areas emphasised the dissemination of urban skills, knowledge and services without taking the human element in the rural areas into account. Tilonia was keen on professionalising volunteerism and using skills already available in the village community.

2. *Lack of accessibility*: The BC considered that numerous needs had to be met and the Tilonia model tries to address these, i.e. the need to bridge gaps in attitudes and facilitate exchange of experiences; the need to bring urban and rural skills closer and learn from each other and jointly plan and implement programmes for families living below the poverty line; the need to bring the rural poor closer to using their skills on how to plan projects, programmes and schemes for their own development.

3. *Poor dissemination of information*: Many of the schemes of the government were misinterpreted by people with vested interests in the village, including village-level government functionaries, with the result that the rural poor were entirely dependent on what the literate people in the village told them. The BC's role was to see that correct information reached the poor through channels they understood and then let them decide for themselves what to do with the information. Knowledge in the hands of a select few was power. The BC wanted to spread this power.

4. *Dependency*: To make communities independent by upgrading the skills existing in the community, by providing the peasants with the correct information, by making their skills more accessible. The BC felt that the peasants would be in a better position to rely on each other rather than on the government: they would then be able to understand the true meaning of cooperation.

5. *Absence of institutional support*: For peasants living in an impoverished state, it is virtually impossible to apply effective pressure on the national political system without the support of an organisation. The location of an organisation close to a village gives confidence and even the courage to resist exploitation, injustice and

misuse. The organisation can help the poor peasants meet senior officials, it can train them for a better and more effective use of laws, it can support them in their administrative and legal endeavours. Moral and even organisational support is not enough.

B. TARGET POPULATION

Initially, the BC was oriented towards providing technical and socio-economic services to all the villages in Silora Block. In India there are castes, there are classes, but very rarely are there actual communities, the only exceptions being the tribal societies. In Tilonia village, for example, there are fourteen different castes, which creates a variety of problems especially for the extremely poor and vulnerable families. In particular because the BC had made its services accessible to all, it found it was being used — often abused — by the richer and more powerful of the village. Obviously, this was not leading to any significant fundamental change of the sort the BC was expecting or considered desirable.

This led, in 1977-79, to a crisis within the BC, because some of the staff considered that persuading the influential individuals in the villages was the best way to contribute to rural development, while others thought that the BC's strategy had to be totally grassroots-oriented. The crisis was precipitated by a case of embezzlement in the Centre. The son of a Tilonia village headman, who had been working with the BC since 1974, was fired because he had stolen funds. He started a campaign against the Centre, which gained momentum and strength after he got elected to the state Legislative Assembly; he was able to institute an inquiry into the working of the BC. It was a difficult time for the Centre, because despite the fact that the BC had been working mainly with the socially vulnerable groups, no scheduled castes or poor peasants dared to testify for it. However, the Centre was able to prevail and the campaign against the BC withered away. This definitely oriented the Centre towards a grassroots strategy.

Since 1979, as a result of a conscious decision, the BC is only working, directly, with the following target groups: small and marginal landless peasants; rural artisans, such as leather workers, potters, carpenters, weavers and blacksmiths; rural women and children; scheduled castes and tribes; harijans (untouchables) and other minorities.

C. STRATEGIES

The strategies can be characterised in the following way:

1. To encourage an integrated approach to rural development. There needed to be an integration between rural skills and urban knowledge, between human and financial resources in urban and rural areas. At the village level, what was crucial was integration between the different services being provided to the peasant and his family. For example, preventive health programmes had to be linked to the provision of drinking water through hand pumps; likewise, the generation of income had to be related to health and education programmes. The process of bringing about this integration resulted in many changes within the BC; the priorities, staffing patterns and evaluation of staff performance had to be adjusted. At the same time, the BC felt even more strongly the need to upgrade the skills of the rural poor themselves.
2. The BC had to be based in a village. It could not and should not be involved in development by proxy or by commuting from an urban base.
3. If the idea was to work with the poorest peasants and to build up their confidence, it was necessary to live simply and in almost the same life-style as they did. The BC members had to set an example if they wanted to convey the impression that the Centre was there for the development of the rural poor. The BC, therefore, on principle, does not depend on electricity from the grid but has electrified the whole campus with solar energy.
4. The interaction within and between the BC and its target populations had to be informal, without hierarchies of any kind. It had to be flexible, the BC members had to be accessible and at the same time knowledgeable. This perforce meant the building of an organisation without degenerating into an institution.
5. If the BC wanted the poorest peasants to participate in their own development, use their own knowledge, skills and experience, then there was a need for the BC to identify skills that needed to be upgraded, knowledge that needed to be percolated, and give this process sanctity and acceptability. This has yielded impressive results today.
6. To mobilise resources from within the community, no service should be given free of charge. There should be no charity in the name of development.

> This realisation came from the endless discussions that BC members had with communities who insisted they did not want to be treated as beggars. This self-respect and dignity is all too often not visible to urban-based development agents.
>
> One indicator of villages or social groups being self-reliant is their paying capacity to support a service. The more the dependence on government, the more the poor peasants are prepared to take its services free, and the more the deterioration of the quality of these services. No service free of charge is valued.
>
> As things now stand (1994), 40 per cent of BC's total financial resources are collected from the peasant target populations from the provision of various services.

The BC feels that such strategies are not universal and fundamental. It is not obvious that they can be replicated in other parts of the country under different socio-economic conditions, such as tribal societies and drought-prone, hilly or coastal areas. While the target populations of the Tilonia Model may be the same as those of other rural development projects, the various approaches, methods and ideologies behind these projects could radically differ from those of the BC. The Tilonia Model encouraged such ideological differences under one umbrella and so far it has worked.

Implementation

Any Indian voluntary agency (VA) is in an unenviable position when it starts working at the village level. The first problem is whether it fits into a set pattern: Is it pro-government? Is it a scheme started by the rural rich? Who sponsors the scheme? Who provides financial support? Which political party does it support?

The first years are spent answering these questions and this process concerns not only the target populations, but also the voluntary agency's members themselves. Depending on how convincing the answers are and depending on how aligned the project and its workers are to parties, ideologies, personalities in the area and to government, the peasants will respond accordingly. Ironically, there is a sense of security in exploitation and the poorest peasants believe the word of the very individuals who exploit them the most. When any project starts, it needs time to settle down; but simultaneously, it must also win over the confidence of the very people whom the project's agents will hopefully be fighting against in years to come.

The first visible objectives of the project must be harmless to the people having vested interests in the village: services are to be provided to the whole village, including the rich; the project's agents have to mix less with the poor and more with the rich. The agents have to pamper the latter's wishes and requests and thus establish contact with the poor through protocol. The BC had to go through this exercise in order to acquire an image, to gain access to the villages it wanted to work with; it had to respond to 'the felt needs of the rural population', which were actually the needs of a few. These were years of preparation with villages at large favouring BC's action.

All voluntary groups including the BC eventually also have to go through a crisis period. The BC had to endure a period of uncertainty and great upheaval when in 1977-79 persons with vested interests wanted to close down the Centre because it was becoming too independent.

From its 1977-79 crisis, the BC learnt several important lessons:

1. It is only when an organisation is challenged that it knows how strong or weak it is. The BC survived the challenge: a member of the State Legislative Assembly had publicly stated that he would finish off the Centre, but he could not succeed.

2. This enhanced the image of the organisation in the eyes of the poorer peasants in the area. They in fact approached the BC later, after the inquiry was over, and asked why the Centre was working through intermediaries. Why did the BC not establish a direct relationship with them? The BC had proved how strong it was and it was obvious from then on that political powers would think twice before challenging it.

3. Changes of any kind come from conflict. In retrospect, this conflict helped the BC immensely in changing attitudes about their work. The target groups for the first time started coming spontaneously to the BC; the very people whom the BC wanted to work with and reach became its strongest supporters.

4. It strengthened the BC members as a group. As a result, the management style became more democratic: decisions that before 1977-79 were taken by the director were now taken by a group.

5. BC's objectives were redefined: the BC decided to work only with the poor in order to increase their level of awareness and make them self-reliant;

development services and training were to be used only to accelerate awareness and bring about social changes.

6. Dependence on any skills from urban areas was reduced drastically and more importance was given to education and literacy and use of technical and human resources from the village itself.

7. Organising farmers and mobilising women's groups to fight for their rights in courts and other groups forums were stepped up.

The reaction of those with vested interests in the villages has been one of caution. They speak disparagingly of the BC as an agency that only supports scheduled castes and harijans, but the BC takes that as a compliment. There is now a feeling among the village elites that the BC is worth using but not worth fighting against; indeed, their experience has shown that the BC is strong enough to refuse an irregular request, which enhances its image with the poor peasants.

In other words, in the whole process of learning by doing, of training to take over responsibilities, in taking decisions that could have unpleasant repercussions, the BC became able to provide the needed support, and this not only in routine day-to-day activities but also during times of crisis.

(a) During the selection process of sites for the installation of hand pumps, the upper castes wanted a pump at a given site; it was refused. The site was finally selected by the scheduled castes, despite the fact that the upper castes were strongly represented. They went to the government and tried to put pressure on the BC to agree to the site selected by them. The pump was installed in the scheduled caste locality. So far the BC has installed over 700 hand pumps only in poorer localities of the village — on payment of a contributions.

(b) In many cases hand pump mechanics had been selected from the lower castes. When the village elites refused to accept them, the BC stood firm and the selection was at the instance of the scheduled castes. Now the hand pump mechanics repair the pumps or the upper castes do not get water through them. Many women hand pump mechanics have been trained and are paid by the government and the community.

(c) By and large, the teachers for evening schools had not been accepted by village councils because their candidates had not been chosen. This, however, had no impact on the process; the councils had either to accept the teachers or not have the schools. Now over 150 night schools are run by 'barefoot' teachers where over 3,000 children come, 400 of them girls.

(d) Women trained by the BC protested against the non-payment of wages in government camps. As a result, lower level officials protested to higher authorities that the BC was not cooperating because it took the side of the women. Eventually the district authorities had to pay; the BC made a lot of enemies in the process. Now women are keeping records and taking measurements on government sites.

(e) In many cases, lands supposedly allotted to landless peasants were in fact nonexistent. The BC took up a number of cases on behalf of the landless and got them land through pressure or influence. These cases have been reported by village people trained by the BC or working with it.

(f) The 21st Century Technology Campus where the Barefoot College is based is a 60,000 sq.ft. complex of buildings built by a villager who can barely sign his name. He cannot read maps or figures. On his own, using his rural skills, he has constructed a rainwater harvesting structure connecting all the roofs to an underground tank of 400,000 litres.

(g) The power for the campus comes from the sun. Solar photovoltaics (SPV) totalling 10 kW using 5 banks of 128 batteries have been installed in the campus by rural youths who have never passed beyond the 10th standard. No solar or electronics engineers were invited nor required. The power is used to run 350 lights required for the library, dining hall, residence, administrative blocks, puppet theatre, soil and water testing laboratory. A total of 8 computers and 2 printers can run day and night. Three SPV-run pumps (140 ft.) distribute 25,000 litres per day. Rural youths, mostly semi-literate, keep all the systems running.

(h) Since 1984, SPVs have been installed in 8 states of India. Tilonia has trained 65 barefoot solar engineers from these states to install 960 solar units. They include adult education centres (300), lighting night schools for boys and girls who cannot afford to go to schools in the morning because they are out grazing sheep and goats (130); domestic lighting to 500 houses over 11,000 ft. up in the Himalayas, cut off by snow for 6 months of the year. The person from Ladakh who has installed these 500 units is Abdul Karim from Gurgurdo village: he can just about sign his name. The units have been working for over 3 years now.

(i) In the field of drinking water the Barefoot College has no paper qualified engineers. Sophisticated India Mark II hand pumps are being repaired by cycle repairers, ordinary farmers, blacksmiths, weavers and housewives. Called Hand Pump Mechanics (HPMs), each one looks after 30 hand pumps within a radius of 5 km from the village. Trained to carry out all major and minor repairs above and below the ground, they carry their tools on cycles and are currently paid less than US $5 a pump per year. When repaired through the government with their trucks, jeeps, engineers and heavy equipment, it was costing over US $50 dollars per pump per year. As a result of this community-based HPM management system, policies have been changed to decentralise operation and maintenance in several states of India. At every step of the way it is the engineers who are opposing the HPM. They find it hard to accept the process of demystification that has made maintenance so absurdly simple.

(j) Boys coming out of night schools have been trained in conducting water tests for contaminated drinking water; they have been trained to carry out geophysical tests with terrameters and read the results before drilling for water and installation of hand pumps take place; they have been trained to run village primary schools and be multipurpose health workers.

Most of the barely 8th standard pass students have shown that the urban-trained engineer, doctor and teacher are not really required.

Problem areas

1. The biggest threat to development and changes in the rural areas is what in the urban areas is called Educated Man. He usually is conservative, inflexible, conceited, arrogant and not open to new ideas; he refuses to work with his hands and he considers anyone less qualified on paper inferior and shows it; he has preconceived notions of development and how to solve problems; he uses knowledge as a tool for exploitation and power; he disseminates information on schemes and subsidies in the form of patronage. Tilonia has never faced any problem in communicating and working with the poorer peasant. But it is the Educated Man who has persistently sabotaged the introduction of innovative and progressive ideas.

2. The concept of self-reliance has not been understood. Or perhaps some have understood it all too clearly and that is why they do not want to see it happening. Among other things, making communities self-sufficient implies that charity would have to be discontinued in the name of development and that the dispensing of patronage would be minimised. Poorer peasants would be less dependent on government and this would hardly be welcomed by some individuals. Voluntary agencies that are working towards peasants' self-sufficiency can expect resistance from the lower bureaucracy every inch of the way; low-level bureaucrats will use every means to discredit the work being done in favour of such a goal.
3. The use of village resources on a larger scale means less coverage and presence of government, greater reliance on each other and more community participation. The problem that the BC has faced is not so much to show what is possible but rather to see that the new opportunities are adequately used. The problem is to get the village to identify, recognise and utilise the available resources for development purposes.
4. It is not easy to demystify technology in order to make it more human, accessible and understandable. The BC's problems in this area has been the technologists and the scientific community at large: the process of simplification has been the most complicated and difficult.

Profile of BC'S human resources

BC began as a professional group bringing specialised services to rural areas. However, by 1979 it had changed its approach. A closer relationship to the rural poor required:

- involvement of a greater number of local people as core workers
- involvement of lower scheduled caste groups
- demystifying technology and delinking education from degrees
- involving an increasing number of women

The following statistical information gives some indication of the extent to which BC has been able to incorporate these ideas in the actual induction of workers.

Table 17.1

Periodical Comparative Statement of BC's Workers

Year	*Total No.*	*Education (%) Up to Secon.*	*BA & Higher*	*Geographical Background (%) Ajmer*	*Other Dist.*	*Caste No. (%) S.C.*	*Others*	*Muslim*	*Women No. (%) PCS*	*NO*	*Total*
1978	59	59	41	42	58	—	—	—	—	—	—
1988	145	91	9	80	20	38(27)	96(65)	11(8)	10(19)	14(10)	24(17)
1993	170	81	19	82	18	30(18)	13(77)	9(5)	7(4)	33(19)	40(24)

Sources: 1. The image and self-image of Tilonia, evaluation report, February 1989.

2. BC reports, 1993.

This gives an overall comparative position of BC workers over 15 years with respect to their education, geographical background, caste and gender. However, in order to get a clearer picture on these issues, we have the following disaggregated information for 1993.

Table 17.2

BC Workers: Placement by Educational Qualification, 1993

(Distribution of Number and Percentage)

Placement	*Literature*	*Primary*	*Middle*	*Secondary/ Hr. Sec.*	*Grad-uate*	*Post Graduate*	*Total*
Field Centre	12(23.1) (35.3)	8(15.4) (38.1)	5(9.6) (20.8)	17(32.7) (29.3)	4(7.7) (28.6)	6(11.5) (31.6)	52(100.0) (30.6)
H.O. Tilonia	22(18.6) (64.7)	13(11.0) (61.9)	19(16.1) (79.2)	41(34.8) (70.7)	10(8.5) (71.4)	13(11.0) (68.4)	118(100.0) (69.4)
Total	34(20.0) (100.0)	21(12.4) (100.0)	24(14.1) (100.0)	58(34.1) (100.0)	14(8.2) (100.0)	19(11.2) (100.0)	170(100.0) (100.0)

Source: BC, Tilonia (1993 records).

The category 'Secondary/Higher Secondary' lists 34 per cent of the total number of workers. The post-graduate group is 11 per cent, which is slightly higher than mere graduates, 8 per cent. However, it is interesting to note that 20 per cent of Tilonia workers are basically literate with no formal educational qualification. This validates the organisation's overall stand that education should not be treated synonymous with formal certification. Respect for other forms of acquiring knowledge is registered in the induction/selection pattern of workers. We find that the head of the Solar Energy Section is not trained in an engineering college. Rural women with minimal formal qualifications are working with computers.

Table 17.3
SWRC Workers: Placement by Geographical Background, 1993
(Distribution of Number and Percentage)

Placement	*Ajmer District*	*Other Districts of Raj.*	*Out of State*	*Total*
Field Centre	45(86.5) (32.4)	5 (9.6) (41.7)	2 (3.9) (10.5)	52(100.0) (30.6)
H.O. Tilonia	94(79.7) (67.6)	7 (5.9) (58.3)	17(14.4) (89.5)	118(100.0) (69.4)
Total	139(81.6) (100.0)	12 (7.0) (100.0)	19 (11.2) (100.0)	170(100.0) (100.0)

Source: SWRC, Tilonia.

Over the year SWRC has encouraged increasing 'taking-over' by local people. The trend since 1978 is increasingly in favour of rural people from Ajmer District. From 42 per cent of its workers in this category, compared to other districts in Rajasthan, the participation from other states is higher now. One reason could be that SWRC has acted as a training centre for social work in which people from different parts of the country have come and gone back to their own state to set up a unit which could be contextually relevant.

Compared with 1988 data, there is a slight shift in the caste composition of workers. SC workers in 1988 were 27 per cent, which is now 18 per cent, and Muslims were 8 per cent, now 5 per cent. It needs to be asked whether the increasing absence of 'outsiders' leads to the emergence of certain age-old features of village pattern, particularly upper-caste dominance.

Table 17.4
SWRC Workers: Placement by Caste, 1993
(Distribution of Number and Percentage)

Placement	*Scheduled Castes*	*Others*	*Muslims*	*Total*
Field Centre	10 (19.2) (33.3)	42(80.8) (32.1)	—	52(100.0) (30.6)
H.O. Tilonia	20 (16.9) (66.7)	89(75.4) (67.9)	9 (7.7) (100.0)	118(100.0) (69.4)
Total	30 (17.6) (100.0)	131(77.1) (100.0)	9 (5.3) (100.0)	170(100.00) (100.0)

Source: SWRC, Tilonia (1993).

Table 17.5
SWRC Workers: Placement by Age Group, 1993
(Distribution of Number and Percentage)

Placement	Age Group in years				
	20-25	26-35	36-45	46 & above	Total
Field Centre	12(23.0) (35.3)	29(55.8) (30.9)	8(15.4) (26.7)	3(5.8) (25.0)	52(100.0 (30.6)
H.O. Tilonia	22(18.6) (64.7)	65(55.1) (69.1)	22(18.6) (73.3)	9(7.7) (75.0)	118(100.0) (69.4)
Total	34(20.0) (100.0)	94(55.3) (100.0)	30(17.6) (100.0)	12(7.1) (100.0)	170(100.0) (100.0)

Source: SWRC, Tilonia.

The largest number of workers fall in the age group 26-45. In a disaggregated analysis, it is clearly brought out that the SWRC is not a repository of superannuated people. Over the last two decades there has been a good deal of turnover, and 124 out of 170 workers are in the age group of 26-45, which can contribute mature energy levels. It is also clear that within this larger category 55 per cent of total workers are in the age category 26-35.

Table 17.6
SWRC Workers: Placement by Sex, 1993
(Distribution of Number and Percentage)

Placement	*Male*	*Female*	*Total*
Field Centre	45(86.5) (34.6)	7(13.5) (17.5)	52(100.0) (30.6)
H.O. Tilonia	85(72.0) (65.4)	33(28.0) (82.5)	118(100.0) (69.4)

Source: SWRC, Tilonia.

Tilonia headquarters has able to induct more women as workers than the field centres. The reasons are obvious. Changes in attitude and social behaviour require a protective nurturing environment. To begin with, a certain insulation is also necessary to ensure survival. Field Centres have a far greater exposure to counter-currents from age-old village traditions, particularly with respect to gender roles. In 1988, the number of women workers at Field Centre was 10 as compared to 7 now. However, at the Tilonia Centre, the number has shown a marked increase from 14 to 33.

Major success factors of the barefoot college model

1. The BC is not influenced or guided by ideological considerations. The Centre feels that every approach is relevant, is important and needs to be tried out by any person who believes in it. So there is room for a Sarvodaya, a Ramakrishna, a Marxist, a social service professional or a believer in charity approaches. To each his own. The BC provides an umbrella for such men and women: it provides the atmosphere and the space for people to test their beliefs, to try their strengths and weaknesses and learn from their experiences.
2. There is unity in diversity in the BC: unity of purpose and diversity in methods and approaches. The purpose is to integrate services, skills,

information and life-styles at the village level. It is to learn from the peasants and go through a process of unlearning ourselves. It is to train the poorer peasants and provide them the tools and skills to become less dependent and hence more responsible citizens. It is to build up the confidence of the poorer peasants and make them demand funds and programmes that will benefit them, in other words make them more aware. It is to demystify technology to the extent desirable and possible and use rural technology — what we have discarded as useless and primitive — for development purposes and make it respectable.

3. In order to make rural development work possible and bring about fundamental changes, the existence of an organisation is essential. The organisation should be accountable to government (registration, audit statement, etc.) as well as to the target populations and there should be flexibility and freedom enough for shifts in thinking, in strategies, in emphasis and in responsibilities (in particular, from the professional to the trained village-based para-professional). For instance, at the end of the year all the members of BC evaluate their own performance. BC's staff members are not encouraged to believe in salary scales or that educational qualifications are more important than experience.

   Organisations tend to become institutions and in due course cease to be either effective or in close touch with their target populations. In order to avoid this, the BC has deliberately formed smaller groups spread far apart so that they do not influence each other if their approaches are different.

4. The BC's definition of community assets in a village differs largely from the conventional version. For the BC, it is wrong to identify 'community' assets with inanimate things like buildings and roads quite apart from the fact that rarely does the whole community use these. In any case, community assets really mean the human assets that the village uses; assets accessible to all human beings like shopkeepers, priests, moneylenders, *dhobis* (washermen) and *lambardars* (traditional keepers of land records). Their community skills in communication, in education, in medicine and in disseminating the right sort of knowledge is grossly underutilised and in fact is not even recognised by government as a community asset. Development organisations are sometimes extremely cut off from reality.

5. The other meaning of participation is village accountability. The agency

must prepare the poorer peasants, must educate them, must be there to guide them, but finally when it comes to testing the system it is the peasant organisation that must do it. Obviously no village level bureaucrat would welcome a system where he has to account for his deeds and performance to someone he has always considered inferior. Already the fact that these bureaucrats have to face a threat from members of the State Legislative Assembly which make them work a trifle harder is a source of much resentment. A rural VA's goal should be that such power of control percolates down from the villages' elites to the villagers at large. This will ensure, for example, that funds reach the right people and that they are well spent, that the keeper of land records does not accept bribes. It implies that it will make local bureaucracy work.

The question of duplicating services at the village level is obviously the first step. India has a private and public sector at the national level, at the state level, at the district level, so why not at the village level? When bureaucrats ask 'why duplicate services?' the answer should be 'where is the job not being done?' There are private practitioners in villages duplicating health services, water diviners virtually taking the place of government geologists, *bal mandirs* and evening schools taking the place of government schools or competing with existing schools. Government cooperatives societies are being run by *banias* (moneylenders) and no one complains. Shopkeepers are actually sponsored by the government to sabotage the consumer societies and everyone keeps silent. The answer is to have supplementary services that offer the poorer peasants a choice, healthy competition so that they start asking questions. How is it that the BC can install a hand pump in one week and it takes the government six months to repair one? The process of questioning is the beginning of awareness.

In the ultimate analysis, the issue is peasant participation. Not the whole village, not the local elites, not the individuals who control public opinion, not the upper and the more influential castes who have abused their position in rural society, but the 40 per cent of those who live below the poverty line. These 40 per cent have never seen or heard, let alone read, the Constitution of India, and they have never been free from hunger and need.

6. The BC has delinked literacy from education, experience from qualification. Linking these elements constitutes a mythical system and the expectation

> of competence deriving from this system has proved to be a colossal failure; alternatives not only need to be found but tried out in the field and given every encouragement. The people against the very idea are the so-called educated who have a vested interest in keeping the system going. Peasants' world-views are very different from those of 'educated' people. Hence, why should development agents contribute to impose national society's world-views on peasants? If one objectively considers what is being taught in rural schools, about the wisest thing poor peasants can do is to keep their children away from morning schools. If 70 per cent of the Silora Block children of primary school age are not going to school, it is not so much a reflection of the peasants' motivation, it is rather a severe indictment of the so-called educated. Obviously, 'educated' individuals refuse to look at it this way. They are literate, how can they be uneducated? Paper degrees give them protection, it safely hides incompetence and generates unemployables.

In Tilonia, the BC has set an example by delinking qualification from experience. For instance, the Centre's Health Programme is run by a village-level health worker who has a degree in an arts subject from a Kishangarh school; Kishangarh, Silora Block's only town, is a small rural centre, but this health worker has — in BC's terms — more relevant knowledge in preventive health and village participation than most physicians, even those who have graduated from the country's leading universities. At BC, physicians have to work under him or the BC will not consider their appointment. Likewise, BC's educational programme, which involves the running of 30 night schools for 1,500 dropout children in 30 villages, is run by a priest who has no degree, and he has trained teachers with bachelors' degrees in education working under him. The Agricultural Extension Programme is looked after by a youth from the village; he has no qualification in agriculture but has produced tremendous results. The Tradition Media Section, where puppetry is the most prominent means of communicating messages, is run by a one-time sheep farmer who has received no training in this art; he just picked it up. The same holds true for the Rural Orientation Programme: it is run by an individual from the village. The new 60,000 sq.ft. campus has been built by a village youth who is illiterate.

The BC's geologists are expert trainers in the repair and maintenance of hand pumps; they have already conducted several courses, thus proving that mechanical engineers are not really required, just common sense. The Women's Programme, the training of traditional midwives, the establishment of *balwadis* are looked after by a widow without any real paper qualification. A social anthropologist with a degree from Jawaharlal Nehru University has to work under her and listen to her when it comes to her experience with women in the area.

Commonalities between BC'S programmes

What do the BC's programmes have in common as far as Tilonia is concerned?

1. They were started by expertise from outside the area by an urban-trained professional who trained someone from the village to take his place. Now all these programmes are run by people from the village who have no formal educational or professional degrees.
2. The move to make these services accessible was made by the people from the village who were trained to take the responsibility of providing services as well as disseminating information.
3. Tilonia wanted to remove the dependency on government to the extent possible. The training of people from the village to take over the provision of services not only increased their confidence but illustrated how it is possible to rely on each other.
4. There were no deadlines to meet, hence development was possible at the pace and speed the peasants wanted. There was no hurry to complete projects. The crucial points were the training and motivation of individuals.

It is a fact that often the peasants do not know precisely what the BC is doing. Is it doing social work? Rural development? Awareness building? Mobilising people against the dominant minority? There is no category that the BC fits into. In the process of explaining to the rural population what the BC is doing, the Centre has learnt the following lessons:

1. If everyone in the village is for a project, then there is something wrong with it. There has to be at least one sector of the village hurt by the implementation of any project; it is only when the right sector for the village objects that the project must be implemented.
2. Change comes only out of conflict. This should not be confused with violence. But only out of a conflict of ideas, experiences and groups can fundamental change of any kind come about. This conflict can and should be non-violent and legal.

3. The success of any project can be judged by the opposition it generates. The survival and continuity of a project depends on the skills of the organisation and on how such opposition can be constructively used to benefit the target group.

Leaders of other established organisations are wary of the interest the BC and its Tilonia Model have generated in the voluntary sector all over India. They cannot believe what they hear and neither can they recognise what they see. They cannot believe that:

1. The SWRC is no longer a one-man show.
2. There has been complete administrative and financial decentralisation in planning, in decision-making, in choice of staff, in deciding on their own emoluments, in selection of areas, in applying for funds.
3. The organisation can be made so flexible and autonomous and in this manner now spreads to 13 states of India with only formal links with the parent organisation.

Lessons to be learnt from the barefoot college

The BC is actually more than a model; it is a process that has stood the test of time and gone through the usual crises of growth and development.

1. The BC encourages people's organising with the aim of performing pressure group functions on the system from below. The organisation would ultimately be controlled by members and services will be provided to these members of rural societies who are not officially part of registered cooperatives. Secondly, the BC works on a no-profit, no-loss basis with social responsibilities instead of generating income for its members alone. The importance the BC gives to economic viability and the generation of profit is really of secondary importance. The BC has found that what is economically viable may not necessarily be socially acceptable.
2. Projects involved in rural development must be based in a village. There is no way of bringing about fundamental changes in the economic and social structure of the village without living and working as close to the poorer peasants as possible. To understand the people without really being accessible to them twenty-four hours a day is expecting the impossible. It is only when urban-based professionals and the ultimate beneficiaries live

and work together, share experiences, go through a learning and 'unlearning' process and show respect for each other that changes are possible. The BC has managed to show this in a tangible way in many fields. But this simple message has yet to be fully understood. Too many VAs still have only a 'village presence', which means that they live in the city but work in a village; in this set-up they expect to organise beneficiaries, get them to oppose people with vested interests, make them aware of their rights and promote their development. It will not work.

3. The BC has developed an identity of its own and does not fall in any category. It is neither Gandhian nor Sarvodaya, nor Marxist, though it has elements of all three. It believes in adopting a non-violent approach and democratic means in promoting development and yet, when it comes to acquiring a certain militancy over critical issues such as women's rights, minimum wages and removal of untouchability, the BC has not compromised and stepped away or pulled back from confronting powers. This has baffled and confused people who like putting labels on organisations.

The process of planning from below and persuading communities to decide their own future and to plan for themselves have resulted in major dilemmas that urban-based 'experts' tend to dismiss as non-issues. In rural development, seen from the village, the question is not one of defining black or white but of clarifying the grey areas.

Replication

The innovative approach of the BC may be seen at its best in how the model was replicated in thirteen other states of India including Rajasthan.

Many VAs in India fight shy of spreading their approaches in other parts of the country because of the many problems they face in the area they started, being persuaded that such problems will always remain. The spread effect actually depends on the orientation of the organisation from the very beginning to want to spread and look for people accordingly.

Not anyone and everyone can start sub-centres under the Tilonia Model. Even if the person has had some field experience in other projects, he/she will have to agree to and satisfy the following conditions:

1. The person will have to stay and work in Tilonia for an indefinite period to feel that he/she is a part of a larger family and that resources exist which

can later be tapped.

2. The person should have had some previous experience in the field of rural development and in the VA sector. Someone coming from a government background, however good, will not be considered.
3. The person will have to be young so that the investment is not short-lived. He/she will have to show grace under pressure (courage), will be tested under different conditions (long working hours, poor salary, etc.) to see if he/she has to capacity and the will to carry on.
4. The person will have to believe strongly in the approach and methodology he/she would like to follow. There is no compulsion that he/she will have to agree to the Tilonia approach. There is room for agreement and disagreement. However, there will have to be underlying areas of agreement like basing the project in a village, adopting an integrated approach to rural development, mobilising local skills and upgrading their knowledge, organising people into groups so that they are in a position to pressurise the system from below. Time plans and methods are left to the project director of the BC in the particular state.
5. It is not necessary that the person have paper qualifications for the assignment he/she takes up in any particular state. The BC gives more importance to field experience than to qualifications.
6. It is important that the person come from the state he/she wants to go back to. But we have had to relax this rule on many occasions without regret.

The Centre in Tilonia helps a person to set up a new sub-centre in the following ways:

1. As and when the person is ready to start a project from the state he/she comes from, funds are provided to (a) visit the village/site/state to decide on the location, (b) prepare a project proposal and loose time plan, (c) identify people from the area to be trained in Tilonia, and (d) meet government officials and inform them of the setting up of the SWRC and seek their support. All this takes time, from 4 to 6 months.
2. Funds are provided for one year, allowing the project to settle down; during this first year, the new sub-centre has to identify important activities and set its priorities. After one year the sub-centre has to be self-sufficient and

totally on its own.

3. Eventually the sub-centre is persuaded to acquire a legal identity of its own and to adopt a name of its choice (not SWRC). This has now happened for several sub-centres.

Summing up

The stand of the Barefoot College in Tilonia is simple. The educational system the world over, especially in the South, has failed the rural poor. It is elitist. It is biased towards people passing exams set by narrow-minded, insensitive people. The only way to meet this approach is to reject it outright, which is what the Barefoot College has done.

Only those people from the rural areas who have been rejected by the present educational system are welcome in Tilonia. Only those who are illiterate or semi-literate, who are socially and economically backward and vulnerable in rural society, can apply and will be accepted in Tilonia.

The Barefoot College respects anyone who is prepared to work with his/her hands; anyone who is prepared to learn; anyone who is prepared to share skills and knowledge and treats others as equals; anyone who has no hang-ups, ego problems and anyone who does not hide behind his/her degree to cover up incompetence, insecurity, and has the courage to say: 'I do not know and I am willing to learn'.

Can this concept be replicated? Of course it can. Wherever there are people from the rural areas who have been rejected by the educational system, where paper qualifications do not matter and are not used to judge the worth, quality and aptitude of people, the Barefoot College concept can work.

List of Contributors

Ram Bapat	2, Prathmesh Apartments Plot No. 157/12, Aundh Pune 411 007 Maharastra
Boedhihartono	Head of the Department of Anthropology University of Indonesia Programme Studi Anthropologi Fakultas Pascasarjna U1, J1 Salemba Raya 4 Jakarta 10430 (Indonesia)
Ashish Bose	I-1777, Chittaranjan Park New Delhi 110 019
Francis Childe	Chief Project Coordination and Section World Decade for Cultural Development Unesco, 7 Place de Fontenoy 75 700 Paris (France)
Tan Chung	Professor Consultant Indira Gandhi National Centre for the Arts Janpath New Delhi 110 001

Sang-Bok Han	Professor of Anthropology Department of Anthropology Seoul National University Seoul 151-742 (South Korea)
Minoru Kasai	Professor of History of Religion International Christian University 3-10-3 Osawa, Mitaka Tokyo 181 (Japan)
Keshav Malik	5/90, Connaught Circus New Delhi 110 001
S.C. Malik	5/90, Connaught Circus New Delhi 110 001
Promode Kumar Misra	Professor in Anthropology and Dean Department of Anthropology North-Eastern Hill University Mayurbhanj Complex Shillong 793 014 Meghalaya
R.P. Misra	17-C, Maurice Nagar Delhi 110 007
Pahalawattage Don Premasiri	Professor of Philosophy and Psychology at the University of Paradeniya C-26, University Park Peradeniya (Sri Lanka)
Amara Raksasataya	161, Mahamek Housing Soi 6 Sathosh District Bangkok 10120 (Thailand)

Sanjit (Bunker) Roy	Director The Social Work and Research Centre Tilonia 305 816 Madanganj, Dist. Ajmer Rajasthan
Sachchidananda	157, Kadam Kuan New Area Patna 800003 Bihar
Baidyanath Saraswati	Unesco Professor Janapada Sampada Indira Gandhi National Centre for the Arts Janpath New Delhi 110 001
Meutia F. Swasono	Dept. of Anthropology University of Indonesia Programme Studi Anthropologi Fakultas Pascasarjna U1, J1 Salemba Raya 4 Jakarta 10430 (Indonesia)
Ngo Duc Thinh	Director of Folklore Institute National Centre for Social and Human Sciences 36 Hang Chuoi Str. Hanoi (Vietnam)
Kapila Vatsyayan	Academic Director Indira Gandhi National Centre for the Arts Janpath New Delhi 110 001